Taxing Sin

Michael Thom

Taxing Sin

palgrave
macmillan

Michael Thom
Sol Price School of Public Policy
University of Southern California
Los Angeles, CA, USA

ISBN 978-3-030-49175-8   ISBN 978-3-030-49176-5   (eBook)
https://doi.org/10.1007/978-3-030-49176-5

Cover illustration: eStudio Calamar

This Palgrave Macmillan imprint is published by the registered company Springer Nature
Switzerland AG
The registered company address is: Gewerbestrasse 11, 6330 Cham, Switzerland

ACKNOWLEDGMENTS

Bringing this book to print was a pain in the you-know-what. There is no other way to describe it.

After an editor at my initial publisher went radio silent, I sent my proposal off to several others. Some editors responded and offered helpful feedback, but not an offer to publish. It was frustrating, to say the least.

Then, a ray of hope. An editor at a large publisher expressed interest in the project and said he would write more in a day or two. He never did. I followed up, but to no avail. That editor ghosted me.

Months later, another ray of hope. An editor at a different academic press said he was interested. I'll respond after Thanksgiving, he wrote. He did not, so I followed up. I'll get a contract to you Monday, he replied. Monday came and went. So did Tuesday, Wednesday, Thursday, and Friday. Then, the Monday after that, a promise to have the contract to me "by tomorrow." That deadline came and went. No contract. No explanation. I inquired but received no response. That editor ghosted me, too.

Neither ghost was not dead, of course. Each one was alive and more than well enough to post on Twitter. (Yes, I checked.)

That is why I have to offer my deepest gratitude and thanks to Nick Barclay, my exceedingly competent—and responsive—senior editor at Palgrave Macmillan. The publishing process could not have gone any better. Nick's professionalism is greatly appreciated. He's no ghost, that's for sure.

Thanks are also due to the many individuals, some known and others unknown, who reviewed this project at various points of completion—even the reviewer who sniffed at my appeal to "layman's logic," as if that were a thing one should not do. Your constructive remarks made the book better.

Thanks are also owed to the many people who were kind enough to ask me how my research was going. There were times when I forgot I was writing a book about sin taxes—or *wanted* to forget I was writing one—but you never did. Thanks, Mom. Thanks, Luis, Luke, Elizabeth, John, and Michael. And thank you, too, Ben. You're awesome.

CONTENTS

CHAPTER 1

Tax Your Sins, Experts Say

Our moral reformers, so often given to intemperate words and contemptuous measures, have been instrumental to a large extent in accustoming the American mind to habits of over-statement and unmitigated rebuke, which are unfortunately now becoming a national disease. *The New York Times*, 1854

Each is the proper guardian of his own health, whether bodily, or mental and spiritual. Mankind are greater gainers by suffering each other to live as seems good to themselves, than by compelling each to live as seems good to the rest. John Stuart Mill, 1859

The word "sin" comes from terms in early Jewish and Christian texts that refer to an individual who committed an error, went astray, o r missed the mark. The notion raises profound questions that theologians have wrestled with for thousands of years. How does an individual know whether a choice is sinful or not, especially if scripture offers no indication? Who makes those judgments? What must a sinner do to reconcile with others and God? Should sinners flounder in imperfection or strive for perfection?

While church and state may be increasingly separate, parallel themes dominate public policymaking. Which choices and behaviors in society are acceptable and unacceptable? Who makes those distinctions? On what basis? What restitution is due from those who make the wrong choice? Should governments aim to help individuals muddle through a world of imperfect choices, or should governments push society toward utopia?

© The Author(s) 2021
M. Thom, *Taxing Sin*,
https://doi.org/10.1007/978-3-030-49176-5_1

If there is a meaningful difference between sacred and secular approaches to those who have committed an error, gone astray, or missed the mark according to their respective standards, it is the path to redemption.

In most religious traditions, atonement comes through repentance and divine mercy. Governments, by contrast, often incarcerate their transgressors to ensure they "pay their debt to society." And although most denominations have abandoned efforts to monetize forgiveness, governments charge some of their sinners for redemption every day.

Taxing Sin is about a particular kind of secular redemption—paying a tax—for a particular kind of secular sin—the choice to buy something the government says you should avoid. Sin taxes have been applied to alcoholic beverages and tobacco products for some time. By the twenty-first century, they spread to soda and marijuana alongside calls to expand the list of tax-worthy items to include plastic bags and meat. Some went further and demanded a tax on robots and carbon.

Against that momentum, *Taxing Sin* argues that classifying certain goods as deserving of a selective tax is a folly—a foolish, ineffective policy for governments to control our choices. To understand why that's the case, it is important to understand the reasons why so many put their faith in the redemptive power of government—and taxation.

* * *

Governments have charged sin taxes for hundreds of years.[1] By the sixteenth and seventeenth centuries, taxes on alcohol, tobacco, and other goods appeared throughout the Americas, Europe, and the Middle East. In 1574, Holland imposed an alcohol tax to fund a revolt against Spain. King James VI of England ordered a tobacco tax in 1604 because he believed smoking was a "foolish vanity." The Ottoman Empire levied

---

[1] Sin taxes have, in the past, been referred to as sumptuary taxes, which were part and parcel of sumptuary laws dating back centuries that sought to discourage choices deemed immoral by governing authorities. In some instances, sumptuary laws did not target intrinsically sinful choices but instead attempted to enforce a class system. For example, certain laws banned the poor from wearing types of clothing that were typically worn by the wealthy. Other laws, particularly during the reign of Edward I in England, sought to curb meat consumption. In 1216, he proclaimed that too many "persons of inferior rank" imitated the "great men" of the time by eating an "outrageous and excessive multitude of meats," which led to "many great evils."

taxes on tobacco and coffee—yes, coffee—in the eighteenth century to finance stipends for the ulema, a group of Islamic scholars. Federal alcohol and tobacco taxes in the United States helped bankroll the Revolutionary War, the War of 1812, and the Civil War.

Those early taxes targeted different choices at the behest of varying motives but had two common traits. First, the tax applied to a small number of goods.[2] And second, it was often temporary. Some taxes ended after military conflict subsided, some ended when regimes changed, and some ended after collection proved difficult.

Neither is true anymore. Sin taxes appear on a growing list of items and are a permanent fixture of government budgets around the world. That shift resulted from an evolution in the relationship between citizens and their government.

The drive for sin taxes now is paternalism, a belief that governments should interfere with an individual's choices for their own good, for the good of society, or both. Those who support paternalism—let's call them paternalists—include experts, policymakers, journalists, special interest groups, philanthropic organizations, and much of the public. Paternalists believe that governments should enact policies to discourage individuals from making choices that experts say are harmful—choices that commit an error, go astray, or miss the mark for assorted secular reasons. The choice can be drinking a soda or an alcoholic beverage. It could be smoking a cigarette or marijuana. Or it might be eating meat, using a plastic bag, or employing robots to eliminate a job.

Paternalists embrace taxation as a way to redeem harmful choices. They view sin taxes as a win-win proposition. The thinking goes something like this: by using a tax to raise the price of harmful goods, individuals buy less of those goods. Their well-being will thus increase, and society overall will benefit. Individuals who purchase the goods anyway pay taxes that fund government programs that benefit society, thus atoning for the harm their choice has created.

In other words, forgiveness is just a tax away.

Paternalism is a thought-provoking viewpoint, one that is simultaneously principled and patronizing. It stems from what economist Thomas

---

[2] That the taxes were often levied on only a few items did not mean the burden was intended to fall on a small number of individuals. In his seminal *Wealth of Nations*, Adam Smith in 1776 remarked that "sugar, rum, and tobacco" were worthy of taxation not only because of their harm, but because they were "objects of almost universal consumption."

Sowell called the "unconstrained vision" of human nature.[3] At their core, paternalists believe most individual choices are flawed, irrational, and perhaps selfish. They believe that those imperfect choices are the root of society's problems. The solution, paternalists say, is to transfer decision-making authority from individuals to experts and government officials, who they trust to use public policy to make better choices for everyone. Only then, according to paternalists, will society embark on an unconstrained path toward utopia.

The paternalism behind today's sin taxes originated in the progressive movement that swept through the United States and Europe beginning in the late nineteenth century, carried by activists, social reformers, and clergy. Social science professors provided the movement's intellectual leadership. Most had studied at German universities, where the prevailing ethos was a leftist political philosophy that prescribed government control as a tonic for the ills of individualism and *laissez-faire* economics.[4]

Most progressives were avowed paternalists, scorning the idea that individuals should be permitted to make their own choices as a freedom that held back society. John C. Calhoun, a former Democratic vice president, argued before the United States Senate as early as 1848 that the belief that all individuals were "born free and equal" was "the most false and dangerous of all political errors."[5] In his 1901 book *Social Control*, prominent sociologist Edward Ross complained that society was "too often the prey of individuals."[6] And Herbert Croly, cofounder of *The New Republic*, a progressive magazine, later wrote that any individual suspicious of government interference in their choices was guilty of "licensed selfishness."[7]

Progressives firmly believed that society's needs took precedence over individual liberty. For some, that deference sprang from a conviction that individuals were merely an appendage of society, a limb inseverable from—and subservient to—the whole body. Charles Cooley, a progressive founding member and later president of the American Sociological

---

[3] Sowell (1995, 2007).

[4] Further examination of progressive thought can be found in Ely (2012), Leonard (2017), and Rodgers (1982).

[5] Quoted from "Speech on the Oregon Bill," delivered June 27, 1848.

[6] Ross (1901).

[7] Croly (1909).

Association, wrote in 1909 that "the notion of a separate and independent ego is an illusion"—in other words, that there was no such thing as an autonomous person.[8] Other progressives granted that individuals existed, but only because society made it possible. A 1915 editorial in *The New Republic* argued that "outside of society" an individual "has never existed and could not exist."[9] Either way, progressives believed that each individual owed a debt of loyalty to society, payable by government allegiance. According to progressive economist E. R. A. Seligman, founder of the American Economic Association, an individual's "very first" obligation in life is "to protect and support the state" because "his life is possible only within the state."[10]

A resentment toward individual choice combined with a belief in the state's importance compelled progressives to argue that society's ideal arrangement was a paternalistic hierarchy. Experts and policymakers responsible for crafting laws and regulations to usher in utopia were at the top of that hierarchy, and below, the masses expected to conform. Within that system, individual liberty and free markets would not be left to their own devices.[11]

Among the upper echelon, however, progressives favored giving experts more authority than elected officials. Experts were thought to be above the political fray, with a keen ability to diagnose and solve social problems through efficient science rather than messy ideology. Frank Goodnow, founding president of the American Political Science Association, argued in 1916 that representative government was inefficient, and only "a greater amount of expert service" would improve societal conditions.[12] Experts were necessary, according to Seligman, to "get people to feel their true needs and acquaint them with the means of their satisfaction," implying that only experts were capable of knowing what was in everyone else's best interest.[13] Once experts had more power,

---

[8] Cooley (1909).

[9] *The New Republic* (1915).

[10] Seligman (1890).

[11] The belief that society should adhere to a hierarchy composed of an elite, ruling few and an ignorant, obedient many did not originate in contemporary progressive thought. Plato's *Republic*, written around 375 BCE, described a society of educated "guardians" presiding over the masses.

[12] Goodnow (1916).

[13] Fink (1997).

predicted progressive economist Irving Fisher, "we begin to see an almost boundless vista for possible human betterment."[14]

The progressive movement ultimately enshrined paternalism in public policy and the social order writ large. The view that individual choices should not be left unchecked attained enough popularity to usher government into nearly every facet of life. Governments around the world erected bureaucracies filled with experts and civil servants to regulate everything from education and employment to banking and finance. Like never before, taxes were imposed to fund those bureaucracies and address other social problems.

* * *

Some of the most enduring progressive influence occurred in public health. Throughout the nineteenth century, most government health programs consisted of little more than initiatives to treat infectious diseases. But by the turn of the twentieth century, progressives leveraged population growth and advances in medicine to promote a much broader concept of public health. It included wide-ranging objectives, including to "prevent epidemics, protect against environmental hazards, promote healthy behaviors, respond to disasters and assist communities in recovery, and assure the quality and accessibility of health care services."[15]

Progressives approached their new public health mandate with paternalistic zeal. To accomplish its lofty goals, progressives saw curtailing individual choice—even the most personal choices—as a necessity. In *Crossing Over the Line*, which examines progressive efforts to regulate sexual behavior, David J. Langum summarizes the attitude:

> By proper use of social engineering, often employing the coercion of the federal government, individual human behavior could be controlled and changed through legislation. Men could be forced to be good and social evils conquered forever.[16]

Under the pretense of improving public health, progressives insisted that the government regulate choices they believed were harmful to society,

---

[14] Fisher (1907).

[15] Epstein (2004); see also Gostin (2016).

[16] Langum (1994).

preferably by banning those choices outright. The justification often blended secular and religious values. Choices that secular progressives believed undermined public health (a secular sin) typically aligned with what religious progressives believed undermined spiritual health (a religious sin).[17] Control over individual choices was viewed by each group as a necessity to serve a higher purpose. For progressives, that purpose was advancing the state; for the religious, who were typically Protestant, that purpose was advancing Christianity.

Examples of their collaboration abound. Social purity groups that demanded bans on prostitution and pornography were supported by secular progressives who argued that both jeopardized public health and by religious progressives who argued that both violated Christian sexual ethics. Groups that demanded alcohol prohibition were backed by secular progressives—including a cadre of economists and other experts—who argued that drinking encouraged social decay. They were joined by religious progressives who maintained drunkenness was an insult to God. Similar coalitions lobbied for restrictions on other choices believed to miss the secular and sectarian marks, such as gambling and smoking marijuana or tobacco.[18]

The social purity movements had some success. Alcohol prohibition became law in several countries, including the United States, Russia, Iceland, Norway, and Finland. Campaigns against tobacco and marijuana also achieved limited victories.

Yet the success was limited. World War I drew attention away from progressive reforms. Many governments that enacted alcohol prohibition reversed course, in part because of public outcry and in part because

---

[17] This seemingly odd pairing was a variation on the "Bootleggers and Baptists" concept of alcohol regulation during the same era. But it should not come as a surprise; progressivism's communitarian emphasis resonated with many Protestant denominations. Progressive minister Washington Gladden wrote that individualism "is not a sound basis for democratic government" and that individuals who failed to embrace the "brotherhood of man" could not believe in God (Gladden 1905). Progressive Baptist theologian Walter Rauschenbusch argued Christian churches should teach believers that they are not individuals with rights, but members of a community. Any emphasis on individualism, he warned, "neutralizes the social consciousness created by Christianity" (Rauschenbusch 1907).

[18] Alston et al. (2002), Blocker (2006), Derthick (2012), Keller (1994), and Kersch (2004).

it did little to curb harmful drinking. Prohibition also imposed unintended consequences, including the growth of organized crime.[19] As smoking grew more popular after World War I and II, most anti-tobacco movements faltered.

But the paternalism that drove progressives to demand government restrictions on choices they believed were harmful did not diminish. Prohibition's failure instilled no humility and no widespread doubt in the ability of experts and policymakers to corral the choices of hundreds of millions of individuals. Proceeding as it does from deeply held beliefs about human nature and the appropriate structure of society, the paternalistic impulse was too powerful.

Progressives merely—and begrudgingly—recognized that bans did not work. They moved from demanding absolute prohibition to demanding that governments adopt a tax-and-control approach to alcohol, tobacco, and other secular sins.[20] This strategy was another win–win. Taxes generated revenue that subsidized government expansion, an item forever at the top of the progressive wish list. And by allowing sinful choices to continue, progressives ensured that their paternalism would have a permanent foil.

The only hitch was how to defend taxes on popular choices. In 1920, the same year many historians coincidentally date as the end of the formal progressive era, economist Arthur Pigou provided a solution. Pigou's book, *The Economics of Welfare*, argued that governments had good reason to tax certain choices. His definitive example was an industrial factory. By polluting the air, a factory imposes harm on individuals living nearby—a spillover, or external, cost known as an externality. Pigou reasoned that this externality warranted a pollution tax, which he felt was an efficient way to oblige the factory to pay the full cost of its choice to pollute. In theory, the tax would also encourage lower pollution.

Pigou extended the argument to alcoholic beverages. Since drinking led to crime and imposed other externalities, including the cost of law enforcement, he wrote that an alcohol tax was justified. Higher prices would also—again, in theory—reduce drinking.

The logic was a stroke of political genius. It had a ring of intuition and fairness and was not obviously partisan. Since it did not rely on moral

---

[19] Miron and Zwiebel (1991).

[20] Morone (2003).

judgments, the logic was embraced by progressives uncomfortable with the social purity movements' religious advocacy. The fact that sin taxes were not coercive sidestepped resistance from those who would typically complain about being forced to pay taxes while free riders did not.[21] Opposition could also be reduced by embedding the tax in a good's price, as Pigou recommended, thereby making it less transparent to taxpayers.

Sin taxes also garnered support that did not exist for other forms of taxation. By targeting the penalty on individuals creating ostensible harm, the strategy appeared consistent with the often-popular ethic of personal responsibility. Some even embraced sin taxes on the assumption that paying them improved their own well-being.[22] Others approved because a relatively small group of individuals paid taxes for the purported benefit of a larger group. That support flourishes when the taxpaying group, like smokers, has lower moral status than the beneficiaries, like women and children.[23]

On the strength of Pigou's logic, sin taxes that were initially legislated as temporary gradually became permanent, and those that were relatively low began to rise. As old justifications for a tax expired, such as that it was necessary to fund a war, a new sensibility took hold: progressives argued that the tax should remain and perhaps rise because the taxed item ultimately created externalities. They did not have to refer to the charges as sin taxes, either. Instead, the levies were called "Pigouvian taxes," a technical term that carried no religious connotation.

That logic eventually hardened into a paternalistic orthodoxy that became conventional wisdom. In essence, some choices impose harm that demand government action. Since bans do not tend to work, only a tax can reasonably redeem that harm. Experts, especially in economics and public health, increasingly made the case to policymakers and the public. It was not hard to convince them to join the crusade for sin taxes; most were already paternalists, and many were already active in the progressive cause.[24]

* * *

[21] Lohmann and Weiss (2002).
[22] Crain et al. (1977).
[23] Carruthers (2016).
[24] Leonard (2017).

The progressive movement may be over, but paternalism is alive and well. It shapes positions taken by every major political party, even parties outwardly committed to protecting freedom of choice. Policy differences across parties often relate to a question of how, not if, governments should attempt to engineer an individual's choices for their own good or the good of society.

Paternalism also remains a dominating force among experts, especially in the social sciences. Many academics have written entire books on its virtues. One such book contends paternalism is the only way to "shake us from our entrenched and destructive ways of living," echoing progressive era sentiments from Goodnow and Seligman.[25] Paternalism is so ingrained in the consciousness of some academics that they view opposition as a cognitive deficiency.[26]

If anything, paternalism is on the rise. Much of its growth can be traced to the development of behavioral economics, a field of study that combines economics and psychology. Like Pigou, behavioral economists view sin taxes and other government interventions as vital to redeem choices that impose externalities. They also argue that public policy should repair internalities, a term devised for self-imposed internal harm that does not necessarily affect anyone else.[27]

According to behavioral economists, sinful choices result from cognitive bias. Perhaps an individual makes an inferior choice because of "status quo bias," a tendency to repeat a familiar behavior even if it is harmful. Or maybe the fault is "hyperbolic discounting," a tendency to prefer short-term over long-term rewards. Or the choice might result from "bounded rationality," the limits faced by an individual when they lack adequate time or information to make the best possible decision.

Those biases, or any one of scores of other flaws that behavioral economists have identified, might lead to a choice that misses the mark. An individual might consume foods that taste good now at the expense of better long-term health or choose a convenient plastic bag at a grocery store without considering the future environmental implications.

---

[25] Quoted from Conly (2012); see also Battaglio et al. (2019), LeGrand and New (2015), and Thaler and Sunstein (2008).

[26] Jolls et al. (1998).

[27] Allcott and Sunstein (2015) and Gruber and Köszegi (2001).

What better way to nudge individuals to less sinful choices, behavioral economists say, than with a harmless tax?

* * *

Paternalism offers an intoxicating narrative about the causes of problems in society and the appropriate solutions. It is both uncomplicated and optimistic; seemingly intractable issues are blamed on flawed choices that expert-developed public policies can solve.

Sin taxes are emblematic of the philosophy. They merely raise the cost of certain items to redeem the harm caused when an individual consumes them. Defenders have taken to calling sin taxes a form of "libertarian paternalism" because nothing is banned completely, and individuals retain the liberty to buy whatever they want. The government has only signaled that the choice is secularly sinful.

But in politics, as in physics, every action provokes a reaction. Paternalism has many critics. Some wince at the self-aggrandizement of one group using the levers of government to manipulate the choices made by another group. That nanny-state social engineering is said to do little more than "infantilize the public."[28] Critics also argue that seemingly benign forms of paternalism, like sin taxes or product warning labels, are a slippery slope toward stricter government controls, like prohibition.[29]

Much of the skepticism is as much a critique of paternalism as it is a critique of progressive philosophy. Many opponents are reluctant to embrace a political system in which experts and policymakers hold significant authority over individual choice and society at large. That is partly motivated by knowledge of history. Without a doubt, experts were behind every government failure, from the eugenics movement championed by progressives to central planning disasters to ill-advised wars.[30]

---

[28] Wright and Ginsburg (2012).

[29] Anderson (1997), Mitchell (2004), Veetil (2011), and Whitman and Rizzo (2007). Tobacco is an instructive case. Taxes on cigarettes and other tobacco products were initially low, only to rise over time. Increases were often enacted alongside minor anti-tobacco nudges, including public health campaigns and laws mandating product warning labels. That evolved into smoking bans, first in limited areas and later nearly everywhere. Many experts now call for total tobacco prohibition, just as experts did during the progressive era. The movement has truly come full circle.

[30] There are too many examples to cite, but four merit a mention: Halberstam (1992) examines how experts led the United States into the Vietnam War, Hall (1982) and

Opposition is also motivated by growing awareness that academic research—which is often used by experts justify public policies like sin taxes—is often flawed. An exhaustive review of over 6000 studies published in economics journals found that nearly 80% of the reported findings were exaggerated.[31] Many results were false, and many others could not be reproduced.[32]

That skepticism illuminates two deeper flaws in paternalism and, by extension, the progressivism that seeks to remake public policy in its image. The first flaw is the assumption that cognitive biases warp choices made by the masses. The assumption implies experts and policymakers are somehow immune to the same choice-distorting biases—a belief deeply embedded in expert circles.[33] One review found 96% of behavioral economics studies that recommend government action—all written by experts—failed to address how cognitive biases might influence the experts and policymakers responsible for designing and implementing those actions.[34]

But policymakers are susceptible to bias. They are human, after all. Studies show that government employees have a range of cognitive biases that affect their decision-making.[35] One of those biases is an overconfidence in their capacity to improve society.[36] Scholars have also argued for decades—and voters have even longer suspected—that government officials tend to make choices that serve their personal interests, not the needs

O'Toole (2007) explore urban planning failures, and Leonard (2017) documents how progressive experts, especially economists, led the American eugenics movement.

[31] Ioannidis et al. (2017).

[32] Chang and Li (2015) and Ioannidis (2005).

[33] Jolls et al. (1998) acknowledge the possibility of bias affecting bureaucrats but nevertheless return to their central argument that bureaucrats pursue soft paternalism.

[34] Berggren (2012); see also discussion in Wright and Ginsburg (2012) and Dudley and Xie (2019).

[35] Bellé et al. (2018). Of the cognitive biases, the authors wrote, "architects of public organizations and services should account for them." Yet no indication was given as to what biases the "architects" might have or how to overcome them. Perhaps that matter is best left to the architect of the architects. See also Cooper and Kovacic (2012), Moynihan and Lavertu (2011), and Roberts and Wernstedt (2019).

[36] Hafner-Burton et al. (2013), Liu et al. (2017), Rachlinski and Farina (2002), and Tasic (2009).

of the public. Studies indicate that the inclination toward self-interest results from "automatic psychological mechanisms."[37]

Making matters worse, compared to the public whose choices they seek to control, policymakers have more ways to avoid the consequences of bad decisions.[38] Elected officials can shift blame for poor outcomes to their political opponents, bureaucrats, and even voters, a tactic that allows them to evade accountability. The net result is that public policy tends to "institutionalize(s) rather than overcome" policymakers' biases.[39]

Experts are not exempt from bias, either. Economist Friedrich Hayek warned about the tendency of experts in the social sciences to utilize simplistic models to explain infinitely complex problems.[40] That choice can originate in confirmation bias, the desire to obtain information that confirms rather than challenges one's initial assumptions. In academic research, confirmation bias also emerges in publication bias, the refusal of journals—reviewed and edited by experts—to publish studies with findings that contradict the typically paternalistic conventional wisdom.[41]

That's not all. Political ideology influences some experts; conflicts of interest with organizations that fund their research prejudice others.[42] Experts also fall prey to "bias bias," the tendency to assume cognitive bias caused a problem even though it did not.[43]

Paternalism's second flaw is the assumption that those who govern can improve on choices made by the governed. In reality, correcting

---

[37] Zamir and Sulitzeanu-Kenan (2018); see also McChesney (1997), Peltzman (1976), and Stigler (1971).

[38] Glaeser (2006) and Klick and Mitchell (2006).

[39] Viscusi and Gayer (2010).

[40] Hayek (1952). One of Hayek's arguments was that early twentieth-century economists introduced a progressive sensibility to their discipline. Instead of viewing society as being composed of free-thinking, unpredictable individuals, they embraced the idea that society was an interconnected organism that could be studied and altered through methods like those used in the natural sciences. Beyond that, social scientists may also have been envious of the speed at which natural sciences developed and improved quality of life. When central planning failed to accomplish the same advancements, many doubled down, furthering their embrace of scientism. See also Haack (2013).

[41] Franco et al. (2014). Knowing that this bias exists, some researchers refrain from even attempting to publish their findings if they contradict or question majority thought, which is known as the "file drawer problem."

[42] Gigerenzer (2015) and Javdani and Chang (2019).

[43] Gigerenzer (2018).

the choices made by billions of individuals would require that experts and policymakers possess and analyze a mind-boggling quantity of data in real-time. That data would include the extent of each individual's biases, which change over time and from one circumstance to another; the extent of each individual's efforts to correct their biases; the net balance among competing biases, since some biases might neutralize others; and the extent to which public policy might affect those biases. Experts and policymakers would also need the capacity to assess all tradeoffs among different strategies to correct bias and have no difficulties implementing, monitoring, and adjusting them.[44]

Hayek argued there is no reason to believe that is even possible in theory, much less in practice.[45] Experts and policymakers simply do not have adequate data. Even if they did, they lack the capacity to make sense of it. As two scholars put it:

> Regardless of how smart they are, and how much information they may assemble, regulators can never know more than a miniscule fraction of the information that is known to the multitude – particularly the internal knowledge and preferences that make each of us unique, as producers, consumers, and as autonomous individuals.[46]

Experts and policymakers nevertheless try to know more than the masses and legislate on that basis. But time and time again, they fail. When that happens, they inevitably resort to "rules of thumb" and "appeal to their own preferences or to socially approved preferences" to make new policies.[47] That is a far cry from the rational decision-making process that paternalism and progressivism require as a prerequisite to utopia.

* * *

A parallel set of criticisms address sin taxes in particular. Sin taxes have long been condemned as regressive—that is, for having a disproportionate impact on the poor, who have less income with which to pay government-imposed higher prices. Policymakers' use of sin taxes also

---

[44] Rizzo and Whitman (2009).

[45] Hayek (1945).

[46] Mannix and Dudley (2015).

[47] Rizzo and Whitman (2009).

raises the question of how to sustain government programs funded by them if individuals stop buying the goods experts and policymakers have told them to avoid.

That, in turn, reveals a peculiar hypocrisy: policymakers condemn a choice on the one hand, but on the other hand, vote for budgets that require that millions of individuals continue to make that very choice.[48] The explanation for that duplicity may be political. Indeed, sin tax revenue attracts interest groups that lobby policymakers for government funding, an inevitability known as rent-seeking.[49]

Most importantly, Pigou's argument that certain goods warrant a tax because of their externalities has critical limitations. Depending on how the data are analyzed, many choices create no externalities at all. Sometimes the supposed externalities are internalities that impose no harm on society. Why, then, tax the choice? Furthermore, as economist Ronald Coase argued in 1960, public policies like sin taxes and prohibition impose unintended consequences and other costs that may exceed their benefits.[50] Under those circumstances, the public would be better off if the government simply left them, and their choices, alone.

That is a recurrent theme across the following chapters.

As Chapter 2 explains, paternalists argue that the choice to drink soda is the leading cause of obesity and a host of other problems. Those problems are said to impose healthcare costs on society, an externality that appears to justify a soda tax. Although a considerable body of research supports soda paternalism, a just-as-considerable body of research weakens its pillars. Several studies reveal no direct route from soda to obesity. They also show that obesity is not the public health burden it is often alleged to be. Both points may be moot, however, because research is clear that soda taxes do not reduce consumption by much, if at all, and may in fact lead to higher sugar intake. That leaves little reason for governments to pursue soda taxes. But they are likely to remain in effect, thanks to tireless support from special interest groups— some of whom receive funding from soda tax revenue—as well an army of experts and public health organizations that proclaim society cannot redeem the sins of obesity without a tax.

---

[48] Dadayan (2019).

[49] Hoffer et al. (2014) and Holcombe (1997).

[50] Coase (1960); see also Dahlman (1979).

Soda is not the only beverage to arouse paternalistic attention. Paternalists have long said that drinking alcohol imposes externalities that justify taxes and other policies intended to discourage individuals from choosing to drink excessively, and perhaps from drinking at all. But as Chapter 3 argues, light and moderate alcohol consumption is beneficial to health. Furthermore, the externalities tied to heavy drinking are exaggerated and, when all costs and benefits are considered, may not exist. Research also suggests that alcohol taxes are self-defeating: those who are likely to drink less because of higher prices are the same light and moderate drinkers whose health improves after they drink. Heavy drinkers, by contrast, are not that responsive to higher prices. But like soda, alcohol taxes are likely to stick around. Too many experts testify to their necessity and too many interest groups echo that refrain, all while receiving government grants.

Paternalists are not only concerned with what individuals choose to drink. They also worry about what individuals inhale. Tobacco products are a longstanding target. Smoking—and increasingly, vaping—is accused of imposing unnecessary healthcare costs on society. Like alcohol, however, tobacco's impact is more complicated than what the conventional wisdom dictates. Chapter 4 shows that many of the health risks from tobacco use are overstated. While they have undeniably shorter life expectancies, tobacco users save governments money—a lot of it. Research is also clear that tobacco taxes have little to no effect on smoking. But thanks to experts and interest groups, tobacco taxes aren't likely going away. Too many government programs cannot afford fewer smokers, nor can experts and interest groups funded with grants from tobacco tax revenue.

As Chapter 5 shows, the case for soda, alcohol, and tobacco taxes is more black-and-white than it is for marijuana. Some paternalists want marijuana prohibited; others want it legalized and taxed to pay for its ostensible harms. Quite a few advocates think marijuana is harmless but are willing to pay a tax if that is the price to pay for legal access. Although paternalists mention alarming studies that tell of marijuana's apparent harms—that it is as a gateway to harmful drugs, mental illness, and crime—innumerable studies question whether those harms occur. They show instead that marijuana is mostly harmless, and that it is an effective treatment for dozens of medical conditions. That leaves no case for taxing it, but those who believe in the necessity of expanding government revenue are not likely to let go of what could be a lucrative money maker.

Chapter 6 illustrates that paternalists have turned their attention toward a host of new sins, including meat, plastic bags, automation, and carbon. Each sin supposedly creates tax-justifying externalities: meat harms the environment and health; plastic bags have a negative environmental impact; automation—whether through artificial intelligence or robots—displaces workers; and carbon inflames climate change. The sins may be new, but the background story is not. Time and time again, experts and policymakers appeal to questionable social science to make a case for a sin tax. But for each sin, the weight of all the evidence—not just what paternalists highlight—suggests that no tax is warranted.

Some of the sins do impose externalities, of course. The succeeding chapters show that there are more effective ways to deal with them. More stringent drunk driving laws and stricter enforcement mitigate impaired driving, for instance, and any individual who imposes higher healthcare costs could simply be charged more for health insurance.

But paternalists are not very enthusiastic about those alternatives, especially if it means moving governments away from taxing sin. That would jeopardize government revenue and, at the same time, reduce the scope of government's control over deciding which choices commit an error, go astray, or miss the mark. In other words, eliminating sin taxes is antithetical to progressivism. If there's another theme across *Taxing Sin*, it's that for all their surface motivations, sin taxes are ultimately a stalking horse for a progressive movement that never really ended.

References

Allcott, Hunt, and Cass R. Sunstein. 2015. "Regulating Internalities." *Journal of Policy Analysis and Management* 34(3): 698–705.

Alston, Lee J., Ruth Dupré, and Tomas Nonnenmacher. 2002. "Social Reformers and Regulation: The Prohibition of Cigarettes in the United States and Canada." *Explorations in Economic History* 39(4): 425–445.

Anderson, Gary M. 1997. "Bureaucratic Incentives and the Transition from Taxes to Prohibition." Pp. 139–167 in *Taxing Choice: The Predatory Politics of Fiscal Discrimination*, edited by William F. Shughart II. New Brunswick, NJ: Transaction Publishers.

Battaglio, R. Paul, Jr., Paolo Belardinelli, Nicola Bellé, and Paola Cantarelli. 2019. "Behavioral Public Administration *ad fontes*: A Synthesis of Research on Bounded Rationality, Cognitive Biases, and Nudging in Public Organizations." *Public Administration Review* 79(3): 304–320.

Bellé, Nicola, Paola Cantarelli, and Paola Belardinelli. 2018. "Prospect Theory Goes Public: Experimental Evidence on Cognitive Biases in Public Policy and Management Decisions." *Public Administration Review* 78(6): 828–840.

Berggren, Niclas. 2012. "Time for a Behavioral Political Economy? An Analysis of Articles in Behavioral Economics." *The Review of Austrian Economics* 25(3): 199–221.

Blocker, Jack S. 2006. "Did Prohibition Really Work? Alcohol Prohibition as a Public Health Innovation." *American Journal of Public Health* 96(2): 233–243.

Carruthers, Bruce G. 2016. "The Semantics of Sin Tax: Politics, Morality, and Fiscal Imposition." *Fordham Law Review* 84(6): 2565–2582.

Chang, Andrew C., and Phillip Li. 2015. "Is Economics Research Replicable? Sixty Published Papers from Thirteen Journals Say 'Usually Not'." Finance and Economics Discussion Series 2015-083. Washington, DC: Board of Governors of the Federal Reserve System.

Coase, Ronald H. 1960. "The Problem of Social Cost." *The Journal of Law & Economics* 3: 1–44.

Conly, Sarah. 2012. *Against Autonomy: Justifying Coercive Paternalism.* Cambridge, MA: Cambridge University Press.

Cooley, Charles H. 1909. *Social Organization: A Study of the Larger Mind.* New York, NY: Charles Scribner's Sons.

Cooper, James C., and William E. Kovacic. 2012. "Behavioral Economics: Implications for Regulatory Behavior." *Journal of Regulatory Economics* 41(1): 41–58.

Crain, Mark, Thomas Deaton, Randall Holcombe, and Robert Tollison. 1977. "Rational Choice and the Taxation of Sin." *Journal of Public Economics* 8(2): 239–245.

Croly, Herbert. 1909. *The Promise of American Life.* New York, NY: Macmillan.

Dadayan, Lucy. 2019. "States' Addiction to Sins: Sin Tax Fallacy." *National Tax Journal* 72(4): 723–754.

Dahlman, Carl J. 1979. "The Problem of Externality." *The Journal of Law & Economics* 22(1): 141–162.

Derthick, Martha A. 2012. *Up in Smoke: From Legislation to Litigation in Tobacco Politics.* 3rd ed. Washington, DC: CQ Press.

Dudley, Susan E., and Zhoudan Xie. 2019. "Designing a Choice Architecture for Regulators." *Public Administration Review* 80(1): 151–156.

Ely, James W., Jr. 2012. "The Progressive Era Assault on Individualism and Property Rights." *Social Philosophy and Policy* 29(2): 255–282.

Epstein, Richard A. 2004. "In Defense of the 'Old' Public Health: The Legal Framework for the Regulation of Public Health." *Brooklyn Law Review* 69: 1421–1470.

Fink, Leon. 1997. *Progressive Intellectuals and the Dilemmas of Democratic Commitment*. Cambridge, MA: Harvard University Press.

Fisher, Irving. 1907. "Why Has the Doctrine of Laissez Faire Been Abandoned?" *Science* 25(627): 18–27.

Franco, Annie, Neil Malhotra, and Gabor Simonovits. 2014. "Publication Bias in the Social Sciences: Unlocking the File Drawer." *Science* 345(6203): 1502–1505.

Gigerenzer, Gerd. 2015. "On the Supposed Evidence for Libertarian Paternalism." *Review of Philosophy and Psychology* 6: 361–383.

Gigerenzer, Gerd. 2018. "The Bias Bias in Behavioral Economics." *Review of Behavioral Economics* 5(3–4): 303–336.

Gladden, Washington. 1905. *The New Idolatry and Other Discussions*. New York, NY: McClure, Phillips, & Company.

Glaeser, Edward L. 2006. "Paternalism and Psychology." *University of Chicago Law Review* 73(1): 133–156.

Goodnow, Frank Johnson. 1916. *The American Conception of Liberty and Government*. Providence, RI: Standard Printing Company.

Gostin, Lawrence O. 2016. *Public Health Law: Power, Duty, Restraint*. 3rd ed. Berkeley, CA: University of California Press.

Gruber, Jonathan, and Botond Köszegi. 2001. "Is Addiction 'Rational'? Theory and Evidence." *The Quarterly Journal of Economics* 116(4): 1261–1303.

Haack, Susan. 2013. "Six Signs of Scientism: Part 1." *Skeptical Inquirer* 37(6): 40–45.

Hafner-Burton, Emilie M., D. Alex Hughes, and David G. Victor. 2013. "The Cognitive Revolution and the Political Psychology of Elite Decision Making." *Perspectives on Politics* 11(2): 368–386.

Halberstam, David. 1992. *The Best and the Brightest*. New York, NY: Ballantine Books.

Hall, Peter. 1982. *Great Planning Disasters*. Berkeley, CA: University of California Press.

Hayek, Friedrich A. 1945. "The Use of Knowledge in Society." *The American Economic Review* 35(4): 519–530.

Hayek, Friedrich A. 1952. *The Counter-Revolution of Science*. New York, NY: Liberty Fund.

Hoffer, Adam J., William F. Shughart II, and Michael D. Thomas. 2014. "Sin Taxes and Sindustry: Revenue, Paternalism, and Political Interest." *The Independent Review* 19(1): 47–64.

Holcombe, Randall G. 1997. "Selective Excise Taxation from an Interest-Group Perspective." Pp. 81–103 in *Taxing Choice: The Predatory Politics of Fiscal Discrimination*, edited by William F. Shughart II. New Brunswick, NJ: Transaction Publishers.

Ioannidis, John P.A. 2005. "Why Most Published Research Findings Are False." *PLoS Medicine* 2(8): e124.

Ioannidis, John P.A., T.D. Stanley, and Hristos Doucouliagos. 2017. "The Power of Bias in Economic Research." *The Economic Journal* 127(605): F236–F265.

Javdani, Mohsen, and Ha-Joon Chang. 2019. "Who Said or What Said? Estimating Ideological Bias in Views Among Economists." IZA Discussion Paper No. 12738.

Jolls, Christine, Cass R. Sunstein, and Richard Thaler. 1998. "A Behavioral Approach to Law and Economics." *Stanford Law Review* 50(5): 1471–1551.

Keller, Morton. 1994. *Regulating a New Society: Public Policy and Social Change in America, 1900–1933*. Cambridge, MA: Harvard University Press.

Kersch, Ken I. 2004. *Constructing Civil Liberties: Discontinuities in the Development of American Constitutional Law*. Cambridge, UK: Cambridge University Press.

Klick, Jonathan, and Gregory Mitchell. 2006. "Government Regulation of Irrationality: Moral and Cognitive Hazards." *Minnesota Law Review* 90(6): 1620–1663.

Langum, David J. 1994. *Crossing Over the Line: Legislating Morality and the Mann Act*. Chicago, IL: University of Chicago Press.

Le Grand, Julian, and Bill New. 2015. *Government Paternalism: Nanny State or Helpful Friend?* Princeton, NJ: Princeton University Press.

Leonard, Thomas C. 2017. *Illiberal Reformers: Race, Eugenics, and American Economics in the Progressive Era*. Princeton, NJ: Princeton University Press.

Liu, Xinsheng, James Stoutenborough, and Arnold Vedlitz. 2017. "Bureaucratic Expertise, Overconfidence, and Policy Choice." *Governance* 30(4): 705–725.

Lohmann, Susanne, and Deborah M. Weiss. 2002. "Hidden Taxes and Representative Government: The Political Economy of the Ramsey Rule." *Public Finance Review* 30(6): 579–611.

Mannix, Brian F., and Susan E. Dudley. 2015. "Please Don't Regulate My Internalities." *Journal of Policy Analysis and Management* 34(3): 715–718.

McChesney, Fred S. 1997. *Money for Nothing: Politicians, Rent Extraction, and Political Extortion*. Cambridge, MA: Harvard University Press.

Miron, Jeffrey A., and Jeffrey Zwiebel. 1991. "Alcohol Consumption During Prohibition." *The American Economic Review* 81(2): 242–247.

Mitchell, Gregory. 2004. "Libertarian Paternalism Is an Oxymoron." *Northwestern University Law Review* 99(3): 1245–1277.

Morone, James A. 2003. *Hellfire Nation: The Politics of Sin in American History*. New Haven, CT: Yale University Press.

Moynihan, Donald P., and Stéphane Lavertu. 2011. "Cognitive Biases in Governing: Technology Preferences in Election Administration." *Public Administration Review* 72(1): 68–77.

O'Toole, Randal. 2007. *The Best-Laid Plans: How Government Planning Harms Your Quality of Life, Your Pocketbook, and Your Future*. Washington, DC: Cato Institute.

Peltzman, Sam. 1976. "Toward a More General Theory of Regulation." *The Journal of Law and Economics* 19(2): 211–240.

Rachlinski, Jeffrey J., and Cynthia R. Farina. 2002. "Cognitive Psychology and Optimal Government Design." *Cornell Law Review* 87(2): 549–615.

Rauschenbusch, Walter. 1907. *Christianity and the Social Crisis*. New York, NY: Macmillan.

Rizzo, Maril J., and Douglas Glen Whitman. 2009. "The Knowledge Problem of New Paternalism." *BYU Law Review* 2009(4): 905–968.

Roberts, Patrick S., and Kris Wernstedt. 2019. "Decision Biases and Heuristics Among Emergency Managers: Just Like the Public They Manage For?" *The American Review of Public Administration* 49(3): 292–308.

Rodgers, Daniel T. 1982. "In Search of Progressivism." *Reviews in American History* 10(4): 113–132.

Ross, Edward Alsworth. 1901. *Social Control: A Survey of the Foundations of Order*. New York, NY: Macmillan.

Seligman, Edwin R.A. 1890. "The General Property Tax." *Political Science Quarterly* 5(1): 24–64.

Sowell, Thomas. 1995. *The Vision of the Anointed: Self-Congratulation as a Basis for Social Policy*. New York, NY: Basic Books.

Sowell, Thomas. 2007. *A Conflict of Visions: Ideological Origins of Political Struggles*. New York, NY: Basic Books.

Stigler, George J. 1971. "The Theory of Economic Regulation." *Bell Journal of Economics and Management Science* 2(1): 3–21.

Tasic, Slavisa. 2009. "The Illusion of Regulatory Competence." *Critical Review* 21(4): 423–436.

Thaler, Richard H., and Cass R. Sunstein. 2008. *Nudge: Improving Decisions about Health, Wealth, and Happiness*. New York, NY: Penguin.

The New Republic. 1915. "The Bill of Rights Again." April 17, pp. 272–273.

Veetil, Vipin P. 2011. "Libertarian Paternalism Is an Oxymoron: An Essay in Defence of Liberty." *European Journal of Law and Economics* 31(3): 321–334.

Viscusi, W. Kip, and Ted Gayer. 2010. "Behavioral Public Choice: The Behavioral Paradox of Government Policy." *Harvard Journal of Law & Public Policy* 38(3): 973–1007.

Whitman, Douglas Glen, and Mario J. Rizzo. 2007. "Paternalist Slopes." *NYU Journal of Law & Liberty* 2(3): 411–443.

Wright, Joshua D., and Douglas H. Ginsburg. 2012. "Behavioral Law and Economics: Its Origins, Fatal Flaws, and Implications for Liberty." *Northwestern University Law Review* 106(3): 1033–1088.

Zamir, Eyal, and Raanan Sulitzeanu-Kenan. 2018. "Explaining Self-Interested Behavior of Public-Spirited Policy Makers." *Public Administration Review* 78(4): 579–592.

CHAPTER 2

Taxing Soda

Sugar and politics have mixed for over ten thousand years. Sugarcane was domesticated in present-day New Guinea as early as 8000 BC before it spread to Persia and the Mediterranean. As demand grew in the fifteenth and sixteenth centuries, Europeans carried sugarcane to the New World, along with colonial governments, slave labor, and the plantation business model. It soon joined other goods on the trade routes that crisscrossed the Atlantic Ocean. Sugar substitutes like high fructose corn syrup—and all the controversies associated with them—developed much later.[1]

Yet it was not until the end of the twentieth century that paternalists turned a critical eye toward sugar. They believed it caused the secular sins of weight gain and obesity, which studies linked to an elevated risk of diabetes, cardiovascular disease, certain types of cancer, and even some mental health conditions. In light of the healthcare costs and other externalities obesity was assumed to impose on society, paternalists called for everything from government dietary guidelines to a tax on foods and beverages they believed were behind the oft-mentioned obesity epidemic.[2]

---

[1] Sugar was not always tax-free during that time; like other commodities, it was often subject to tariffs. More comprehensive discussions of sugar's political history are found in Abbott (2008), Parker (2012), and Taubes (2016).

[2] It may seem like mere semantics, but the sustained increase in obesity means that it is a pandemic, not an epidemic.

© The Author(s) 2021
M. Thom, *Taxing Sin*,
https://doi.org/10.1007/978-3-030-49176-5_2

But not all foods and beverages. Paternalists were especially sour on sugar-sweetened drinks. And while some beverages such as fruit juices and flavored coffee escaped heavy scrutiny, soda was not so lucky. Before long, obesity was rarely discussed without reference to soda. Instead of banning it, however, paternalists argued for a soda tax. They said a tax would nudge consumers toward less sinful beverage choices, reduce sugar consumption, and generate government revenue to counteract obesity's externalities. The tax was also pitched as an effective way to break an unhealthy habit rooted in cognitive biases, and as a way to fight back against the beverage industry—pejoratively nicknamed "big soda"—and its heartless exploitation of thirsty consumers.

Soda paternalism spread like wildfire. The World Health Organization urged policymakers to fight obesity with taxes. A press release issued by the Organization on World Obesity Day 2016 even provided suggestions on how policymakers might rally public opinion.[3] Other public health groups, including the American Medical Association, the American Heart Association, and the American Academy of Pediatrics, also endorsed soda taxes.

Experts championed soda paternalism in academic journals.[4] One expert wrote a book about "taking on big soda."[5] Three others argued in a *Los Angeles Times* column that a tax could save "millions of lives."[6] In the *New York Times*, Nobel Prize-winning economist Paul Krugman chided United States presidential candidate Bernie Sanders for opposing a soda tax. It may hurt the poor, Krugman conceded, but "soda consumption really is destructive" and the revenue will pay for "more important" things.[7]

Media coverage largely agreed with the experts. One study found that pro-soda tax arguments in news stories outnumbered anti-tax arguments by a margin of over two-to-one. According to another survey, major media outlets in the United Kingdom published 930 stories about the

---

[3] The press release, "WHO Urges Global Action to Curtail Consumption and Health Impacts of Sugary Drinks," was issued October 11, 2016.

[4] For two of many examples of experts extolling the virtues of soda taxes, see Brownell and Frieden (2009) and Brownell et al. (2009).

[5] Nestle (2015).

[6] Allcott et al. (2019).

[7] Krugman (2016).

merits of soda taxes in one year alone compared to only 182 stories on portion control.[8]

Philanthropic organizations chipped in financial support. The Robert Wood Johnson Foundation contributed millions of dollars to soda tax activism.[9] Bloomberg Philanthropies spent nearly $20 million to push a soda tax in Mexico.[10] Bloomberg also funded "Advocating for Sugar-Sweetened Beverage Taxation," a full-color, 36-page report issued by the Bloomberg School of Public Health at Johns Hopkins University. The report offered a list of strategies paternalists should use to lobby policymakers to enact a soda tax.

But the collective impact of public health groups, experts, media, and philanthropists was practically inert compared to special interest groups, which framed soda taxes as something much broader. The Children's Food Campaign, a British organization dedicated to "children's rights, parent power and government action," argued that a tax was essential to "protect children," "save lives," and "save taxpayers' money." Policymakers must act, they said, to oppose powerful forces against soda taxes, including "big soda," "big food," "big tobacco," "lobbyists for the tobacco industry," "obesity-deniers," "anti-science ideologues," and "Twitter trolls." After the tax became law, the Campaign publicly thanked various labor unions and environmental groups for their support.[11]

***

[8] Niederdeppe et al. (2013) and McKinsey Global Institute (2014), respectively.

[9] The Robert Wood Johnson Foundation has argued that it never adopted a position on soda taxes, but that's not true. After a 2016 *Reason* magazine article noted the Foundation's relationship with pro-tax initiatives, a representative complained that characterizing them as "a supporter of soda taxes" was "inaccurate," claiming instead that the Foundation had "not taken a position on the issue." But in 2009, the Foundation donated $3.5 million to the Campaign for Healthy Kids, which lobbied for soda taxes in three states (Mississippi, New Mexico, and Washington) as well as the city of Philadelphia. When the Campaign shifted tactics away from tax advocacy, Foundation officials were reportedly "disappointed" because they had "encouraged" the group "to advocate for soda taxes." For more information, see Linnekin (2016) and Neuman (2010).

[10] Evich (2015) and Rosenberg (2016). Other elements of billionaire Michael Bloomberg's empire also lent help to soda paternalism. After a soda took effect in Mexico, *Bloomberg News* published an editorial praising the tax's "success." When California policymakers enacted a law to restrict local beverage taxes, a *Bloomberg News* editorial criticized them. See *Bloomberg News* (2016, 2018).

[11] Quotes taken from the Coalition's website; see also http://sustainweb.org/news/apr16_anatomy_campaign_win/.

Stateside, the Healthy Child Coalition, a group formed to promote a soda tax in Berkeley, California, was even more explicit about framing soda taxes as a fight against "big soda." Their website—quite literally berkeleyvsbigsoda.com—depicted a cross-section of society, with each of the pictured activists holding one of two signs, one that read "Berkeley vs. Big Soda" and the other "Protect Our Children." Several progressive organizations, including the American Civil Liberties Union, and labor unions, including the California Nurses Association, California Federation of Teachers, and the Berkeley Federation of Teachers, supported the tax.

That "for the children" rallying cry metastasized throughout the United States. The Coalition Against Hunger, a group based in Philadelphia, Pennsylvania, promoted a soda tax with an editorial that described it as "an investment in Philly's children."[12] They were joined by the Greater Philadelphia Cultural Alliance, which described the tax as an investment in "children, families, and neighborhoods" with revenue for "high-quality pre-K education, parks, rec centers, and libraries." The picture chosen to accompany the Alliance's editorial in local media depicted children of color sitting at a table upon which pieces of multicolored clay spelled out "I have a dream."[13] Like the Berkeley initiative, several public sector labor unions supported the tax.[14]

Other American groups parroted the approach. Pre-K for Santa Fe, New Mexico, said a soda tax was necessary to fund "high quality early learning programs." Healthy Boulder Kids, which campaigned for a tax in Boulder, Colorado, promoted it as critical to "improving the health of children and families." After voters approved the tax, a campaign manager declared it "a major victory" for "all our children."[15] The Coalition for Healthy Kids and Education, a group formed to promote a tax in and around Portland, Oregon, said it was necessary to "ensure our kids grow up healthy and strong."[16]

---

[12] Fisher (2016).

[13] Lyon (2016).

[14] The unions included two UNITE HERE locals, three American Federation of State, County, and Municipal Employees locals, and four Service Employees International Union locals.

[15] Burness (2016).

[16] Quotes taken from each group's respective website.

Advocacy from all corners undoubtedly affected public opinion. A 2017 poll conducted for Politico and Harvard University found 57% of adults in the United States supported a soda tax.[17] Other surveys showed support was higher among those who believe soda causes obesity.[18]

Policymakers responded in kind, translating soda paternalism into law worldwide.[19] Over 30 countries tax soda at the national level, including France, Hungary, Ireland, Mexico, Nauru, Chile, the United Arab Emirates, and the United Kingdom. Although the United States federal government enacted soda and other beverage taxes during World War I and the Great Depression, they were later repealed. Democrats in 2009 considered a new federal tax to generate revenue for public healthcare programs, but the proposal failed to gain traction.[20] Local governments instead levy most soda taxes in the United States.

* * *

Soda paternalism rests on an assumption is that soda is a culprit—arguably *the* culprit—behind rising obesity. Without question, multiple government data sources report that both the adolescent and adult obesity rates have sharply increased.[21] Reflecting expert opinion on the matter, a study funded by the American Heart Association in 2006 concluded that policymakers should "discourage consumption of sugary drinks" because they

[17] Evich (2017).

[18] Donaldson et al. (2015).

[19] Some taxes took effect prior to widespread concern over soda's effect on obesity or human health in general. Regardless of the original motivations, however, any movement to reduce or eliminate soda taxes is now challenged by invoking the paternalistic conventional wisdom that soda consumption is deleterious to health.

[20] Adamy (2009).

[21] The body mass index ("BMI"), which compares a person's weight to their height, is something of an official way to determine their obesity status. The BMI is used by government agencies, including the Centers for Disease Control and Prevention, and health groups, including the American Cancer Society, to measure obesity and report population-wide statistics about the obesity epidemic (or pandemic). The index was originally developed in 1835 by Adolphe Quetelet, a Belgian social scientist. Among other flaws, the BMI formula does not incorporate waist size or differentiate between fat and muscle mass. A great many healthy individuals are classified as obese by their government.

are "associated with weight gain and obesity."[22] Since its publication, that study has been cited over 2900 times.

But data trends directly undermine the notion that there is a direct connection from drinking soda to tipping the scale into obese territory. Soft drink consumption in the United States more than doubled from 1960 to 1980, yet over that two-decade period, the obesity rate was flat.[23] Between 2005 and 2010, the number of calories in beverages sold in schools plunged by 90%—mostly because of voluntary action taken by "big soda"—but the adolescent obesity rate rose 10%.[24] Studies also show that obesity's latter-day surge occurred alongside plummeting soda consumption.[25]

Those contradictions beg the question of whether the causal link between soda and weight gain is as strong as paternalists say.

In fact, a growing body of research contradicts that conventional wisdom. In one review of studies on the relationship between soda and obesity, more than two-thirds reported no evidence that the former affects the latter.[26] Another review of the research stated that the association between soda and obesity was "near zero" among children and adolescents.[27] An analysis of diets over five years likewise found "no association between sugar-sweetened beverage consumption, juice consumption, and adolescent weight gain."[28] Based on that evidence, it is no wonder that the authors of yet another study concluded that reducing beverage consumption would not reduce obesity.[29]

What does explain obesity's well-documented rise? Studies have identified several factors that encourage weight gain, both directly and

[22] Malik et al. (2006).

[23] Marlow and Shiers (2010a, b).

[24] Turner and Chaloupka (2012) and Wescott et al. (2012). Adolescent obesity rates are drawn from the Centers for Disease Control and Prevention's National Health and Nutrition Examination Survey, which reported a rate in the United States of 15.4% in 2005–2006 and 16.9% in 2009–2010.

[25] Bleich et al. (2018), Rehm et al. (2016), and Welsh et al. (2011).

[26] Vartanian et al. (2007).

[27] Forshee et al. (2008). The authors subsequently corrected a minor error in their analysis, but the correction did not change their findings. See also Trumbo and Rivers (2014).

[28] Vanselow et al. (2009).

[29] Mattes et al. (2011).

indirectly, such as economic conditions, agricultural subsidies, declining physical activity, and technological change.[30]

Paternalism is another factor. Experts and policymakers spent decades urging the public to eat a carbohydrate-rich diet with daily servings of pasta, rice, bread, and cereal. Dietary guidelines developed and publicized by goveragencies, like the United States Department of Agriculture's infamous "food pyramid," conveyed the message. But over-consumption of grains and starches promotes weight gain.[31]

Experts further encouraged a diet low in fat. That spurred demand for "low fat" foods in restaurants and grocery stores. But studies show "low fat" product labels entice people into overeating.[32]

Studies also link weight gain to a decline in cigarette smoking, which is facilitated in part by paternalistic public health campaigns against the sin of tobacco use. Because smokers tend to consume fewer calories and have a higher metabolism than nonsmokers, increasing the ranks of nonsmokers has, according to the authors of one study, "contributed to the upward trend in obesity."[33]

* * *

Despite evidence to the contrary, paternalists remain firm in the conviction that drinking soda causes obesity and other problems. That hundreds of millions of people are overweight would not be cause for concern, they say, except that those same people impose externalities, especially through added, avoidable healthcare costs. In 2020, the Centers for Disease Control and Prevention, a federal health agency in the United States, listed as an "adult obesity fact" that the condition is responsible

---

[30] Cutler et al. (2003), Lakdawalla and Philipson (2009), Posner and Philipson (2003), Rosen (2008), Wallinga (2010), and Zhao and Kaestner (2010).

[31] Carden and Carr (2013) and Choo et al. (2015). In 2020, the header image on the World Health Organization's obesity fact sheet website (https://www.who.int/en/news-room/fact-sheets/detail/obesity-and-overweight) depicted a smiling, but overweight person (wearing a shirt with buttons pushed to the brink) sitting at a table upon which the following foods were shown: toast (with and without avocado), yogurt, two bowls of fruit, and glasses of what appear to be juice. All are loaded with carbohydrates.

[32] Chandon and Wansink (2007), Provencher et al. (2009), and Wansink and Chandon (2006).

[33] Chou et al. (2004).

for healthcare costs of nearly $150 billion annually, an estimate drawn from a 2009 study.[34]

That estimate and others like it should be viewed with skepticism. While the study's authors controlled for a variety of confounding factors that might impact a person's healthcare costs, including five different categories for race, they failed to control for other important variables, such as overall fitness, exercise levels, and diet quality. But those factors play a definite role in a person's health and, ultimately, their healthcare costs.

The study's more significant flaw was a failure to include obesity's financial benefits to society. While the obese have higher healthcare costs in life, they also have shorter life expectancies. Morbid as it may be, premature death among the obese yields cost savings, including expenses for healthcare and other programs like pensions and long-term care that are avoided entirely by dying at age 75, for instance, instead of age 85.[35] Multiple studies confirm this tradeoff: the nonobese—not the obese—impose higher lifetime healthcare costs.[36]

That completely undermines the argument for taxing soda or any other food or beverage because of its supposed role in imposing externalities and it raises questions about the wisdom of other governmental approaches to reducing obesity.

It is reasonable to wonder why the tradeoff is not widely acknowledged. The explanation is simple: few experts ever conduct a full accounting of obesity's lifetime costs and benefits. One review found only a single study that had done so.[37] The typical approach, like that taken in the study cited by the Centers for Disease Control and Prevention, is to estimate population-wide healthcare costs that might stem from obesity and report that figure as its externality. But by leaving out costs avoided because of premature death, those estimates are wrong. Those estimates also leave out the new healthcare and other government program costs that would result from reducing premature death.

Ironically, reducing obesity imposes externalities.

[34] See "Adult Obesity Facts," available at https://www.cdc.gov/obesity/data/adult.html. The study referenced is Finkelstein et al. (2009). The estimate was for the United States only.

[35] See discussion in Bhattacharya and Sood (2011).

[36] Allison et al. (1999), McPherson (2008), and van Baal et al. (2008).

[37] van Baal et al. (2008).

Even conceding paternalists' argument that obesity imposes a burden on society, evidence suggests that most of that burden is an internality confined to the obese. Many studies conclude that employers transfer perceived obesity-related costs to obese employees via lower wages, not to the workforce at large. Hiring discrimination against the obese is not an externality, either, because the nonobese benefit from added employment opportunities.[38]

Of course, paternalists argue that soda and obesity have other negative consequences, such as an increased risk of diabetes. Writing in the *New York Times* in 2017, two self-described "healthy food advocates" triggered that alarm by referring to a study that concluded drinking one or two sodas per day increased a person's risk of type 2 diabetes by 26%.[39] An effective way to address the "major public health threat" created by sugary beverages was, they suggested, a soda tax.

That 26% figure deserves the same skepticism applied to estimates of obesity's apparent externalities. The number reported in the study was a relative risk, not an absolute risk. That means that if Person A drinks no soda and Person B drinks one or two servings per day, Person B's diabetes risk is 26% higher than Person A's. If Person A's risk is 20%, then Person B's risk is 25.2%.[40] Or, from a different vantage point, Person A's chance of never developing diabetes is 80%, while Person B's chance is about 75%. The twice-daily soda drinker still has a higher diabetes risk, but it's not even close to double that of a nondrinker—and it hardly makes soda appear to be "major public health threat."

The rush to stigmatize soda and sugar with fears of obesity, disease, and lost wages has distracted attention from a basic but essential question: why do people drink it in the first place? Is it because they are overwhelmed b y ġnorance and cognitive biases? Is it because they can't resist the temptation of "big soda" and its exploitative marketing techniques?

[38] Atella et al. (2008), Bhattacharya and Bundorf (2009), Cawley (2004), and Han et al. (2009); see also Nortan and Han (2008).

[39] Lappé and Bronsing-Lazalde (2017); the study referenced is Malik et al. (2010). That study was a meta-analysis of eight studies on the risk of metabolic syndrome and diabetes risk imposed by sugar-sweetened beverages, but two of the eight actually looked at diet soda.

[40] The math is straightforward: 26% of 20% is 5.2 percentage points; therefore, 26% more than 20% is 25.2%. A person who drinks no soda already has a 20–30% likelihood of developing the disease at some point in their life (Narayan et al. 2003). Risk varies by age, gender, and race, and by several lifestyle factors.

Not exactly. Paternalists may not want to hear it, but sugar serves a biological purpose. The brain depends on glucose for a majority of its energy.[41] Soda may not be the best source of that energy, but it is nevertheless a source, and an affordable one.

And that is not the only need soda may fulfill.

Many people consume soda and other sugary foods and beverages because they feel disconnected from the world around them. Studies show individuals that feel lonely, that lack supportive friends, family, and coworkers, and that lack other emotional supports consume more sugar-sweetened beverages, but not more artificially sweetened beverages. The relationship is present in both men and women, across age groups, and in diverse cultural settings.[42] The reason why is that feelings of isolation and loneliness are cognitively demanding and prompt the brain to signal that it needs more energy. Once again, soda may not be the best source of that energy, and it is definitely not the best substitute for connectedness, but it still fulfills a genuine—and very human—need.[43]

* * *

Setting aside the debate over soda and obesity, what about soda taxes? Do they work? At first glance, a wealth of evidence supports the contention that soda taxes pay public health dividends, redeeming the sinful choice to imbibe a sugary drink.

One study reported that a small tax would reduce weight, lower health-care costs, and generate government revenue, compelling its authors to call it "a promising public health response to the obesity epidemic."[44] Other studies conclude that a tax could reduce consumption by up to 25%.[45] Research on the effectiveness of a 20% tax estimate that it may reduce obesity in countries as varied as South Africa, Australia, and

---

[41] Studies show that our blood sugar level drops immediately after completing cognitively-demanding tasks (Scholey et al. 2001).

[42] Ein-Dor et al. (2015), Henriksen et al. (2014), and Laitinen et al. (2002).

[43] Taking it for granted that soda drinkers consume soda because of cognitive biases and not because of other reasons is an illustration of the "bias bias" mentioned in Chapter 1—i.e., the prejudice many paternalists have that compels them to blame choices they don't like on cognitive biases.

[44] Long et al. (2015).

[45] Andreyeva et al. (2011) and Wang et al. (2012).

the United Kingdom. The authors of the United Kingdom study christened the soda tax a "promising population measure to target population obesity."[46]

But each of these studies and many others that report comparable findings has a common weakness: the analysis relies on a simulation. In a simulation study, experts model the impact of a soda tax that could have been implemented in the past or that might take effect in the future. The alternative to a simulation is an observational study in which experts estimate the impact of a real tax. Think of them as a natural experiment that absorbs real-world conditions that statistical simulations may leave out. The difference is subtle but important: simulation studies forecast what might have or might happen, and observational studies suggest what really occurred.

Studies in each category usually report different findings. Simulations tend to predict that soda taxes improve health. But observational studies tend to find, as one research team described it, "no statistically significant associations between sugar-sweetened beverage taxes and weight gain."[47]

They also differ in prevalence. Across soda tax research, simulations outnumber observational studies by a margin of about three-to-one.[48]

The relative dearth of observational studies on soda taxes is regrettable because they are much more revealing about their real-world impact. One study took advantage of a short-lived tax in Ohio. The authors found that, although the percentage of Ohioans considered overweight declined slightly after the tax took effect, it rebounded one year later, and the obesity rate never fell. They concluded there was "very little evidence that the large tax … had any detectable effect on population weight." They also reported that each percentage-point increase in soda taxes elsewhere in the United States had increased, not reduced, calorie intake.[49]

Several other observational studies also report that soda taxes have little to no public health impact. One discovered that each percentage-point tax increase in the United States from 1990 through 2006 reduced obesity by just one-hundredth of one percent. According to that study,

---

[46] Briggs et al. (2013), Manyema et al. (2014), and Nomaguchi et al. (2017).

[47] Bes-Rastrollo et al. (2016).

[48] Bes-Rastrollo et al. (2016), Niebylski et al. (2015), and Shemilt et al. (2013) also report bias in favor of simulation studies but do not report a ratio.

[49] Fletcher et al. (2015).

raising soda taxes to a level comparable with tobacco taxes, a change sought by paternalists that argue soda taxes are too low to elicit significant behavioral change, would reduce the obesity rate by less than one percentage-point.[50] Another study examined a soda tax in Maine and a second tax in Ohio by analyzing beverage sales data in each state. The authors concluded that neither tax "had a statistically significant impact on the consumption of soft drinks."[51] Echoing so many others, a study of Philadelphia's soda tax failed to "detect a significant reduction in calorie and sugar intake."[52]

The contrast between simulation and observational studies is striking when comparing their findings for a specific country.

Take Mexico, where the Bloomberg-supported soda tax aimed at curbing obesity and diabetes took effect in 2014. A simulation predicted the tax would reduce sugar consumption enough to eliminate hundreds of thousands of cases of diabetes, stroke, heart attack, and premature death.[53] Although an observational study found consumption declined after the tax, the authors limited their evaluation to changes to store-bought beverages. They failed to incorporate the possibility that individuals responded to the tax by substituting for non-store-bought drinks, including homemade lemonade or aguas frescas, a popular sugary beverage. The authors also failed to control for outside factors that may have contributed to lower consumption, including a public health campaign that coincided with the tax.[54] An observational study that addressed these and other factors concluded the Mexican soda tax did not influence obesity.[55]

Chile may be an even better illustration. In 2014 the Chilean government increased its tax on beverages with a high sugar concentration. A simulation concluded the tax would lead to "meaningful" and "significant" reductions in sugar consumption across socioeconomic groups.[56] But an observational study conducted after the tax increase—written by

[50] Fletcher et al. (2010a).

[51] Colantuoni and Rojas (2015).

[52] Seiler et al. (2019).

[53] Sánchez-Romero et al. (2016).

[54] Colchero et al. (2016).

[55] Aguilar et al. (2015).

[56] Caro et al. (2017).

some of the same experts behind the simulation—revealed that it reduced consumption by just four percent, far from the "meaningful" and "significant" level simulated. Furthermore, most of the decline occurred in high-income households, where obesity and diabetes rates were already lower. The effect was not, as simulated, consistent across socioeconomic groups. When drawing on Chile's real-world experience and not its simulated experience, the observational study's authors concluded that soda taxes "are unlikely to promote the changes" in sugar consumption needed to reduce obesity and related health conditions.[57]

Admittedly, simulation and observational studies are not the only kind of research used to justify soda taxes. Experimental studies that try to recreate real-world conditions are common but have flaws of their own.

Consider a study from the Netherlands, in which researchers recruited 102 university students and staff to purchase a week's worth of groceries at a virtual supermarket, a computer-based facsimile of a real grocery store. Participants were assigned to either a control group for whom prices were typical or a treatment group for whom prices reflected a substantial tax on sugar-sweetened beverages. Because participants in the treatment group purchased about one fewer litres of sugar-sweetened beverages than the control group, the study's authors concluded that the tax was "effective" and "had no negative side-effects."[58]

While the experts deserve credit for designing an experiment—something that is never easy in the social sciences—their approach had several problems. One issue is that participants did not reflect the Dutch population, or any population for that matter. Another problem is that purchases were not made in a real grocery store, but a virtual facsimile, and fake money, not real money, was spent. Yet another issue was that purchases were evaluated once, not over weeks, months, or years.

The use of a limited timeframe in any study is especially troublesome. A different experiment that used a more representative sample and collected data on actual purchases made in real grocery stores found that a tax on high-calorie beverages reduced consumption, but only temporarily. The effect vanished within three months.[59]

---

[57] Caro et al. (2018).

[58] Waterlander et al. (2014).

[59] Hanks et al. (2013).

Given these findings, it is no surprise that a review of over 800 studies concluded the effects of soda taxes and other policies intended to alter dietary choices are "less compelling than some proponents have claimed" and that, in the future, experts "should include measurement of people's actual behavioral responses."[60]

It also comes as no surprise that a McKinsey Global Institute analysis ranked beverage taxation as one of the least effective strategies to reduce obesity. The most effective was portion control.[61]

* * *

The information presented thus far presents a jarring reality that does not conform to the conventional wisdom about soda, obesity, and soda taxes. How is it possible that so much research and so many experts could be so wrong? After all, most of the influential studies on the relationship between soda and obesity, and on the merits of soda taxes, appear in highly respected peer-reviewed academic journals. Many are written by experts with advanced degrees, some of whom don trust-inspiring white lab coats.

That's all true. But it's also true that many of those studies have fundamental errors. Whether their research draws on a simulation models or observational methods, experts routinely fail to incorporate characteristics of the environment in which individuals chose to consume soda, and that leads experts to draw conclusions that bear little semblance to reality.[62] At the risk of being unduly harsh, when garbage goes into an academic study, then garbage will inevitably come back out.

One flaw is the assumption that soda buyers will happily comply with a tax that raises the cost of a product they like—a tax that also carries the unsolicited message that soda is socially unacceptable. In reality, most people do not relish being on the receiving end of paternalism, and some respond to efforts to control a particular behavior by increasing that very behavior, a process known as reactance.[63] Inspired by New

---

[60] Shemilt et al. (2013).

[61] McKinsey Global Institute (2014).

[62] Simulation models also tend to ignore corporate reactions. For example, most fail to anticipate beverage industry responses, such as product reformulations, designed to help products escape soda taxes and other regulations. See Shemilt et al. (2013).

[63] Brehm and Brehm (1981).

York City's failed attempt to limit soda sizes under then-Mayor Michael Bloomberg, a group of researchers used an experiment to determine how people respond to such constraints. They found that trying to limit soda sizes led to higher consumption. Thus, stigmatizing soda can lead to an unintended consequence: individuals drink more of it, not less.[64]

Another flaw is the failure to account for substitution, another unintended consequence. A simulation might estimate the effect of a 20% soda tax and conclude that it will lower sugar consumption while ignoring that in most locations where soda is available, there are dozens of other sugary products an individual may choose to buy instead. If the tax only applies to soda, they might buy a sugar-sweetened coffee or dairy product, such as chocolate-flavored milk. If the tax applies to all sugar-sweetened beverages, they might buy a fruit juice, which many governments exempt from taxation. If the tax truly applies to all sugary drinks, they might buy candy, ice cream, a pastry, or another baked good. If the tax applies to all sugary foods, they might buy another item high in other carbohydrates. The tax could also be avoided altogether by purchasing soda where there is no tax, or from a store that breaks the law and doesn't collect it.

The failure to address substitution may be the fatal flaw in any soda tax study because it is how individuals respond to higher prices. One observational study found that although a soda tax led to a moderate decline in soft drink consumption among children and adolescents, the reduction was "completely offset" by increased consumption of other high-calorie beverages.[65] Another study concluded that adolescents in schools that banned soda responded by purchasing more energy drinks and other sugar-sweetened beverages.[66] Even a simulation—but one that modeled a variety of possible substitutions—found that taxes lowered soda consumption but also nudged individuals toward foods that led to higher overall fat and sodium intake.[67] A study on Berkeley's soda tax found after the levy went into effect that the average resident consumed six fewer calories per day from taxable beverages, but 32 more calories per day from nontaxable drinks, like milkshakes and smoothies.[68]

---

[64] Wilson et al. (2013).

[65] Fletcher et al. (2010b).

[66] Taber et al. (2015); see also Capacci et al. (2018).

[67] Zhen et al. (2014).

[68] Silver et al. (2017).

A far more frustrating mistake across soda tax research is experts' penchant for interpreting correlation as proof of causation. That's an inexcusable mistake for any person who has ever completed a single statistics course. Many experts conduct studies that conclude that higher soda taxes lead to lower soda consumption, but in many of those studies, taxes can't be said to have caused lower consumption because the decline started before the tax took effect. In other studies, including many encompassed in the oft-cited American Heart Association Study that urged governments to reduce soda consumption, experts failed to control for other factors that affect weight and failed to track study participants for long periods. Those mistakes lead to a "false positive" conclusion that soda taxes are effective.

What these errors have in common is what Hayek observed in 1945: the tendency among experts to approach complex problems with excessively simplistic assumptions and statistical models. Across the board, that leads to findings that support rather than contradict paternalism.

* * *

Paternalists do not take kindly to evidence that undermines any campaign for soda taxes, whether its "for the children" or another socially-valued constituency. A common rebuttal to contradictory perspectives is to allege that the evidence is somehow tied to the soda industry and is therefore not to be taken seriously. According to the expert who wrote a book about "taking on big soda," industry-funded research causes a prejudice among those conducting that research that is "almost always unconscious, unintentional, and unrecognized"—invisible to all except, apparently, that particular expert.[69]

The industry bias storyline is often conveyed uncritically in the media. A 2015 front-page article in the *New York Times*, one that spurred follow-up coverage from National Public Radio, described the industry's troubling role in sponsoring academic research. The article referenced a report that concluded industry-funded studies were "five times more likely to find no link between sugary drinks and weight gain."[70] It quoted two experts—one identified as a "professor" and the other as an "author,"

---

[69] Nestle (2016).

[70] O'Connor (2015); the report referenced is Bes-Rastrollo et al. (2013).

even though both were industry critics and soda tax advocates—troubled by Coca-Cola's preference toward emphasizing physical activity as a way to reduce obesity.

The article left out a few caveats. For starters, the report in question assessed only 17 studies out of thousands. Furthermore, perhaps confusing correlation with causation, its authors did not prove industry sponsorship biased a study's results. They also failed to consider how bias could have persistently escaped notice from peer reviewers and the editors at academic journals that published the research.

Interestingly enough, and without any *New York Times* or National Public Radio coverage on bias, the report's authors later published a study that concluded policymakers should impose a soda tax even though it would have little effect on obesity.[71]

Although the media has yet to take notice, fair evaluations of industry-sponsored research undermine the charge that it is biased. One study concluded that in terms of "protocol, statistical analysis, and presentation of results," studies that disclosed industry funding were no different than studies without it.[72] That finding was reinforced by another study four years later.[73]

That's not to say there aren't some differences. Industry-funded studies are more likely to acknowledge that soda's health impact is ambiguous, which is consistent with any review of existing research—all of the research, not just the studies that support paternalism.[74]

Industry-funded studies are also more likely to dissect their critics' research methods. Far from welcoming scientific scrutiny, however, the authors of a study that alleged industry funding was a problem complained that "shaping the debate around scientific methods can be another strategy that corporations use for their benefit."[75]

If directing attention toward research methods benefits the industry, what does that indicate about the quality of anti-industry studies, including those used to justify soda taxes? The industry, and the public,

---

[71] Bes-Rastrollo et al. (2016).

[72] Kaiser et al. (2012).

[73] Chartres et al. (2016).

[74] Massougbodji et al. (2014).

[75] Fabbri et al. (2018).

have good reason to scrutinize the research used to advance soda pater-nalism. The problems are much deeper than relying on simulation studies, ignoring behavioral responses and substitution, overlooking long-term effects, and confusing correlation and causation.

Bias is one issue, but not the type paternalists fret over. An investiga-tion of obesity journals found publication bias in favor of soda paternalism "in the service of what may be perceived to be righteous ends." The investigation also found that when referring to prior research, experts tend to "describe results in a misleadingly positive way" such as by claiming a causal relationship exists when it does not.[76] That overreach has become more frequent and is more prevalent in studies conducted without beverage industry support.[77]

Other types of bias are also a problem. A review that concluded "strong evidence" showed soda taxes improve public health—that has since been cited over 100 times—arrived at that conclusion after its authors excluded studies they felt "failed to document any outcomes of interest," a textbook case of confirmation bias.[78]

Another more nefarious issue is that far too much soda-related research is a lazy social science. An analysis of studies that claimed to document a relationship between soda and obesity found that "surprisingly few" satis-fied best practices.[79] About one-quarter of the articles in peer-reviewed obesity journals misinterpret common statistical measures.[80]

Some experts also resort to using misleading statistics. A seminal article in *The New England Journal of Medicine* by Kelly Brownell, accurately labeled a "soda-tax advocate" in the *New York Times*, recommended policymakers enact a soda tax. Brownell and his coauthors—including two professors from Harvard University, the then-current surgeon general

---

[76] Cope and Allison (2010); note that Forshee et al. (2008) also find evidence of "publication bias against studies that do not report statistically significant findings." As an example, a revealing study funded by the Robert Wood Johnson Foundation suggested soda taxes would need to be significantly higher to influence consumption, even though the study's analysis offered no evidence to suggest that recommendation (Powell et al. 2009).

[77] Menachemi et al. (2013).

[78] Niebylski et al. (2015).

[79] Weed et al. (2011).

[80] Tajeu et al. (2012).

of Arkansas, and then-current health commissioner of New York City—argued that government action was necessary because, through 2002, the "intake of caloric beverages doubled in the United States."[81]

Whether or not that's true is beside the point: the statistic was seven years old. Why use an out-of-date number? Because if the paternalists that wrote the article had used an up-to-date number, then they would have had to report that soda consumption *declined* by 16% without taxation, yet obesity continued to rise.[82]

* * *

The problems that afflict research cited to support soda paternalism could be set aside if the revenue generated by soda taxes was at least put to productive use. But that's rarely, if ever true.

Far from a critical revenue source, initial soda tax revenue in Berkeley, California, represented just one percent of the city's general fund budget.[83] The city allocated about 15% of the revenue to administrative costs; two full-time employees were hired for tax administration alone. The remainder went to nonprofit organizations that the city's "panel of experts" believed would use the funding to implement programs that lessened soda consumption or improved public health in some other way.

Strangely, Berkeley's evaluation of tax-supported programming did not assess whether either objective was achieved. Funding distributions instead imply that many recipients successfully engaged in rent-seeking. Several organizations awarded soda tax-funded grants previously lobbied for the tax, including the Berkeley Unified School District, Berkeley Youth Alternatives, the Ecology Center, Healthy Black Families, Lifelong Medical Care, Options Recovery Services, Youth Spirit Artworks, and the YMCA.[84]

---

[81] The study is Brownell et al. (2009) and the *New York Times* article is Sanger-Katz (2016). Although the *Times* has quoted Brownell over 70 times, its reporters rarely identify him as a soda tax advocate or beverage industry critic.

[82] Drenkard (2011). Note that Drenkard's timeframe continues through 2010, one year after the Brownell et al. (2009) was published.

[83] For FY 2017-FY 2019, the city projected soda tax revenue of between $1.60 million and $1.75 million out of total revenue of between $163.7 and $174.6 million.

[84] See "Healthy Berkeley Program Evaluation: Executive Summary," prepared by John Snow, Inc. and issued in January 2018.

A similar pattern occurred in Boulder, Colorado. Jeff Zayach, Executive Director of Boulder County's Public Health Department, editorialized in favor of soda taxes, calling sugar-sweetened beverages "a major contributor to the country's obesity epidemic." But he did not disclose that his department received nearly $1 million in grants funded by the city's soda tax. Among other programs, grant funding was used to subsidize the purchase of fruits and vegetables at Whole Foods, promote breastfeeding, buy "children's gardening books," and target mobile home residents with an anti-sugar campaign.[85]

That wasn't the only instance of an organization funded with soda tax revenue lobbying for the tax. Jorge De Santiago, Executive Director of Boulder's El Centro Amistad, opined in 2016 that soda "contributes ... to the obesity epidemic" and that a soda tax was "an effective way of communicating its harm to all residents." His organization later received $325,000 in tax-funded grants to cover operating expenses and "educate the Latino community about health equity."[86]

Other local organizations in Boulder used grants for a wide-ranging set of initiatives, including a "rewards program for taking alternate transportation to school," gardening classes for homeless youth, and cooking classes for senior citizens.[87]

Like Berkeley, soda tax revenue did not contribute much to Philadelphia's budget, either, and markedly less than supporters promised while building public support for the tax. After collections ran 15% below initial forecasts, the city's budget director commented that he was "pretty proud of the fact that we came within fifteen percent."[88] Proud or not, dramatically lower revenue had consequences. Although the city's mayor lobbied for the tax by promising that it would fund free, universal prekindergarten—helping secure the support of teachers unions—the city was forced to reduce the number of "free" openings by 1000. And whereas the mayor had initially promised 25 new schools, the city was only able to move forward with 20.

---

[85] See Zayach (2018) and the Boulder Health Equity Advisory Committee's Health Equity Fund Allocation reports for 2018 and 2019.

[86] De Santiago (2016); see also the Boulder Health Equity Advisory Committee's Health Equity Fund Allocation reports for 2017, 2018, and 2019.

[87] See the Boulder Health Equity Advisory Committee's Health Equity Fund Allocation reports for 2018 and 2019.

[88] Loeb (2018).

Rent-seeking might be excusable if it at least funded effective programs—"more important" things, as Krugman called them—but the types of initiatives usually supported by soda tax revenue are not. Early childhood programs like the universal pre-kindergarten initiative in Philadelphia are often described as a remedy for all sorts of problems, but research on their effectiveness is ambiguous.[89]

Circumstances are no better for gardening and healthy eating initiatives. An evaluation of a school-based nutrition program in Los Angeles, California, found that participating adolescents increased their fiber intake—certainly a positive outcome—but also gained weight.[90] A review of similar programs elsewhere concluded that evidence of their value was "mixed."[91] Other school-based programs, such as those that encourage more physical activity, may succeed on that front but can also lower academic performance.[92]

Informative as it is, excursions into how governments spend soda tax revenue leaves unresolved the question of why soda drinkers should pay a disproportionate share of the cost of any public program. Many interest groups propose soda taxes as a way to pay for ostensibly public goods, like education, without ever making a strong case for why a higher share of the burden should fall on those who buy soda. It's also not clear why soda drinkers should have to pay a disproportionate share of the cost of other initiatives, like breastfeeding promotion, gardening books, or cooking classes. That also begs the more important question of how paternalists plan to continue funding those programs if soda consumption continues to fall. Budget cuts seem less likely than tax increases on something—or someone—else.

* * *

Despite the material offered in this chapter, political inertia is on soda paternalism's side. Until that changes, soda drinkers and their non-sinning peers should demand that current and future taxes incorporate specific

---

[89] Wong (2014).

[90] Davis et al. (2011). Despite evidence of weight gain, the study's authors still concluded the program reduced obesity.

[91] Savoie-Roskos et al. (2017).

[92] Golsteyn et al. (2020).

reforms. One reform would ban any individual or organization that campaigned or otherwise lobbied for a soda tax from benefiting from the revenue generated by that tax if it becomes law. If those individuals or organizations are sincerely concerned about improving public health, then they should have no problem with a ban on rent-seeking. Another reform would require that policymakers reduce future healthcare spending by an amount equal to the savings that experts claim will result from lower, tax-induced soda consumption. Sunset provisions should also be attached to each soda tax, granting voters a perpetual option to keep or repeal it.

Still, these reforms miss a more significant point. If paternalists remain convinced that obesity imposes massive externalities—even though evidence suggests it does not—then they need not resort to taxes as a solution. A more efficient approach would allow greater variability in the price of health insurance.[93] Just as drivers with a bad safety record pay more for vehicle insurance and groups with a higher risk of death pay more for life insurance, the obese should pay more for health insurance. That avoids the intrinsic unfairness of a soda or other food or beverage tax inflicted on both the obese and non-obese. After all, isn't the tax supposed to compensate the nonobese for their share of obesity's burden?

Strangely, few soda paternalists "support adjusting health insurance premiums."[94] Under nationalized healthcare systems, of course, discriminating premiums are impossible. And in the United States, the Affordable Care Act—otherwise known as Obamacare—mostly prevents private health insurers from establishing premiums based on an individual's health status. There are exceptions, though: age and tobacco use. If obesity is truly the costly epidemic paternalists claim it to be, why not add excessive weight to the list of characteristics that trigger a higher health insurance premium?

The answer to that question, and the reason why experts rarely, if ever, lobby for higher premiums on the obese, is political. The evidence on soda paternalism—from the interest groups that support it to the experts that produce the social science to justify it—suggests that its real motive

[93] See discussion in Bhattacharya and Sood (2007).
[94] Marlow and Shiers (2010a, b).

is not necessarily to improve public health, but to increase government revenue and broaden the scope of its influence over individual choice.[95]

Soda paternalism is, in other words, progressivism.

If there is any doubt, look no further than the Rudd Center for Food Policy and Obesity, funded by the pro-soda tax Rudd Foundation.[96] The Center hosts an interactive calculator on its website into which users can select a year, location, soda tax amount, and other parameters to estimate the tax's potential impact on society. The calculator does not determine any public health effects of the tax, nor does it calculate the healthcare costs it will save. The calculator only shows how much extra tax revenue the government will collect.

As the next chapter shows, soda is not unique in that regard. Alcohol paternalism, which targets the sinful choice to drink beer, wine, or distilled spirits, has nearly-identical contours. That includes the online calculators funded by interest groups that seek to increase government revenue.

REFERENCES

Abbott, Elizabeth. 2008. *Sugar: A Bittersweet History*. London, UK: Duckworth Publishers.

Adamy, Janet. 2009. "Soda Tax Weighed to Pay for Health Care." *The Wall Street Journal*. Retrieved March 4, 2020 (https://www.wsj.com/articles/SB1 24208505896608647).

Aguilar, Arturo, Emilio Gutiérrez, and Enrique Seira. 2015. "Taxing Calories in Mexico." Mexico Institute of Technology Center for Economic Research. Retrieved March 4, 2020 (http://cie.itam.mx/sites/default/files/cie/15-04.pdf).

Allcott, Hunt, Benjamin B. Lockwood, and Dmitry Taubinsky. 2019. "The Cigarette Tax Has Saved Millions of Lives. A Soda Tax Could Too." *The Los Angeles Times*. Retrieved June 3, 2019 (https://www.latimes.com/opinion/op-ed/la-oe-allcott-lockwood-taubinsky-soda-tax-economics-20190603-story.html).

Allison, David B., Raffaella Zannolli, and K.M. Venkat Narayan. 1999. "The Direct Health Care Costs of Obesity in the United States." *American Journal of Public Health* 89(8): 1194–1199.

---

[95] See discussion in Chouinard et al. (2007), Craven et al. (2012), Mueller et al. (2017), and Snowdon (2013).

[96] See uconnruddcenter.org/revenue-calculator-for-sugary-drink-taxes.

Andreyeva, Tatiana, Frank J. Chaloupka, and Kelly D. Brownell. 2011. "Estimating the Potential of Taxes on Sugar-Sweetened Beverages to Reduce Consumption and Generate Revenue." *Preventative Medicine* 52(6): 413–416.

Atella, Vincenzo, Noemi Pace, and Daniela Vuri. 2008. "Are Employers Discriminating with Respect to Weight? European Evidence Using Quantile Regression." *Economics & Human Biology* 6(3): 305–329.

Bes-Rastrollo, Maira, Carmen Sayon-Orea, Miguel Ruiz-Canela, and Miguel A. Martinez-Gonzalez. 2016. "Impact of Sugars and Sugar Taxation on Body Weight Control: A Comprehensive Literature Review." *Obesity* 24(7): 1410–1426.

Bes-Rastrollo, Maira, Matthias B. Schulze, Miguel Ruiz-Canela, and Miguel A. Martinez-Gonzalez. 2013. "Financial Conflicts of Interest and Reporting Bias Regarding the Association Between Sugar-Sweetened Beverages and Weight Gain: A Systematic Review of Systematic Reviews." *PLoS Medicine* 10(12): e1001578.

Bhattacharya, Jay, and M. Kate Bundorf. 2009. "The Incidence of the Healthcare Costs of Obesity." *Journal of Health Economics* 28(3): 649–658.

Bhattacharya, Jay, and Neeraj Sood. 2007. "Health Insurance and the Obesity Externality." *Advances in Health Economics and Health Services Research* 17: 279–318.

Bhattacharya, Jay, and Neeraj Sood. 2011. "Who Pays for Obesity?" *Journal of Economic Perspectives* 25(1): 139–158.

Bleich, Sara N., Kelsey A. Vercammen, Jonathan Wyatt Koma, and Zhonghe Li. 2018. "Trends in Beverage Consumption Among Children and Adults, 2003–2014." *Obesity* 26(2): 432–441.

Bloomberg News. 2016. "Mexico's Soda Tax Success." Retrieved March 4, 2020 (https://www.bloomberg.com/opinion/articles/2016-01-08/mexicos-soda-tax-success).

Bloomberg News. 2018. "California's Ban on Soda Taxes Should Not Stand." Retrieved July 23, 2018 (https://www.bloomberg.com/opinion/articles/2018-07-23/california-soda-tax-ban-should-not-stand).

Brehm, Sharon S., and Jack W. Brehm. 1981. *Psychological Reactance: A Theory of Freedom and Control*. New York, NY: Academic Press.

Briggs, Adam D.M., Oliver T. Mytton, Ariane, Kehlbacher, Richard Tiffin, Mike Rayner, and Peter Scarborough. 2013. "Overall and Income Specific Effect on Prevalence of Overweight and Obesity of 20% Sugar Sweetened Drink Tax in UK: Econometric and Comparative Risk Assessment Modelling Study." *BMJ* 347: f6189.

Brownell, Kelly D., and Thomas R. Frieden. 2009. "Ounces of Prevention—The Public Policy Case for Taxes on Sugared Beverages." *The New England Journal of Medicine* 360: 1805–1808.

Brownell, Kelly D., Thomas Farley, Walter C. Willett, Barry M. Popkin, Frank J. Chaloupka, Joseph W. Thompson, and David S. Ludwig. 2009. "The Public Health and Economic Benefits of Taxing Sugar-Sweetened Beverages." *The New England Journal of Medicine* 361(16): 1599–1605.

Burness, Alex. 2016. "Boulder Becomes Nation's Second City to Vote in a Soda Tax." *Daily Camera.* Retrieved March 4, 2020 (https://www.dailycamera.com/2016/11/08/boulder-becomes-nations-second-city-to-vote-in-a-soda-tax/).

Capacci, Sara, Mario Mazzocchi, and Bhavani Shankar. 2018. "Breaking Habits: The Effect of the French Vending Machine Ban on School Snaking and Sugar Intakes." *Journal of Policy Analysis and Management* 37(1): 88–111.

Carden, Trevor J., and Timothy P. Carr. 2013. "Food Availability of Glucose and Fat, but Not Fructose, Increased in the US Between 1970 and 2009: Analysis of the USDA Food Availability Data System." *Nutrition Journal* 12: 130.

Caro, Juan Carlos, Shu Wen Ng, Lindsey Smith Taillie, and Barry M. Popkin. 2017. "Designing a Tax to Discourage Unhealthy Food and Beverage Purchases." *Food Policy* 71: 86–100.

Caro, Juan Carlos, Camila Corvalán, Marcela Reyes, Andres Silva, Barry Popkin, and Lindsey Smith Taillie. 2018. "Chile's 2014 Sugar-Sweetened Beverage Tax and Changes in Prices and Purchases of Sugar-Sweetened Beverages: An Observational Study in an Urban Environment." *PLoS Medicine* 15(7): e1002597.

Cawley, John. 2004. "The Impact of Obesity on Wages." *Journal of Human Resources* 39(2): 451–474.

Chandon, Pierre, and Brian Wansink. 2007. "The Biasing Health Halos of Fast-Food Restaurant Health Claims: Lower Calorie Estimates and Higher Side-Dish Consumption Intentions." *Journal of Consumer Research* 34(3): 301–314.

Chartres, Nicholas, Alice Fabbri, and Lisa A. Bero. 2016. "Association of Industry Sponsorship with Outcomes of Nutrition Studies." *JAMA Internal Medicine* 176(12): 1769–1777.

Choo, V.L., V. Ha, and J.L. Sievenpiper. 2015. "Sugars and Obesity: Is It the Sugars or the Calories?" *Nutrition Bulletin* 40(2): 88–96.

Chou, Shin-Yi, Michael Grossman, and Henry Saffer. 2004. "An Economic Analysis of Adult Obesity: Results from the Behavioral Risk Factor Surveillance System." *Journal of Health Economics* 23(3): 565–587.

Chouinard, Hayley H., David E. Davis, Jeffrey T. LaFrance, and Jeffrey M. Perloff. 2007. "Fat Taxes: Big Money for Small Change." *Forum for Health & Economics Policy* 10(2): 1–28.

Colantuoni, Francesca, and Christian Rojas. 2015. "The Impact of Soda Sales Taxes on Consumption: Evidence from Scanner Data." *Contemporary Economic Policy* 33(4): 714–734.

Colchero, M. Arantxa, Barry M. Popkin, Juan A. Rivera, and Shu Wen Ng. 2016. "Beverage Purchases from Stores in Mexico Under the Excise Tax on Sugar Sweetened Beverages: Observational Study." *BMJ* 352: h6704.

Cope, Mark B., and David B. Allison. 2010. "White Hat Bias: Examples of Its Presence in Obesity Research and a Call for Renewed Commitment to Faithfulness in Research Reporting." *International Journal of Obesity* 34(1): 84–88.

Craven, Barrie M., Michael L. Marlow, and Alden F. Shiers. 2012. "Fat Taxes and Other Interventions Won't Cure Obesity." *Economic Affairs* 32(2): 36–40.

Cutler, David, Edward Glaeser, and Jesse Shapiro. 2003. "Why Have Americans Become More Obese." *Journal of Economic Perspectives* 17(3): 93–118.

Davis, Jaimie, Emily E. Ventura, Lauren T. Cook, Lauren E. Gyllenhammer, Nicole M. Gatto. 2011. "LA Sprouts: A Gardening, Nutrition, and Cooking Intervention for Latino Youth Improves Diet and Reduces Obesity." *Journal of the American Diabetic Association* 111(8): 1224–1230.

De Santiago, Jorge. 2016. "Join Healthy Boulder Kids Ballot Initiative." *Daily Camera*. Retrieved March 4, 2020 (https://www.dailycamera.com/2016/06/25/jorge-de-santiago-join-healthy-boulder-kids-ballot-initiative/).

Donaldson, Elisabeth A., Joanna E. Cohen, Lianie Rutkow, Andrea C. Villanti, Norma F. Kanarek, and Colleen L. Barry. 2015. "Public Support for a Sugar-Sweetened Beverage Tax and Pro-Tax Messages in a Mid-Atlantic State." *Public Health Nutrition* 18(12): 2263–2273.

Drenkard, Scott. 2011. "Overreaching on Obesity: Governments Consider New Taxes on Soda and Candy." The Tax Foundation Special Report No. 196.

Ein-Dor, Tsachi, James A. Coan, Abira Reizer, Elizabeth B. Gross, Dana Dahan, Meredyth A. Wegener, Rafael Carel, Claude R. Cloninger, and Ada H. Zohar. 2015. "Sugarcoated Isolation: Evidence That Social Avoidance Is Linked to Higher Basal Glucose Levels and Higher Consumption of Glucose." *Frontiers in Psychology* 6: 492.

Evich, Helena Bottemiller. 2015. "War Over Soda Taxes Coming to a Polling Place Near You." *Politico*. Retrieved March 1, 2020 (https://www.politico.com/story/2015/11/war-over-soda-taxes-coming-to-a-polling-place-near-you-216216).

Evich, Helena Bottemiller. 2017. "POLITICO-Harvard Poll: Majority Support Soda Taxes to Fund Pre-K, Health Programs." *Politico*. Retrieved September 21, 2017 (https://www.politico.com/story/2017/09/21/politico-harvard-poll-soda-taxes-pre-k-health-programs-242996).

Fabbri, Alice, Taylor J. Holland, and Lisa A. Bero. 2018. "Food Industry Sponsorship of Academic Research: Investigating Commercial Bias in the Research Agenda." *Public Health Nutrition* 21(18): 3422–3480.

Finkelstein, Eric A., Justin G. Trogdon, Joel W. Cohen, and William Dietz. 2009. "Annual Medical Spending Attributable to Obesity: Payer- And Service-Specific Estimates." *Health Affairs* 28(S1). Online publication.

Fisher, Kathy. 2016. "'Soda Tax' an Investment in Philly's Children." *The Philadelphia Inquirer*. Retrieved April 27, 2016 (https://www.inquirer.com/philly/opinion/20160427_Commentary___Soda_tax__an_investment_in_P hilly_s_children.html).

Fletcher, Jason M., David Frisvold, and Nathan Tefft. 2010a. "Can Soft Drink Taxes Reduce Population Weight?" *Contemporary Economic Policy* 28(1): 23–35.

Fletcher, Jason M., David E. Frisvold, and Nathan Tefft. 2010b. "The Effects of Soft Drink Taxes on Child and Adolescent Consumption and Weight Outcomes." *Journal of Public Economics* 94(11–12): 967–974.

Fletcher, Jason M., David E. Frisvold, and Nathan Tefft. 2015. "Non-Linear Effects of Soda Taxes on Consumption and Weight Outcomes." *Health Economics* 24(5): 566–582.

Forshee, Richard A., Patricia A. Anderson, and Maureen L. Storey. 2008. "Sugar-Sweetened Beverages and Body Mass Index in Children and Adolescents: A Meta-Analysis." *The American Journal of Clinical Nutrition* 87(6): 1662–1671.

Golsteyn, Bart H.H., Maria W.J. Jansen, Dave H.H. Van Kann, and Annelore M.C. Verhagen. 2020. "Does Stimulating Physical Activity Affect School Performance?" *Journal of Policy Analysis and Management* 39(1): 64–95.

Han, Euna, Edward C. Norton, and Sally C. Stearns. 2009. "Weight and Wages: Fat Versus Lean Paychecks." *Health Economics* 18(5): 535–548.

Hanks, Andrew S., Brian Wansink, David R. Just, John Cawley, Harry Kaiser, Laura E. Smith, Jeff Sobal, Elaine Wethington, and William Schulze. 2013. "From Coke to Coors: A Field Study of a Fat Tax and Its Unintended Consequences." *Journal of Nutrition Education and Behavior* 45(4): S40.

Henriksen, Roger Ekeberg, Torbjørn Torsheim, and Frode Thuen. 2014. "Lone-liness, Social Integration and Consumption of Sugar-Containing Beverages: Testing the Social Baseline Theory." *PLoS ONE* 9(8): e104421.

Kaiser, Kathryn A., Stacey S. Cofield, Kevin R. Fontaine, Stephen P. Glasser, Lehana Thabane, Rong Chu, Samir Ambrale, Ashish D. Dwary, Ashish Kumar, Gaurav Nayyar, Olivia Affuso, Mark Beasley, and David B. Allison. 2012. "Is Funding Source Related to Study Reporting Quality in Obesity or Nutri-tion Randomized Control Trials (RCTs) in Top Tier Medical Journals?" *International Journal of Obesity* 36(7): 977–981.

Krugman, Paul. 2016. "A Note on the Soda Tax Controversy." *The New York Times*. Retrieved April 25, 2016 (https://krugman.blogs.nytimes.com/2016/04/25/a-note-on-the-soda-tax-controversy/).

Laitinen, Jaana, Ellen Ek, and Ulla Sovio. 2002. "Stress-Related Eating and Drinking Behavior and Body Mass Index and Predictors of This Behavior." *Preventive Medicine* 34(1): 29–39.

Lakdawalla, Darius, and Tomas Philipson. 2009. "The Growth of Obesity and Technological Change." *Economics and Human Biology* 7(3): 283–293.

Lappé, Anna, and Christina Bronsing-Lazalde. 2017. "How to Win Against Big Soda." *The New York Times*. Retrieved October 15, 2017 (https://www.nytimes.com/2017/10/15/opinion/soda-tax-chicago-sugar.html).

Linnekin, Baylen. 2016. "Is Mexico's Soda Tax Really Working?" *Reason*. Retrieved February 13, 2016 (https://reason.com/2016/02/13/is-mexicos-soda-tax-working/).

Loeb, Pat. 2018. "Universal Pre-K Takes a Hit in Mayor's Five Year Plan." CBS3 Philadelphia. Retrieved March 1, 2018 (https://philadelphia.cbslocal.com/2018/03/01/universal-pre-k-takes-hit-in-mayors-five-year-plan/).

Long, Michael W., Steven L. Gortmaker, Zachary J. Ward, Stephen C. Resch, Marj L. Moodie, Gary Sacks, Boyd A. Swinburn, Rob C. Carter, and Y. Clare Wang. 2015. "Cost Effectiveness of a Sugar-Sweetened Beverage Excise Tax in the U.S." *American Journal of Preventative Medicine* 49(1): 112–123.

Lyon, Maud. 2016. "Soda Tax Presents Opportunity for Greater Access to The Arts." WHYY. Retrieved May 31, 2016 (https://whyy.org/articles/soda-tax-presents-opportunity-for-greater-access-to-the-arts/).

Malik, Vasanti S., Matthias B. Schulze, and Frank B. Hu. 2006. "Intake of Sugar-Sweetened Beverages and Weight Gain: A Systematic Review." *The American Journal of Clinical Nutrition* 84(2): 274–288.

Malik, Vasanti S., Barry M. Popkin, George A. Bray, Jean-Pierre Després, Walter C. Willett, and Frank B. Hu. 2010. "Sugar-Sweetened Beverages and Risk of Metabolic Syndrome and Type 2 Diabetes: A Meta-Analysis." *Diabetes Care* 33(11): 2477–2483.

Manyema, Mercy, Lennert J. Veerman, Lumbwe Chola, Aviva Tugendhaft, Benn Sartorius, Demetre Labadarios, and Karen J. Hofman. 2014. "The Potential Impact of a 20% Tax on Sugar-Sweetened Beverages on Obesity in South African Adults: A Mathematical Model." *PLoS ONE* 9(8): e105287.

Marlow, Michael L., and Alden F. Shiers. 2010a. "Does Government Have a Role in Curbing Obesity?" *Journal of American Physicians and Surgeons* 15(3): 75–77.

Marlow, Michael L., and Alden Shiers. 2010b. "Would Soda Taxes Really Yield Health Benefits"? *Regulation* 33(3): 34–38.

Massougbodji, José, Yann Le Bodo, Ramona Fratu, and Philippe De Wals. 2014. "Reviews Examining Sugar-Sweetened Beverages and Body Weight." *The American Journal of Clinical Nutrition* 99(5): 1096–1104.

Mattes, Richard D., James M. Shikany, Kathryn A. Kaiser, and David B. Allison. 2011. "Nutritively Sweetened Beverage Consumption and Body Weight: A

Systematic Review and Meta-Analysis of Randomized Experiments." *Obesity Reviews* 12(5): 346–365.

McKinsey Global Institute. 2014. "Overcoming Obesity: An Initial Economic Analysis." Discussion Paper.

McPherson, Klim. 2008. "Does Preventing Obesity Lead to Reduced Health-Care Costs?" *PLoS Medicine* 5(2): e37.

Menachemi, Nir, Gabriel Tajeu, Bisakha Sen, Alva O. Ferdinand, Chelsea Singleton, Janic Utley, Olivia Affuso, and David B. Allison. 2013. "Overstatement of Results in the Nutrition and Obesity Peer-Reviewed Literature." *American Journal of Preventative Medicine* 45(5): 615–621.

Mueller, Laurent, Anne Lacroix, Jayson L. Lusk, and Bernard Ruffieux. 2017. "Distributional Impacts of Fat Taxes and Thin Subsidies." *The Economic Journal* 127(604): 2066–2092.

Narayan, K.M. Venkat, James P. Boyle, Theodore J. Thompson, Stephen W. Sorensen, and David F. Williamson. 2003. "Lifetime Risk for Diabetes Mellitus in the United States." *Journal of the American Medical Association* 290(14): 1884–1890.

Nestle, Marion. 2015. *Soda Politics: Taking on Big Soda (and Winning)*. New York, NY: Oxford University Press.

Nestle, Marion. 2016. "Corporate Funding of Food and Nutrition Research: Science or Marketing?" *JAMA Internal Medicine* 176(1): 13–14.

Neuman, William. 2010. "Save the Children Breaks With Soda Tax Effort." *The New York Times*. Retrieved March 5, 2020 (https://www.nytimes.com/2010/12/15/business/15soda.html).

Niebylski, Mark L., Kimbree A. Redburn, Tara Duhaney, and Norm R. Campbell. 2015. "Healthy Food Subsidies and Unhealthy Food Taxation: A Systematic Review of the Evidence." *Nutrition* 31(6): 787–795.

Niederdeppe, Jeff, Sarah E. Gollust, Marian P. Jarlenski, Ashley M. Nathanson, and Colleen L. Barry. 2013. "News Coverage of Sugar-Sweetened Beverage Taxes: Pro- and Antitax Arguments in Public Discourse." *American Journal of Public Health* 103(6): e92–e98.

Nomaguchi, Takeshi, Michelle Cunich, Belen Zapata-Diomedi, and J. Lennert Veerman. 2017. "The Impact of a Hypothetical Tax on Sugar- Sweetened Beverages." *Health Policy* 121(6): 715–725.

Norton, Edward C., and Euna Han. 2008. "Genetic Information, Obesity, and Labor Market Outcomes." *Health Economics* 17(9): 1089–1104.

O'Connor, Anahad. 2015. "Coca-Cola Funds Effort to Alter Obesity Battle." *The New York Times*. Retrieved March 5, 2020 (https://well.blogs.nytimes.com/2015/08/09/coca-cola-funds-scientists-who-shift-blame-for-obesity-away-from-bad-diets/).

Parker, Matthew. 2012. *The Sugar Barons*. New York, NY: Walker & Company.

Posner, Richard A., and Tomas J. Philipson. 2003. "The Long-Run Growth in Obesity as a Function of Technological Change." *Perspectives in Biology and Medicine* 46(3): S87–S107.

Powell, Lisa M., Jamie Chriqui, and Frank J. Chaloupka. 2009. "Associations Between State-level Soda Taxes and Adolescent Body Mass Index." *Journal of Adolescent Health* 45(3): S57–S63.

Provencher, Veronique, Janet Polivy, and C. Peter Herman. 2009. "Perceived Healthiness of Food: If It's Healthy, You Can Eat More!" *Appetite* 52(2): 340–344.

Rehm, Colin D., José L. Peñalvo, and Ashkan Afshin. 2016. "Dietary Intake Among US Adults, 1999–2012." *Journal of the American Medical Association* 325(23): 2542–2553.

Rosen, Odelia. 2008. "The Economic Causes of Obesity." *Journal of Economic Surveys* 22(4): 617–647.

Rosenberg, Tina. 2016. "How One of the Most Obese Countries on Earth Took on the Soda Giants." *The Guardian*. Retrieved March 5, 2020 (https://www.theguardian.com/news/2015/nov/03/obese-soda-sugar-tax-mexico).

Sánchez-Romero, Luz Maria, Joanne Penko, Pamela G. Coxson, Alicia Fernández, Antoinette Mason, Andrew E. Moran, Leticia Ávila-Burgos, Michelle Odden, Simón Barquera, and Kirsten Bibbins-Domingo. 2016. "Projected Impact of Mexico's Sugar-Sweetened Beverage Tax Policy on Diabetes and Cardiovascular Disease: A Modeling Study." *PLoS Medicine* 13(11): e1002158.

Sanger-Katz, Margot. 2016. "Novel Strategy Puts Big Soda Tax Within Philadelphia's Reach." *The New York Times*. Retrieved March 4, 2020 (https://www.nytimes.com/2016/06/09/upshot/novel-strategy-puts-big-soda-tax-within-philadelphias-reach.html).

Savoie-Roskos, Mateja R., Heidi Wengreen, and Carrie Durward. 2017. "Increasing Fruit and Vegetable Intake among Children and Youth Through Gardening-Based Interventions: A Systematic Review." *Journal of the Academy of Nutrition and Dietetics* 117(2): 240–250.

Scholey, Andrew B., Susan Harper, and David O. Kennedy. 2001. "Cognitive Demand and Blood Glucose." *Physiology & Behavior* 73(4): 585–592.

Seiler, Stephan, Anna Tuchman, and Song Yao. 2019. "The Impact of Soda Taxes: Pass-through, Tax Avoidance, and Nutritional Effects." Stanford University Graduate School of Business, Research Paper No. 19–12.

Shemilt, Ian, Gareth J. Hollands, Theresa M. Marteau, Ryota Nakamura, Susan A. Jebb, Michael P. Kelly, Marc Suhrcke, and David Ogilvie. 2013. "Economic Instruments for Population Diet and Physical Activity Behaviour Change: A Systematic Scoping Review." *PLoS ONE* 8(9): e75070.

Silver, Lynn D., Shu Wen Ng, Suzanne Ryan-Ibarra, Lindsey Smith Taillie, Marta Induni, Donna R. Miles, Jennifer M. Poti, and Barry M. Popkin. 2017.

"Changes in Prices, Sales, Consumer Spending, and Beverage Consumption in Berkeley, California, US: A Before-and-After Study." *PLoS Medicine* 14(4): e1002283.

Snowdon, Christopher. 2013. "The Proof of the Pudding: Denmark's Fat Tax Fiasco." Institute for Economic Affairs, Current Controversies Paper No. 42.

Taber, Daniel R., Jamie F. Chriqui, Renee Vuillaume, Steven H. Kelder, and Frank J. Chaloupka. 2015. "The Association Between State Bans on Soda and Adolescent Substitution with Other Sugar-Sweetened Beverages: A Cross-Sectional Study." *International Journal of Behavioral Nutrition and Physical Activity* 12(Supplement 1): S7.

Tajeu, Gabriel S., Bisakha Sen, David B. Allison, and Nir Menachemi. 2012. "Misuse of Odds Ratios in Obesity Literature: An Empirical Analysis of Published Studies." *Obesity* 20(8): 1726–1731.

Taubes, Gary. 2016. *The Case Against Sugar*. New York, NY: Knopf.

Trumbo, Paula R., and Crystal R. Rivers. 2014. "Systematic Review of the Evidence for an Association Between Sugar-Sweetened Beverage Consumption and Risk of Obesity." *Nutrition Reviews* 72(9): 566–574.

Turner, Lindsey, and Frank J. Chaloupka. 2012. "Encouraging Trends in Student Access to Competitive Beverages in U.S. Public Elementary Schools, 2006–2007 to 2010–2011." *Archives of Pediatrics and Adolescent Medicine* 166(7): 673–675.

van Baal, Pieter H.M., Johan J. Polder, G. Ardine de Wit, Rudolf T. Hoogenveen, Talitha L. Feenstra, Hendriek C. Boshuizen, Peter M. Engelfriet, and Werner B.F. Brouwer. 2008. "Lifetime Medical Costs of Obesity: Prevention No Cure for Increasing Health Expenditure." *PLoS Medicine* 5(2): e29.

Vanselow, Michelle S., Mark A. Pereira, Dianne Neumark-Sztainer, and Susan K. Raatz. 2009. "Adolescent Beverage Habits and Changes in Weight Over Time: Findings from Project EAT." *American Journal of Clinical Nutrition* 90(6): 1489–1495.

Vartanian, Lenny R., Marlene B. Schwartz, and Kelly D. Brownell. 2007. "Effects of Soft Drink Consumption on Nutrition and Health: A Systematic Review and Meta-Analysis." *American Journal of Public Health* 97(4): 667–675.

Wallinga, David. 2010. "Agricultural Policy and Childhood Obesity: A Food Systems and Public Health Commentary." *Health Affairs* 29(3): 405–410.

Wang, Y. Claire, Pamela Coxson, Yu-Ming Shen, Lee Goldman, and Kirsten Bibbins-Domingo. 2012. "A Penny-Per-Ounce on Sugar-Sweetened Beverages Would Cut Health and Cost Burdens of Diabetes." *Health Affairs* 31(1): 199–207.

Wansink, Brian, and Pierre Chandon. 2006. "Can 'Low-Fat' Nutrition Labels Lead to Obesity?" *Journal of Marketing Research* 43(4): 605–617.

Waterlander, Wilma Elzeline, Cliona Ni Mhurchu, and Ingrid H.M. Steenhuis. 2014. "Effects of a Price Increase on Purchases of Sugar Sweetened Beverages. Results from a Randomized Control Trial." *Appetite* 78: 32–39.

Weed, Douglas L., Michelle D. Althuis, and Pamela J. Mink. 2011. "Quality of Reviews on Sugar-Sweetened Beverages and Health Outcomes: A Systematic Review." *American Journal of Clinical Nutrition* 94(5): 1340–1347.

Welsh, Jean A., Andrea J. Sharma, Lisa Grellinger, and Miriam B. Vos. 2011. "Consumption of Added Sugars Is Decreasing in the United States." *American Journal of Clinical Nutrition* 94(3): 726–734.

Wescott, Robert F., Brendan M. Fitzpatrick, and Elizabeth Phillips. 2012. "Industry Self-Regulation to Improve Student Health: Quantifying Changes in Beverage Shipments to Schools." *American Journal of Public Health* 103(10): 1928–1935.

Wilson, Brent M., Stephanie Stolarz-Fantino, and Edmund Fantino. 2013. "Regulating the Way to Obesity: Unintended Consequences of Limiting Sugary Drink Sizes." *PLoS ONE* 8(4): e61081.

Wong, Alia. 2014. "The Case Against Universal Preschool." *The Atlantic*. Retrieved November 18, 2014 (https://www.theatlantic.com/education/arc hive/2014/11/the-case-against-universal-preschool/382853/).

Zayach, Jeff. 2018. "Sugary Drink Tax Surplus Should Stay in Boulder, Not Go to Industry." *Daily Camera*. Retrieved July 28, 2018 (https://www.dailyc amera.com/2018/07/28/jeff-zayach-sugary-drink-tax-surplus-should-stay-in-boulder-not-go-to-industry/).

Zhao, Zhenxiang, and Robert Kaestner. 2010. "Effects of Urban Sprawl on Obesity." *Journal of Health Economics* 29(6): 778–787.

Zhen, Chen, Eric A. Finkelstein, James M. Nonnemaker, Shawn A. Karns, and Jessica E. Todd. 2014. "Predicting the Effects of Sugar-Sweetened Beverage Taxes on Food and Beverage Demand in a Large Demand System." *American Journal of Agricultural Economics* 96(1): 1–25.

CHAPTER 3

Taxing Alcohol

Alcoholic beverages have had an ever-present role in human experience across time and culture. Archeological evidence indicates that beer was served in Israel at least 13,000 years ago.[1] Alcoholic drinks were also a part of life in ancient China, Egypt, Greece, Iran, and Mexico. Christian worship services included wine from the beginning, and the Bible depicts alcohol—but not drunkenness—in a positive light.

Thanks to persistent consumption, alcohol taxes are among the oldest means to pay for government expenses.[2] In many areas, enough people drank, and did so consistently, that the tax burden diffused widely and revenue was usually stable. Holland enacted an alcohol tax in 1574. New York and Connecticut taxed alcohol as early as 1644 and 1650, respectively. In 1791, a tax on distilled spirits took effect in the United States.

That's not to say the drinking public looked favorably at alcohol taxes. Many viewed higher prices the way they saw alcohol and the government itself: as a necessary but inconvenient evil. Others, however, were more forceful i n heir opposition. A group of Pennsylvania men—some in blackface and some wearing dresses—tarred and feathered a tax collector

---

[1] Liu et al. (2018); see also Forsyth (2017) and Phillips (2014).

[2] Reliance on alcohol taxes was also a practical matter. Before it was commonplace to work in exchange for a wage, an income tax was not a useful source of revenue. The same could not be said about an alcohol tax.

© The Author(s) 2021
M. Thom, *Taxing Sin*,
https://doi.org/10.1007/978-3-030-49176-5_3

not long after the federal spirits tax took effect, launching what was later known as the Whiskey Rebellion.[3]

Paternalists were never enthused with alcohol taxes, either.

As the temperance movement gained traction alongside the progressive movement in the late nineteenth century, paternalists argued alcohol taxes did not go far enough to eliminate a litany of secular and religious sins that they said drinking caused, such as laziness, poverty, and domestic abuse.[4] Paternalists demanded that governments impose prohibition, and they realized some success. Many local and state governments enacted "dry laws" that barred the sale or consumption of alcohol on certain days and times, if not altogether.

But nationwide prohibition was a political challenge because many governments could not sustain the loss of alcohol tax revenue. That was especially true of the United States federal budget, which relied on alcohol taxes to supply about 30% of revenue from 1910 through 1916 alone. Elements of the temperance movement lobbied for an income tax on the assumption that, if the federal government were less dependent on alcohol taxes, then prohibition would be easier to legislate.

They were correct. Once the United States Congress authorized an income tax in 1916, a significant barrier to nationwide prohibition collapsed. By early 1919, thirty-six state governments ratified a constitutional amendment on prohibition. It took effect in 1920, but did not last. Having created several problems of its own, American prohibition was repealed at the end of 1933. Other countries that enacted forms of prohibition, including Finland, Iceland, Norway, and Russia, also repealed them.

Alcohol paternalism endured. Dry activists moved from a prohibition stance to pressing governments to implement tax-and-control policies designed to reduce the ease with which anyone could drink. That scheme also found success. In the depression era, policymakers were amenable to revenue provided by higher alcohol taxes. They also embraced the paternalistic notion that alcohol taxes and regulation were a way to realize

---

[3] Hodgeland (2015) and Hu (1950).

[4] McGirr (2019) notes that racial and anti-immigrant undertones also marked the temperance movement, just as it marked campaigns against marijuana.

"effective social control."[5] According to a 1950 report from alcohol control officials in the United States:

> The principle is well established that certain anti-social conditions will inevitably flow from the operation of this business if uncontrolled by government, and that the lowest elements of society will attach themselves to it as parasites unless prevented from so doing by vigilant and resolute action by government.[6]

Today's alcohol paternalism is not altogether different from what it was over a century ago. Paternalists argue that drinking imposes externalities, including additional healthcare costs and impaired driving. They say alcohol taxes are an effective way to redeem those sins and reduce drinking, just as Pigou wrote in 1920, and perhaps reduce alcoholism.

Public health groups largely concur with alcohol paternalism. The World Health Organization advises policymakers to reduce drinking through taxes and other policies.[7] The American Public Health Association has also called for an increase in alcohol taxes.[8] The Thai Center for Alcohol Studies and the Canadian Centre for Addiction and Mental Health likewise contend that alcohol taxes provide benefits to society, including lower alcohol consumption and higher government revenue.[9]

Experts agree. One academic wrote a book that argued higher alcohol prices are needed "to lower rates of underage drinking, traffic fatalities, and sexually transmitted disease."[10] After Republicans proposed lower federal alcohol taxes in 2017, experts at the Brookings Institution, an American think tank, issued a report that claimed the cuts would lead to 1600 deaths each year.[11] The National Academies of Sciences, a professional organization composed of over 2000 experts, called for higher alcohol taxes in 2018, reasoning that current levies fail to compensate

[5] Fosdick and Scott (1933).

[6] Joint Committee of the States to Study Alcoholic Beverage Laws (1950).

[7] The press release, "Harmful Use of Alcohol Kills More Than 3 Million People Each Year, most of them Men," was issued September 21, 2018.

[8] See Policy Number 20041, "Reducing Underage Alcohol Consumption," and Policy Number 8613, "Alcohol Tax Policy Reform."

[9] Sornpaisarn et al. (2017).

[10] Cook (2007).

[11] Looney (2017).

for alcohol's externalities.[12] That plea echoed one from the same group 15 years earlier.[13]

Philanthropic organizations provide alcohol paternalism with financial support. For example, the Pew Charitable Trusts and the Robert Wood Johnson Foundation fund the Center on Alcohol Marketing and Youth, which backs alcohol taxes. The Center hosts a calculator on its website wherein a user can select a state and an alcohol tax and generate estimates of the revenue raised and the number of government jobs created. But as with the Rudd Center's soda tax calculator, this one does not produce estimates of any public health benefits from higher alcohol taxes.

As they do with soda, a cottage industry of interest groups aides and abets the spread of alcohol paternalism. Alcohol Change UK, a self-described "leading UK alcohol charity," decries alcohol's purported role in crime and "antisocial behavior." To curb drinking, the group promotes initiatives like Dry January, a campaign that urges adults to abstain from drinking that month. The group argues that alcohol taxes "save lives."[14]

Alcohol Justice, a California-based group that aims to "promote evidence-based public health policies and organize campaigns with diverse communities and youth against the alcohol industry's harmful practices," lobbies for higher alcohol taxes in the United States. Their "Charge for Harm" campaign urges supporters to join the movement because products sold by "big alcohol" inflict harm that taxation counters. Like the Center on Alcohol Marketing and Youth, their website features a calculator—branded an "advocacy tool"—in which a user selects a state government and inputs a tax on beer, wine, and spirits to estimate how much additional tax revenue that state would collect. Once again, the calculator does not provide estimates of the public health benefits facilitated by higher taxes. Evidently, more government revenue is benefit enough.

These groups are far from alone. Mothers Against Drunk Driving ("MADD") maintains that taxes on beer and wine, which are usually low,

---

[12] Teutsch et al. (2018).

[13] The report, "Reducing Underage Drinking: A Collective Responsibility," was issued by the National Research Council and the Institute of Medicine of the National Academies in 2003. It recommended alcohol tax increases, especially on beer.

[14] For example, Alcohol Change UK issued a press release in October 2017 announcing the group's support for minimum pricing in Wales that "will improve health and save lives."

should climb to reach parity with taxes on spirits, which tend to be higher. Texans Standing Tall, a group that aims "to create healthier and safer communities," urges the public to demand higher alcohol taxes. They provide a list of policy "action steps" that, if successful, will "improve public health (and) increase revenue."

Widespread promotion is not without effect. Hundreds of governments around the world tax alcoholic beverages, and most apply different levies on beer, wine, and spirits. In some areas, alcohol is subject to a tax at multiple levels of government. Alcoholic beverages in the United States are taxed at the federal and state level and sometimes by local governments. The combination can yield an effective tax rate of over 100%, and sometimes as high as 150%.[15] In a far cry from the Whiskey Rebellion, a majority of the public favors taxing alcohol.[16]

* * *

A wide-ranging research literature supports paternalists' argument that drinking alcoholic beverages imposes externalities, including additional healthcare costs and the too often fatal consequences of impaired driving.[17] Multiple studies report a similar estimate of alcohol's burden on society: about $2 for each drink.[18] That has led some experts to take a position not widely seen since the progressive era. A 2018 report signed by hundreds of experts concluded that policymakers should increase alcohol control because no amount of drinking is safe.[19] Less drastically, other experts argue that current alcohol taxes fail to cover its costs to society and should therefore increase.[20]

When it comes to evaluating alcohol's externalities, however, the effects of light and moderate drinking must be separated from the effects

---

[15] See illustration on page 170 of Thom (2017).

[16] Callinan et al. (2014) and Li et al. (2017).

[17] For a general discussion, see Chaloupka et al. (2002).

[18] Bates et al. (2015), Bouchery et al. (2011), Cesur and Kelly (2014), Herrnstadt et al. (2015), Manning et al. (1989), Pogue and Sgontz (1989), Stahre et al. (2014), and Sacks et al. (2015).

[19] Authors (2018) and Burton and Sheron (2018).

[20] Blanchette et al. (2019).

of heavy drinking.[21] That's because a growing number of studies indicate that light and moderate drinking contribute to positive, not negative, health outcomes. One review of 84 studies published between 1950 and 2009 concluded that drinking one or two alcoholic beverages per day was associated with a lower risk of cardiovascular disease.[22] Other studies have shown that light and moderate drinking reduce a person's risk of type 2 diabetes, stroke, arthritis, Alzheimer's disease, and some mental health conditions.[23]

While far too many studies cite little more than the correlation between drinking and health outcomes, some research indicates that alcoholic beverages do indeed cause better health. For example, studies show that light and moderate drinking is conducive to molecular changes in the body that protect against cardiovascular disease.[24] Drinking alcohol has also been shown to increase levels of "good" HDL cholesterol, improve sleep quality, increase metabolism, enhance the immune system, and reduce the risk of complications following a heart attack.[25]

Those positive outcomes can hardly be considered externalities, and that challenges the argument that the choice to drink light or moderate amounts of alcohol should be discouraged with taxes and other regulations. Those outcomes also undermine the view held by some experts and paternalists that no amount of drinking is safe. The evidence is clear that alcoholic beverages can be very good to drinkers—and thus very good for society overall.

The impact of excessive drinking, however, is completely different. Binge drinkers and chronic heavy drinkers have a higher risk of developing several health problems, including cirrhosis and other liver diseases, pancreatitis, certain types of cancer, and brain damage. The expense of treating those conditions inevitably spreads beyond the drinker, an apparent tax-justifying externality.

---

[21] Stockwell et al. (2016).

[22] Ronksley et al. (2011); see also Corrao et al. (2000) and Di Castelnuovo et al. (2006).

[23] Dasgupta (2019) and Kim et al. (2020); see also van den Brandt and Brandts (2020).

[24] Brien et al. (2011).

[25] Authors (2015), de Lorgeril et al. (2002), Fragopoulou et al. (2018), and Romeo et al. (2007).

Yet the magnitude of that externality is unclear, and estimates vary substantially.[26] The methods used to develop such estimates have been described as "highly speculative and without foundation" as well as "flawed empirically and conceptually."[27] Among other errors, experts habitually combine internalities and externalities to amplify alcohol's purported burden, just as they do when analyzing obesity to make the case for a soda tax.[28]

For example, a 2015 study supported by the Centers for Disease Control and Prevention, the American health agency that also warns of obesity's externalities, estimated that the annual burden of excessive drinking in the United States amounted to $249 billion. The authors reported that estimate as a justification for higher alcohol prices and stricter government control of the alcohol supply. "Several evidence-based strategies can help reduce excessive drinking and related costs," they wrote, "including increasing alcohol excise taxes."[29]

But the externality was exaggerated. Seventy-two percent of the $249 billion figure was tied to lower productivity among drinkers—and that's an internality, not an externality. As one critic noted:

> This, overwhelmingly, is a private cost and not an external cost. If individuals' alcohol consumption affects their work performance, or their human capital accumulation, or the length of their working life, the vast proportion of that cost would ultimately be borne by the individual themselves through worse employment prospects and lower wages.[30]

Besides that, the internality may not even exist. Some research indeed links drinking with lower productivity, reduced wages, and a higher probability of unemployment. But it is difficult to separate the role alcohol

---

[26] Wagner (1997) and Woodfield (1988).

[27] Wagner (1997); see also Crampton et al. (2011).

[28] Gant and Ekelund (1997), Heien and Pittman (1989), and Stringham (2009).

[29] Sacks et al. (2015).

[30] Bourne (2019).

plays in those outcomes from other factors.[31] And the effect is contradicted in numerous studies that find light and moderate drinking leads to higher wages, perhaps by increasing drinkers' social capital.[32]

That undermines the argument for taxing alcohol.

Conflating internalities and externalities was not the only strategy the study's authors employed to inflate their estimate of alcohol's social burden. They also used an exaggerated definition of excessive drinkers, one that combined individuals belonging to three different drinking categories into one:

- Underage drinkers, defined by the study's authors as any alcohol consumption by a person under 21 years old; thus, a 20 year old who reported drinking one beer per month was classified in the study as an excessive drinker.
- Heavy drinkers, defined as more than 1.1 or 2.1 drinks per day for the average woman or man, respectively; thus, a woman who reported drinking one glass of wine with dinner each night was, according to the study's authors, dangerously close to being classified as a heavy drinker.
- Binge drinkers, defined as having at least four or five drinks per occasion for the average woman or man, respectively.

The decision to pool these drinkers together greatly overstated the number of "excessive" drinkers for whom healthcare and other costs could be inferred as resulting from drinking. While the decision to not differentiate among drinking levels strains credulity, it is consistent with Centers for Disease Control and Prevention guidelines and is a common practice in alcohol research.[33]

More problematically, the study and many others like it failed to recognize that chronic heavy drinkers have shorter life expectancies. Their premature death creates cost savings that compensate for at least some of whatever externalities their drinking imposes. A chronic heavy drinker

---

[31] Dave and Kaestner (2002), Chaloupka et al. (2019), Jarl and Gerdtham (2010), Jones and Richmond (2006), MacDonald and Shields (2004), and Peters (2004).

[32] Auld (2005), Heien (1996a, b), and van Ours (2004); see also Peters and Stringham (2006).

[33] Bouchery et al. (2011); see also Stringham (2009).

may present above-average healthcare costs that stem from treating liver disease, for instance, but that person is also likely to die several years, if not one or more decades, prematurely. Those are years or decades over which the drinker imposes no routine healthcare costs and no costs for treating old-age conditions like dementia that never have a chance to develop. Thanks to shorter life expectancies, heavy drinkers also have lower pension and social security expenses.[34] Some studies thus report that heavy drinkers do not burden society any more heavily than nondrinkers.[35]

That, too, weakens the case for taxing alcohol.

But like analyses of obesity, most estimates of alcohol's externalities do not incorporate the tradeoff between lifetime costs and benefits. The latter is often left out entirely. The reason is simple—and revealing. According to guidance from the World Health Organization, if the goal of experts conducting alcohol research is to "show that alcohol is a major social and economic problem," then they should ignore its benefits.[36]

Paternalists very reasonably point out that alcohol's externalities are not entirely related to employment impacts or healthcare costs—that alcohol does contribute to other social problems. Alcohol-impaired driving is one externality that deserves careful consideration.[37] Given the emotion involved with the issue, it's necessary to put impaired driving fatalities in perspective. Motor vehicle accidents, including those that are not alcohol-related, are not among the ten leading causes of death in the United States. Pneumonia and influenza are responsible for about five times as many deaths as accidents in which alcohol was a factor.[38] Nearly

[34] While arguing that the pension impact would be minor, Horlings and Scoggins (2006) note that it is understudied. See also Meltzer (1997).

[35] Heise (2010) and Polen et al. (2001).

[36] See Møller and Matic (2010). Although the authors argue that all costs and benefits should be considered, they go to great lengths to explain how difficult the benefits are to estimate.

[37] According to the National Highway Traffic Safety Administration, an impaired driving accident is one in which the driver has a blood alcohol concentration above 0.08.

[38] See Centers for Disease Control and Prevention National Vital Statistics Reports, Volume 68, Number 6, and the same agency's "Impaired Driving: Get the Facts" issued in June 2019.

25 times as many people die from medical errors than drunk driving.[39] Several other behaviors, including the use of a cellular phone or a vehicle's infotainment system, are far more dangerous than driving while under the influence of alcohol.[40]

It is also not widely recognized that, at least in the United States, just one-quarter of drunk driving fatalities are occupants in other vehicles or bystanders. Drunk drivers represent about 60% of all deaths. Drunk passengers in the same vehicle represent another 15%.[41]

Still, drunk driving inflicts raw harm on victims, their families, and their property. But the externality is confined to those victims and their families, who can and should seek redress in civil court, just as governments should pursue justice in criminal court. That targets the sanction to the person or persons involved in imposing harm, which avoids the unfairness of spreading the cost to the entire drinking population through an alcoholic beverage tax. Taxing every drink because a small number of drinkers might drive drunk makes as much sense as taxing all knives because a few knife owners might use it stab someone.

* * *

Contradictory evidence about alcohol's harms does not sway paternalists, nor does research that challenges the virtues of alcohol taxation.

Historical inertia from the progressive era onward has fed the development of a conventional wisdom that alcohol taxes succeed at reducing drinking and its externalities. That alcohol taxes have been around for so long is easily confused as an indicator of their success. But there should be no doubt that, over time, alcohol paternalism has also accumulated strong backing in the research literature. Paternalists appeal to that literature whenever they lobby policymakers for stricter alcohol controls or higher alcohol taxes.

Experts have conducted quite literally thousands of studies on alcohol taxes. Most conclude that taxes work as intended. A review of over 100 different studies found that taxes and other policies that raise alcohol's

[39] The Centers for Disease Control and Prevention reported 10,497 deaths in 2016 from motor vehicle accidents where alcohol was a factor; estimates of medical error-induced mortality are discussed in Makary and Daniel (2016).

[40] Ramnath et al. (2020).

[41] National Highway Traffic Safety Administration (2018).

price "are an effective means to reduce drinking" and, by extension, reduce its externalities.[42] According to another study, doubling alcohol taxes could lead to an 11% reduction in traffic-related deaths, a 6% reduction in sexually-transmitted infections, a 2% reduction in violence, and a small decrease in crime.[43] Another study found that higher alcohol taxes in the European Union would "postpone" tens of thousands of deaths and eliminate tens of thousands of cases of diabetes, stroke, and cancer.[44] The authors of an Australian study went as far as to proclaim that taxation had a 100% chance of reducing alcohol's harmful effects.[45] Research on alcohol taxes in New York City claimed that they could reduce the homicide rate and save up to 1200 lives annually.[46]

But like the experts that study soda taxes, those who research alcohol taxes tend to eschew observational studies in favor of simulation models.[47] The study that claimed alcohol taxes would save lives and reduce diabetes, stroke, and cancer drew on simulations, and so did the study that claimed alcohol taxes would reduce New York City's homicide rate. The study that guaranteed alcohol taxes would reduce its externalities was likewise based on simulations. The simulations were not even run in a sophisticated software application, but with spreadsheet program Microsoft Excel.

More importantly, several studies contradict conventional wisdom about alcohol taxes. A review of research on taxes in Australia, Denmark, Finland, Hong Kong, Iceland, Russia, Sweden, Switzerland, and the United States concluded that while alcohol taxes are perceived as a successful policy to reduce drinking, "the confidence placed on this measure is too high."[48]

That's because not all drinkers are affected by higher prices. According to one review, only two out of 19 studies reported that higher prices

---

[42] Wagenaar et al. (2009).

[43] Wagenaar et al. (2010).

[44] Lhachimi et al. (2012).

[45] Cobiac et al. (2009).

[46] Keyes et al. (2019).

[47] It should be noted that some methodologies (e.g., the Sheffield Alcohol Policy Model) have attempted to incorporate more dynamic modeling.

[48] Nelson and McNall (2016).

discouraged excessive drinking.[49] Studies that conclude higher taxes lead to lower drinking often show that the reduction occurs among light and moderate drinkers. But those drinkers the least likely to endanger others and the most likely to experience alcohol-related health benefits.[50] If those studies' findings are correct, then alcohol taxes have the unintended consequence of reducing the prevalence of alcohol's health benefits in society while not reducing heavy drinking. Alcohol taxes accomplish the exact opposite of what one assumes public health advocates would want them to.

Research also challenges the belief that alcohol taxes have other positive public health impacts. Many paternalists argue that higher alcohol prices are key to minimizing drinking among minors. But studies show that beer taxes, for example, have a "relatively small and statistically insignificant impact on teen drinking" and no effect on vehicle fatalities.[51] Drawing on the National Longitudinal Survey of Adolescent to Adult Health, a group of researchers found that drinking among high school and college students is instead shaped by peer pressure, not price.[52]

Funnily enough, a more effective policy to reduce the sin of excessive drinking may be greater availability of another sin: marijuana.[53]

* * *

If the contradictions in alcohol research are reminiscent of those in soda research, it is because they are remarkably similar. That is no accident: much of the evidence for alcohol paternalism has comparable flaws.

A fundamental issue that afflicts many studies is experts' reliance on incomplete data. One data source often used to evaluate the connection between alcohol taxes and drinking excludes purchasing activity in some areas and contains sales of only a single brand of beer, wine, and whiskey. Studies show that when more comprehensive data sources are

---

[49] Nelson (2013); see also Manning et al. (1995).

[50] Ayyagari et al. (2013).

[51] Quoted from Dee (1999); see also Mast et al. (1999), Nelson (2014b), and Young and Likens (2000).

[52] Ajilore et al. (2016) and Guo et al. (2015).

[53] Alley et al. (2020).

used instead, the purported link between alcohol prices and drinking weakens.[54]

Another issue is a presumption that short-term effects will not change over time. A 2015 study concluded that an alcohol tax increase in Illinois reduced fatal vehicle accidents in that state by 26%. The study's authors argued that implementing tax increases elsewhere "could save thousands of lives."[55] But an analysis from the Tax Policy Center, an American think tank, contradicted those findings. It found the tax increase had not "led to a long-term reduction in alcohol-related traffic fatalities."[56] One reason for the discrepancy was that the first study relied on data collected over a shorter period, suggesting that any impact from the tax increase was temporary.

The first study had other flaws as well. The authors chose to focus their analysis on the number of accidents involving alcohol, without adjusting for important factors, such as changes in vehicle ownership, driving behavior, or overall accident rates. They also classified accidents involving a driver with any blood alcohol concentration above zero, even 0.01, as alcohol-related.

Those mistakes barely scratch the surface.

Like soda tax research, experts conducting alcohol tax studies have a penchant for ignoring substitution that may occur after price increases. At one extreme, a drinker may consume less alcohol but substitute for illicit drugs or other risky behaviors to satisfy whatever underlying needs drinking satisfied, an unintended consequence of alcohol taxation. Less drastically, a drinker may switch to a cheaper brand with the same alcohol content.[57] They may also change from spirits to wine, or from wine to beer.[58]

Or they may shop in another jurisdiction. Common sense dictates that people living in an area with high prices may decide to avoid them by buying alcohol in a neighboring area where prices are lower. But experts who study alcohol taxes often overlook this possibility.

---

[54] Ruhm et al. (2012). The data set in question is the Council for Community and Economic Research's ACCRA Cost of Living Index.

[55] Wagenaar et al. (2015).

[56] McClelland and Iselin (2017).

[57] Beard et al. (1997), Beatty et al. (2009), and Stehr (2007).

[58] Gant and Ekelund (1997).

Consider a study on Maryland's 2011 alcohol sales tax increase, which found "increased alcohol sales taxes may be as effective as excise taxes in reducing alcohol consumption and related problems."[59] The authors did not use data on alcohol consumption; they used data on alcohol sales, which missed the effect of cross-border shopping. In response to the tax increase, anyone could have purchased alcohol in nearby Pennsylvania, New Jersey, Delaware, Virginia, or West Virginia and taken it back to Maryland to drink at home. The study's authors acknowledged this possibility—yet left it out of their research design—and stated in the article's conclusion that they "cannot be certain that there was an overall reduction in alcohol consumption." Strangely, however, their abstract stated higher taxes "may be as effective … in reducing alcohol consumption."

Questionable research choices mar other studies. Many studies that appear to connect higher alcohol taxes to lower vehicle fatalities fail to control for confounding factors that may affect fatality rates, such as other alcohol control policies. They also fail to control for varying levels of law enforcement and the severity of legal and civil penalties for impaired driving. For example, the authors of a 2020 study concluded that taxes reduce beer consumption but conceded that their analysis failed to control for "laws related to drunk-driving, such as blood alcohol content limits and license revocation policies"—laws that undoubtedly have an impact.[60] Evidence suggests that once these salient features are accounted for, the supposed influence of alcohol taxes on drinking declines or vanishes altogether.[61]

A failure to control for all relevant factors was undoubtedly a problem with a 1998 report issued by the National Institutes of Health, a public health agency in the United States. The report concluded that drinking alcohol lowered wages among men, but the analysis failed to control for an important trait that affects anyone's salary: their level of education. When the model included education, alcohol's negative wage impact disappeared.[62]

[59] Esser et al. (2016).

[60] For example, Subbaraman et al. (2020) report that alcohol taxes reduce beer consumption, but also concede that they failed to control for "laws related to drunk-driving, such as blood alcohol content limits and license revocation policies."

[61] Benson et al. (1999) and Mast et al. (1999).

[62] The report is titled, "Economic Costs of Alcohol and Drug Abuse in the United States—1992."

Likewise, a study that concluded a tax on beer was among the "most effective" policies to discourage drunk driving failed to control for fixed characteristics of each state that are hard to measure. The reason for that omission, the experts clarified in a footnote, was that while they had initially controlled for those characteristics, they declined to report the results because they were not "meaningful."[63]

But perhaps the least forgivable flaw in alcohol tax research is experts' conflation of correlation and causation. The review that concluded alcohol taxes were an "effective means to reduce drinking" did not establish whether they caused a reduction in alcohol consumption; in fact, the words "cause" and "causation" do not appear in the article's text. The authors merely gathered results reported in a group of other studies, and those studies typically reported nothing more than a correlation between taxes and drinking. No rigorous determination was made as to whether the former affected the latter.

The research that linked higher alcohol taxes with lower traffic deaths, fewer sexually-transmitted infections, and a slight reduction in violence is another example. The authors of that study merely documented an "inverse relationship." They did not warn readers that because the study failed to determine cause and effect, its findings should be interpreted with caution.

* * *

Alcohol paternalists often respond to contradictory evidence with the same tactic used by soda paternalists: deflection. They claim that the evidence is poisoned by biased information funded by the alcohol industry. "Alcohol Companies Are Funding Research to Convince You Drinking Is Healthy" warned a headline in the Huffington Post. "We don't trust nutrition studies funded by soda companies," the author noted. "Why would we trust alcohol studies funded by the booze industry?"[64] The narrative is aided by media coverage of purported

---

[63] The study in question is Chaloupka et al. (1993); see discussion in Benson et al. (1999). Dee (1999) also reports that including fixed effects eliminates taxes' statistical significance.

[64] Almendrala (2018).

conflicts of interest, such as a controversy in 2018 involving an industry-sponsored research study at the National Institutes of Health, the American health agency.

Assessments of industry-funded research undermine those allegations. The authors of a review of 84 studies on the health benefits of alcohol found "no specific grounds for concern that alcohol industry funding has biased what is known about the protective effects of alcohol on cardiovascular disease."[65] Overlooked in the National Institutes of Health brouhaha was that the alcohol industry—"big alcohol"—had not sought out a favorable venue for its research. Rather, government experts had sought industry funding.[66]

Paternalists should instead direct their concerns about bias toward the social science used to justify alcohol taxes. Countless studies in that canon are biased in the direction of supporting a pro-tax argument. Like the research that links soda to obesity, studies have found evidence of publication bias within alcohol research. Academic journals are more likely to publish studies that report alcohol taxes have an effect on drinking than studies that report no connection.[67] Correcting for publication bias alone—without addressing other errors in the research—reduces the estimated size of price's effect on drinking by about 50%.[68]

Bias also surfaces in experts' propensity toward exaggeration. The Centers for Disease Control and Prevention study that used a rather generous definition of excessive drinking is one example. Or take a 2002 study from the National Center on Addiction and Substance Abuse, an American group now called the Center on Addiction, that reported teenagers consumed 25% of all alcohol in the United States. To reduce underage drinking, the group called for higher alcohol taxes and other government interventions. Upon further review, it was discovered that

---

[65] McCambridge and Hartwell (2015). The authors note there may be some bias with respect to the relationship between alcohol consumption and stroke, but there were too few studies to make a definitive conclusion one way or the other. One of the authors of that paper later argued that the subject of industry bias was understudied (McCambridge and Mialon 2018).

[66] Rabin (2018) and Thacker (2018).

[67] Fogarty (2010) and Nelson (2011).

[68] Nelson (2014a).

the Center improperly handled their data. The real figure was not 25%; it was 11%.[69]

That was not the first time the Center embellished statistics to justify higher taxes. A 1994 report claimed that almost 30% of welfare recipients had alcohol problems when the actual figure was closer to 5%. And it wouldn't be the Center's last. According to the *New York Times*, a 2003 report "assumed that everyone from 12-year-olds in junior high school to 20-year-old college juniors had the same drinking rate."[70]

The inclination to embellish is closely related to dissemination bias, the selective use of research findings to support alcohol paternalism. That may include overstating studies' results and ignoring their flaws and limitations. Evidence suggests this occurs in research published by the pro-tax Center on Alcohol Marketing and Youth, located at the Bloomberg School of Public Health at Johns Hopkins University.[71] That's the same school that published a 36-page report on how to campaign for soda taxes.

Unfortunately, if it were not already clear from how the Centers for Disease Control and Prevention approaches alcohol research, government agencies are not unbiased, either.

After completing a study that found men who drank moderately had a lower risk of cardiovascular disease—a finding consistent with many studies—a scientist was reportedly told by an associate director at the National Heart and Lung Institute, a division of the National Institutes of Health, that the finding was "scientifically misleading and socially undesirable." He was encouraged to write a revised study based on older data so that his conclusion would instead state there was no relationship between alcohol and cardiovascular health.[72]

Taken together, alcohol tax research does not inspire much confidence—and is a weak foundation for alcohol paternalism. Luckily, its deficiencies have caught some experts' notice. A review of alcohol control research, which included studies on alcohol taxes and other policies

[69] Lewin (2002).

[70] McNeil (2003).

[71] Nelson (2011).

[72] See Seltzer (1997). Note that the former National Heart and Lung Institute is now called the National Heart, Lung, and Blood Institute.

designed to reduce drinking, reported that it is "characterised by inadequate methodology." Among other problems, the review's authors found that the field lacks studies with proper controls. "Robust and well-reported research synthesis is deficient," they concluded, "despite the availability of clear methodological guidance."[73]

* * *

Flaws in alcohol research could be tolerated if, at the very least, alcohol tax revenue funded programs that reduce the harms purportedly caused by drinking. But the majority of tax revenue does no such thing.

About one half of 1% of federal alcohol tax revenue in the United States is sufficient to cover the entire Alcohol and Tobacco Tax and Trade Bureau budget.[74] The Bureau has several responsibilities tied to alcohol control, such as collecting taxes, issuing permits, and regulating product labels. But reducing alcohol consumption is not in the agency's mission—doing so would jeopardize the Bureau's very existence. The remaining 99.5% of revenue subsidizes overall federal spending. No funds are set aside for programs that aim to reduce drinking. None reimburses healthcare providers for any financial burden supposedly created by alcohol-related conditions.[75]

American state governments largely mirror the federal pattern. In most cases, alcohol tax revenue funds the agency or agencies tasked with collecting it, and the remainder goes to the state's general fund. Alcohol tax revenue in California transfers into the state's Alcohol Beverage Control Fund, which supports California's overall budget. Likewise, alcohol tax revenue in Texas goes to the state's general fund.

There are exceptions. In Washington, about 60% of alcohol tax revenue transfers into the state's general fund. The remainder is awarded to local governments to "meet community needs," including at least some money for alcohol education, as well as for substance abuse programs

---

[73] Siegfried and Parry (2019).

[74] In 2018, the Bureau collected nearly $21 billion in revenue from alcohol, tobacco, and firearm taxes against a total agency budget of just over $111 million. About $8 billion of that revenue was from alcohol excise taxes.

[75] Notably, the United States federal government does not handle some other excise taxes in a similar fashion. Revenue from firearm and ammunition taxes is transferred to the Fish and Wildlife Restoration Fund, which uses the proceeds to fund grants for hunter education and wildlife restoration.

and miscellaneous endeavors.[76] Among the programs receiving support from alcohol taxes is the Washington Wine Commission, whose mission is to "raise awareness *and demand* for Washington State wine" (emphasis added). Thus, in Washington, alcohol taxes promote drinking while also subsidizing substance abuse programs.

Although it is not often derived from alcohol tax revenue per se, governments earmark limited funding for alcohol-related initiatives, but the programs are often ineffective. For several years, federal funding in the United States buoyed Drug Abuse Resistance Education ("DARE"), a school-based curriculum that urged youth to avoid drug and alcohol abuse. Despite its ubiquity across American schools, DARE is now widely understood to have had little to no impact.[77]

Governments also award substantial funding as grants to interest groups that encourage alcohol paternalism, the very same rent-seeking dynamic that occurs with soda tax revenue. Alcohol Change UK receives financial support from government grants and investment income from an endowment established with alcohol license fees. Alcohol Justice—the California group with an interactive calculator that estimates how much extra government revenue higher alcohol taxes could generate—received government grants amounting to nearly $500,000 from 2015 through 2017 alone.[78] Over the same period, the Center on Addiction—the group with a documented history of using misleading statistics to exaggerate the severity of alcohol abuse—received $5.1 million in government funding.[79]

Those organizations are not alone. The pro-tax Texans Standing Tall received $1 million in government grants in 2017, about 75% of their total revenue.[80] The same year, MADD received $8.8 million in government funding, about 25% of its total revenue. MADD also collected another $7.1 million in fees for "victim impact panels," which the organization has lobbied some jurisdictions to force drunk drivers to

[76] The percentages vary from year to year and can be calculated based on data reported in the Washington State Liquor and Cannabis Board's annual reports.

[77] Pan and Bai (2009). The federal government was biased against evidence that contradicted DARE's efficacy. When a study funded by the Department of Justice concluded that DARE was a flop, the department refused to publish it (Ingraham 2017).

[78] Based on figures reported in Alcohol Justice's 2015 through 2017 Form 990.

[79] Based on figures reported in the Center on Addiction's 2017 Form 990.

[80] Based on figures reported in Texans Standing Tall's 2017 Form 990.

attend—and pay for.[81] Although the panels generate literal millions of dollars for MADD, studies show that they are ineffective at reducing alcohol abuse.[82]

What these groups have in common, other than their promotion of alcohol paternalism and dependence on government funding, is their support for higher alcohol taxes. As one opponent of this arrangement observed, "taxpayers are paying to help activists lobby to ... impose higher excise taxes on the very same taxpayers."[83]

The larger issue is why those who drink alcohol are forced to pay a disproportionate share of the cost of government, especially when there is little to no rigorous evidence that drinkers impose any externalities. Alcohol taxes are not as regressive as other sin taxes, but that's not the point.[84] Why should drinkers pay to forgive a sin they didn't commit?

* * *

Despite evidence that alcohol taxes are poorly justified and sometimes counterproductive, they are so widespread—and have such broad-based support from experts, public health organizations, and interest groups— that they are not likely to evaporate anytime soon. But like soda taxes, a few basic reforms are worth pursuing. At a minimum, individuals and organizations that lobby for alcohol taxes should be barred from profiting from the revenue those taxes generate. Taxpayers should also hold paternalists to account and demand that policymakers enact cuts to healthcare programs equal to whatever savings experts claim result from alcohol taxes. They should also seek sunset provisions on existing taxes so that voters may continually evaluate whether the tax should be continued or repealed.

If alcohol paternalists want to reduce alcohol abuse and its attendant externalities, research suggests that several other policies are more effective than taxation. Their focus should be targeting sanctions on individuals who abuse alcohol without penalizing light and moderate drinkers who present no risk to public health and who benefit from drinking. The most direct way to target those who cause harm, other than through the

---

[81] Based on figures reported in MADD's 2017 Form 990.

[82] Crew and Johnson (2011) and Wheeler et al. (2004).

[83] Bandow (1995).

[84] Vandenberg and Sharma (2016).

justice system, is with higher vehicle insurance premiums, a strategy that reduces impaired driving.[85]

Research also consistently shows that law enforcement reduces impaired driving. Four specific laws are especially useful:

- Dram-shop laws that make establishments that serve alcohol to intoxicated patrons liable for any harm they may cause
- Social host laws that extend dram-shop liabilities to individuals who serve alcohol on private property, such as at home parties
- Open container laws that make it illegal to possess or drink from an unsealed alcohol container in certain areas, such as inside a motor vehicle, and
- Laws that reduce the blood alcohol concentration considered impaired, perhaps from 0.10 to 0.08.[86]

Expanded use of breathalyzers and sobriety checkpoints, mandatory arrest and expedited conviction statutes, and severe penalties also deter impaired driving.[87] Having these laws "on the books" is not sufficient for them to work; governments have to commit adequate funding to enforcement.[88]

These policies do not necessarily target youth drinking, but fortunately, that is in decline—and without any substantial alcohol tax increases. According to the Youth Risk Behavior Survey, 82% of American high school students in 1991 reported having ever consumed alcohol, but just 60% reported the same in 2017. Current alcohol use over the same period, defined as one or more drinks in the previous month, fell over from 51% in 1991 to 30% in 2017. Fewer high school students also report having had their first drink before age 13.[89]

---

[85] Sloan and Githens (1994) and Sloan et al. (1995).

[86] Benson et al. (1999), Dee (2001), Dills (2010), Rammohan et al. (2011), Scherer et al. (2015), Whetten-Goldstein et al. (2000), and Young and Likens (2000).

[87] Bertelli and Richardson (2008), Chaloupka and Wechsler (1996), Evans et al. (1991), Kenkel (1993), and Wagenaar and Maldonado-Molina (2007).

[88] Benson et al. (2000). To illustrate this point, Lenk et al. (2016) found that open container laws might not have an effect per se, but that open container *enforcement* does.

[89] See "Trends in the Prevalence of Alcohol Use National YRBS: 1991–2017," a data summary published by the Centers for Disease Control and Prevention.

Alcohol education is key to maintaining those trends, providing that it is designed to avoid the pitfalls that undermined DARE.[90] Setting the minimum legal drinking age at 21 has been shown to lower rates of alcohol abuse among teenagers in the United States; thus, proposals to lower the age to 18 or 19 should be carefully evaluated.[91] Evidence also suggests that another way to reduce teenage drinking is through more stringent high school graduation requirements, especially in mathematics and science.[92]

Many alcohol paternalists embrace these suggestions. But they aren't likely to embrace any cut or repeal of alcohol taxes. For them, that would be too costly. Doing so would reduce government revenue so helpfully calculated on pro-paternalism interest group websites. It would also reduce the government's control over an individual's choice to drink alcohol, jeopardize government jobs, and undermine funding for experts and interest groups. In other words, cutting alcohol taxes would not advance progressivism—and that is another sin that paternalists will not tolerate.

References

Ajilore, Olugbenga, Aliaksandr Amialchuk, and Keven Egan. 2016. "Alcohol Consumption by Youth: Peers, Parents, or Prices?" *Economics & Human Biology* 23: 76–83.

Alley, Zoe M., David C.R. Kerr, and Harold Bae. 2020. "Trends in College Students' Alcohol, Nicotine, Prescription Opioid and Other Drug Use After Recreational Marijuana Legalization, 2008–2018." *Addictive Behaviors* 102: 106212.

Almendrala, Anna. 2018. "Alcohol Companies Are Funding Research to Convince You Drinking Is Healthy." The Huffington Post. Retrieved April 15, 2018 (https://www.huffingtonpost.com/entry/alcohol-companies-want-you-to-drink-more-and-theyre-funding-research-to-make-it-happen_us_5ad123bce4b077c89ce8a835).

Auld, M. Christopher. 2005. "Smoking, Drinking, and Income." *The Journal of Human Resources* 40(2): 505–518.

[90] Carpenter et al. (2019).

[91] Dee (1999).

[92] Hao and Cowan (2019).

Authors. 2015. "Effect of Initiating Moderate Alcohol Intake on Cardiometabolic Risk in Adults with Type 2 Diabetes: A 2-Year Randomized, Controlled Trial." *Annals of Internal Medicine* 163(8): 569–579.

Authors. 2018. "Alcohol Use and Burden for 195 Countries and Territories, 1990–2016: A Systematic Analysis for the Global Burden of Disease Study 2016." *The Lancet* 392(10152): 1015–1035.

Ayyagari, Padmaja, Partha Deb, Jason Fletcher, William Gallo, and Jody L. Sindelar. 2013. "Understanding Heterogeneity in Price Elasticities in the Demand for Alcohol for Older Individuals." *Health Economics* 22(1): 89–105.

Bandow, Doug. 1995. "Direct and Indirect Taxpayer Support for Lobbying." Congressional Testimony. Retrieved March 5, 2020 (https://www.cato.org/publications/congressional-testimony/direct-indirect-taxpayer-support-lobbying).

Bates, Laurie J., Resul Cesur, and Rexford E. Santerre. 2015. "Short-Run Marginal Medical Costs from Booze and Butts: Evidence from the States." *Southern Economic Journal* 81(4): 1047–1095.

Beard, T. Randolph, Paula A. Grant, and Richard P. Saba. 1997. "Border-Crossing Sales, Tax Avoidance, and State Tax Policies: An Application to Alcohol." *Southern Economic Journal* 64(1): 293–306.

Beatty, Timothy K.M., Erling Larsen, and Dag Einar Sommervoll. 2009. "Driven to Drink: Sin Taxese Near a Border." *Journal of Health Economics* 28(6): 1175–1184.

Benson, Bruce L., David W. Rasmussen, and Brent D. Mast. 1999. "Deterring Drunk Driving Fatalities: An Economics of Crime Perspective." *International Review of Law and Economics* 19(2): 205–225.

Benson, Bruce L., Brent D. Mast, and David W. Rasmussen. 2000. "Can Police Deter Drunk Driving?" *Applied Economics* 32(3): 357–366.

Bertelli, Anthony M., and Lilliard E. Richardson Jr. 2008. "The Behavioral Impact of Drinking and Driving Laws." *Policy Studies Journal* 36(4): 545–569.

Blanchette, Jason G., Frank J. Chaloupka, and Timothy S. Naimi. 2019. "The Composition and Magnitude of Alcohol Taxes in States: Do They Cover Alcohol-Related Costs?" *Journal of Studies on Alcohol and Drugs* 80(4): 408–414.

Bouchery, Ellen E., Henrick J. Harwood, Jeffrey J. Sacks, Carol J. Simon, and Robert D. Brewer. 2011. "Economic Costs of Excessive Alcohol Consumption in the U.S., 2006." *American Journal of Preventative Medicine* 41(5): 516–524.

Bourne, Ryan. 2019. "The Case for Economics When Considering Alcohol Tax Levels." The Cato Institute. Retrieved January 10, 2020 (https://www.cato.org/blog/case-economics-when-considering-alcohol-tax-levels).

Brien, Susan E., Paul E. Ronksley, Barbara J. Turner, Kenneth J. Mukamal, and William A. Ghali. 2011. "Effect of Alcohol Consumption on Biological Markers Associated with Risk of Coronary Heart Disease: Systematic Review and Meta-Analysis of Interventional Studies." *BMJ* 342: d636.

Burton, Robyn, and Nick Sheron. 2018. "No Level of Alcohol Consumption IS Safe." *The Lancet* 392(10152): 987–988.

Callinan, Sarah, Robin Room, and Michael Livingston. 2014. "Changes in Australian Attitudes to Alcohol Policy: 1995–2010." *Drug and Alcohol Review* 33(3): 227–234.

Carpenter, Christopher S., Tim A. Bruckner, Thurston Domina, Julie Gerlinger, and Sara Wakefield. 2019. "Effects of State Education Requirements for Substance Use Prevention." *Health Economics* 28(1): 78–86.

Cesur, Resul, and Inas Rashad Kelly. 2014. "Who Pays the Bar Tab? Beer Consumption and Economic Growth in the United States." *Economic Inquiry* 52(1): 477–494.

Chaloupka, Frank J., and Henry Wechsler. 1996. "Binge Drinking in College: The Impact of Price, Availability, and Alcohol Control Policies." *Contemporary Economic Policy* 14(4): 112–124.

Chaloupka, Frank J., Henry Saffer, and Michael Grossman. 1993. "Alcohol-Control Policies and Motor-Vehicle Fatalities." *Journal of Legal Studies* 22(1): 161–186.

Chaloupka, Frank J., Michael Grossman, and Henry Saffer. 2002. "The Effects of Price on Alcohol Consumption and Alcohol-Related Problems." *Alcohol Research & Health* 26(1): 22–34.

Chaloupka, Frank J., Lisa M. Powell, and Kenneth E. Warner. 2019. "The Use of Excise Taxes to Reduce Tobacco, Alcohol, and Sugary Beverage Consumption." *Annual Review of Public Health* 40: 187–201.

Cobiac, Linda, Theo Vos, Christopher Doran, and Angela Wallace. 2009. "Cost-Effectiveness of Interventions to Prevent Alcohol-Related Disease and Injury in Australia." *Addiction* 104(10): 1646–1655.

Cook, Philip J. 2007. *Paying the Tab: The Costs and Benefits of Alcohol Control.* Princeton, NJ: Princeton University Press.

Corrao, Giovanni, Luca Rubbiati, Vincenzo Bagnardi, Antonella Zambon, and Kari Poikolainen. 2000. "Alcohol and Coronary Heart Disease: A Meta-Analysis." *Addiction* 95(10): 1505–1523.

Crampton, Eric, Matt Burgess, and Brad Taylor. 2011. "The Cost of Cost Studies." Working Paper No. 29/2011, College of Business and Economics, Department of Economics and Finance, University of Canterbury.

Crew, Benjamin Keith, and Sarah Emily Johnson. 2011. "Do Victim Impact Programs Reduce Recidivism for Operating a Motor Vehicle While Intoxicated? Findings from an Outcomes Evaluation." *Criminal Justice Studies* 24(2): 153–163.

Dasgupta, Amitava. 2019. "Alcohol: Pharmacokinetics, Health Benefits with Moderate Consumption and Toxicity." Pp. 1–26 in *Critical Issues in Alcohol and Drugs of Abuse Testing*, 2nd ed. London, UK: Academic Press.

Dave, Dhaval, and Robert Kaestner. 2002. "Alcohol Taxes and Labor Market Outcomes." *Journal of Health Economics* 21(3): 357–371.

de Lorgeril, Michel, Patricia Salen, Jean-Louis Martin, François Boucher, François Paillard, and Joël de Leiris. 2002. "Wine Drinking and Risks of Cardiovascular Complications After Recent Acute Myocardial Infarction." *Circulation* 106(12): 1465–1469.

Dee, Thomas S. 1999. "State Alcohol Policies, Teen Drinking and Traffic Fatalities." *Journal of Public Economics* 72(2): 289–315.

Dee, Thomas S. 2001. "Does Setting Limits Save Lives? The Case of 0.08 BAC Laws." *Journal of Policy Analysis and Management* 20(1): 111–128.

Di Castelnuovo, Augusto, Simona Costanzo, Vincenzo Bagnardi, Maria Benedetta Donati, Licia Iacoviello, and Giovanni de Gaetano. 2006. "Alcohol Dosing and Total Mortality in Men and Women: An Updated Meta-Analysis of 34 Prospective Studies." *Archives of Internal Medicine* 166(22): 2437–2445.

Dills, Angela K. 2010. "Social Host Liability for Minors and Underage Drunk-Driving Accidents." *Journal of Health Economics* 29(2): 241–249.

Esser, Marissa B., Hugh Waters, Mieka Smart, and David H. Jernigan. 2016. "Impact of Maryland's 2011 Alcohol Sales Tax Increase on Alcoholic Beverage Sales." *American Journal of Drug and Alcohol Abuse* 42(4): 404–411.

Evans, William N., Doreen Neville, and John D. Graham. 1991. "General Deterrence of Drunk Driving: Evaluation of Recent American Policies." *Risk Analysis* 11(2): 279–289.

Fogarty, James. 2010. "The Demand for Beer, Wine and Spirits: A Survey of the Literature." *Journal of Economic Surveys* 24(3): 428–478.

Forsyth, Mark. 2017. *A Short History of Drunkenness: How, Why, Where, and When Humankind Has Gotten Merry from the Stone Age to the Present*. New York, NY: Three Rivers Press.

Fosdick, Raymond B., and Albert L. Scott. 1933. *Toward Liquor Control*. New York, NY: Harper & Brothers.

Fragopoulou, Elizabeth, Maria Choleva, Smaragdi Antonopoulou, and Constantinos A. Demopoulos. 2018. "Wine and Its Metabolic Effects. A Comprehensive Review of Clinical Trials." *Metabolism* 83(6): 102–119.

Gant, Paula A., and Robert B. Ekelund Jr. 1997. "Excise Taxes, Social Costs, and the Consumption of Wine." Pp. 247–269 in *Taxing Choice: The Predatory Politics of Fiscal Discrimination*, edited by William F. Shughart II. New Brunswick, NJ: Transaction Publishers.

Guo, Guang, Yi Li, Craig Owen, Hongyu Wang, and Greg J. Duncan. 2015. "A Natural Experiment of Peer Influences on Youth Alcohol Use." *Social Science Research* 52: 193–207.

Hao, Zhuang, and Benjamin W. Cowan. 2019. "The Effects of Graduation Requirements on Risky Health Behaviors of High School Students." *American Journal of Health Economics* 5(1): 97–125.

Heien, Dale. 1996a. "The Relationship Between Alcohol Consumption and Earnings." *Journal of Studies on Alcohol* 57(5): 536–542.

Heien, Dale M. 1996b. "Do Drinkers Earn Less?" *Southern Economic Journal* 63(1): 60–68.

Heien, Dale M., and David J. Pittman. 1989. "The Economic Costs of Alcohol Abuse: An Assessment of Current Methods and Estimates." *Journal of Studies on Alcohol* 50: 567–679.

Heise, Barbara. 2010. "Healthcare System Use by Risky Alcohol Drinkers: A Secondary Data Analysis." *Journal of the American Academy of Nurse Practitioners* 22(5): 256–263.

Herrnstadt, Evan, Ian W.H. Parry, and Juha Siikamäki. 2015. "Do Alcohol Taxes in Europe and the US Rightly Correct for Externalities?" *International Tax and Public Finance* 22(1): 73–101.

Hodgeland, William. 2015. *The Whiskey Rebellion: George Washington, Alexander Hamilton, and the Frontier Rebels Who Challenged America's Newfound Sovereignty.* New York, NY: Simon & Schuster.

Horlings, Edwin, and Amanda Scoggins. 2006. "An Ex Ante Assessment of the Economic Impacts of EU Alcohol Policies." RAND Europe Technical Report. Retrieved March 5, 2020 (https://www.rand.org/content/dam/rand/pubs/technical_reports/2006/RAND_TR412.pdf).

Hu, Tun Yuan. 1950. "The Liquor Tax in the United States, 1791–1947: A History of the Internal Revenue Taxes Imposed on Distilled Spirits by the Federal Government." New York, NY: Columbia University Graduate School of Business.

Ingraham, Christopher. 2017. "A Brief History of DARE, the Anti-drug Program Jeff Sessions Wants to Revive." *The Washington Post.* Retrieved February 1, 2020 (https://www.washingtonpost.com/news/wonk/wp/2017/07/12/a-brief-history-of-d-a-r-e-the-anti-drug-program-jeff-sessions-wants-to-revive/).

Jarl, Johan, and Ulf Gerdtham. 2010. "Wage Penalty of Abstinence and Wage Premium of Drinking—A Misclassification Bias Due to Pooling of Drinking Groups?" *Addition Research & Theory* 18(3): 284–297.

Joint Committee of the States to Study Alcoholic Beverage Laws. 1950. "Alcoholic Beverage Control: An Official Study." Report.

Jones, Alison Snow, and David W. Richmond. 2006. "Causal Effects of Alcoholism on Earnings: Estimates from the NLSY." *Health Economics* 15(8): 849–871.

Kenkel, Donald S. 1993. "Drinking, Driving, and Deterrence: The Effectiveness and Social Costs of Alternative Policies." *The Journal of Law & Economics* 36(2): 877–913.

Keyes, Katherine M., Aaron Shev, Melissa Tracy, and Magdalena Cerdá. 2019. "Assessing the Impact of Alcohol Taxation on Rates of Violent Victimization in a Large Urban Area: An Agent-Based Modeling Approach." *Addiction* 114(2): 236–247.

Kim, Jee Wook, Min Soo Byun, Dahyun Yi, Jun Ho Lee, Kang Ko, So Yeon Jeon, Bo Kyung Sohn, Jun-Young Lee, Yu Kyeong Kim, Seong A Shin, Chul-Ho Sohn, and Dong Young Lee. 2020. "Association of Moderate Alcohol Intake with in Vivo Amyloid-Beta Deposition in Human Brain: A Cross-Sectional Study." *PLoS Medicine* 17(2): e1003022.

Lenk, Kathleen M., Toben F. Nelson, Traci L. Toomey, Rhonda Jones-Webb, and Darin J. Erickson. 2016. "Sobriety Checkpoint and Open Container Laws in the United States: Associations with Reported Drinking-Driving." *Traffic Injury Prevention* 17(8): 782–787.

Lewin, Tamar. 2002. "Teenage Drinking a Problem but Not in Way Study Found." *The New York Times*. Retrieved December 1, 2019 (https://www.nytimes.com/2002/02/27/us/teenage-drinking-a-problem-but-not-in-way-study-found.html).

Lhachimi, Stefan K., Katie J. Cole, Wilma J. Nusselder, H.A. Smit, Paolo Balli, Kathleen Bennett, Joceline Pomerleau, Martin McKee, Kate Charlesworth, Margarete C. Kulik, Johan P. Mackenbach, and Hendriek Boshuizen. 2012. "Health Impacts of Increasing Alcohol Prices in the European Union: A Dynamic Projection." *Preventative Medicine* 55(3): 237–243.

Li, Jessica, Melanie Lovatt, Douglas Eadie, Fiona Dobbie, Petra Meier, John Holmes, Gerard Hastings, and Anne Marie MacKintosh. 2017. "Public Attitudes Towards Alcohol Control Policies in Scotland and England: Results from a Mixed-Methods Study." *Social Science & Medicine* 177: 177–189.

Liu, Li, Jiajing Wang, Danny Rosenberg, Hao Zhao, György Lengyeld, and Dani Nadele. 2018. "Fermented Beverage and Food Storage in 13,000y-Old Stone Mortars at Raqefet Cave, Israel: Investigating Natufian Ritual Feasting." *Journal of Archeological Science: Reports* 21(10): 783–793.

Looney, Adam. 2017. "Measuring the Loss of Life from the Senate's Tax Cuts for Alcohol Producers." The Brookings Institution. Retrieved December 1, 2019 (https://www.brookings.edu/research/measuring-the-loss-of-life-from-the-senates-tax-cuts-for-alcohol-producers/).

MacDonald, Ziggy, and Michael A. Shields. 2004. "Does Problem Drinking Affect Employment? Evidence from England." *Health Economics* 13(2): 139–155.

Makary, Martin A., and Michael Daniel. 2016. "Medical Error—The Third Leading Cause of Death in the US." *BMJ* 353: i2139.

Manning, Willard G., Emmett B. Keeler, and Joseph P. Newhouse. 1989. "The Taxes of Sin: Do Smokers and Drinkers Pay Their Way?" *Journal of the American Medical Association* 261(11): 1604–1609.

Manning, Willard G., Linda Blumberg, and Lawrence H. Moulton. 1995. "Demand for Alcohol: The Differential Response to Price." *Journal of Health Economics* 14(2): 123–148.

Mast, Brent, Bruce L. Benson, and David W. Rasmussen. 1999. "Beer Taxation and Alcohol-Related Traffic Fatalities." *Southern Economic Journal* 66(2): 214–249.

McCambridge, Jim, and Greg Hartwell. 2015. "Has Industry Funding Biased Studies of the Protective Effects of Alcohol on Cardiovascular Disease? A Preliminary Investigation of Prospective Cohort Studies." *Drug and Alcohol Review* 34(1): 58–66.

McCambridge, Jim, and Melissa Mialon. 2018. "Alcohol Industry Involvement in Science: A Systematic Review of the Perspectives of the Alcohol Research Community." *Drug and Alcohol Review* 37(5): 565–579.

McClelland, Robert, and John Iselin. 2017. "Do Alcohol Excise Taxes Reduce Motor Vehicle Fatalities? Evidence from Two Illinois Tax Increases." Tax Policy Center.

McGirr, Lisa. 2019. "How Prohibition Fueled the Klan." *The New York Times*. Retrieved December 1, 2019 (https://www.nytimes.com/2019/01/16/opinion/prohibition-immigration-klan.html).

McNeil, Donald G., Jr. 2003. "Liquor Industry and Scientists at Odds Over Alcohol Study." *The New York Times*. Retrieved March 5, 2020 (https://www.nytimes.com/2003/02/26/us/liquor-industry-and-scientists-at-odds-over-alcohol-study.html).

Meltzer, David. 1997. "Accounting for Future Costs in Medical Cost-Effectiveness Analysis." *Journal of Health Economics* 16(1): 33–64.

Møller, Lars, and Srdan Matic. 2010. "Best Practice in Estimating the Costs of Alcohol—Recommendations for Future Studies." World Health Organization for Europe.

National Highway Safety Traffic Administration. 2018. "Alcohol-Impaired Driving." Report.

Nelson, Jon P. 2011. "Alcohol Marketing, Adolescent Drinking and Publication Bias in Longitudinal Studies: A Critical Survey Using Meta-Analysis." *Journal of Economic Surveys* 25(2): 191–232.

Nelson, Jon P. 2013. "Does Heavy Drinking by Adults Respond to Higher Alcohol Prices and Taxes? A Survey and Assessment." *Economic Analysis and Policy* 43(3): 265–291.

Nelson, Jon P. 2014a. "Estimating the Price Elasticity of Beer: Meta-Analysis of Data with Heterogeneity, Dependence, and Publication Bias." *Journal of Health Economics* 33: 180–187.

Nelson, Jon P. 2014b. "Gender Differences in Alcohol Demand: A Systematic Review of the Role of Prices and Taxes." *Health Economics* 23(10): 1260–1280.

Nelson, Jon P., and Amy D. McNall. 2016. "Alcohol Prices, Taxes, and Alcohol-Related Harms: A Critical Review of Natural Experiments in Alcohol Policy for Nine Countries." *Health Policy* 120(3): 264–272.

Pan, Wei, and Haiyan Bai. 2009. "A Multivariate Approach to a Meta-Analytic Review of the Effectiveness of the D.A.R.E. Program." *International Journal of Environmental Research and Public Health* 6(1): 267–277.

Peters, Bethany L. 2004. "Is There a Wage Bonus from Drinking? Unobserved Heterogeneity Examined." *Applied Economics* 36(20): 2299–2315.

Peters, Bethany L., and Edward Stringham. 2006. "No Booze? You May Lose: Why Drinkers Earn More than Nondrinkers." *Journal of Labor Research* 27(3): 411–421.

Phillips, Rod. 2014. *Alcohol: A History*. Chapel Hill, NC: University of North Carolina Press.

Pogue, Thomas F., and Larry G. Sgontz. 1989. "Taxing to Control Social Costs: The Case of Alcohol." *American Economic Review* 79(1): 235–243.

Polen, Michael R., Carla A. Green, Donald K. Freeborn, John P. Mullooly, and Frances Lynch. 2001. "Drinking Patterns, Health Care Utilization, and Costs Among HMO Primary Care Patients." *Journal of Behavioral Health Services & Research* 28(4): 378–399.

Rabin, Roni Caryn. 2018. "Federal Agency Courted Alcohol Industry to Fund Study on Benefits of Moderate Drinking." *The New York Times*. Retrieved December 1, 2019 (https://www.nytimes.com/2018/03/17/health/nih-alcohol-study-liquor-industry.html).

Rammohan, Veda, Robert A. Hahn, Randy Elder, Robert Brewer, Jonathan Fielding, Timothy S. Naimi, Traci L. Toomey, Sajal K. Chattopadhyay, and Carlos Zometa. 2011. "Effects of Dram Shop Liability and Enhanced Over-service Law Enforcement Initiatives on Excessive Alcohol Consumption and Related Harms: Two Community Guide Systematic Reviews." *American Journal of Preventative Medicine* 41(3): 334–343.

Ramnath, R., N. Kinnear, S. Chowdhury, and T. Hyatt. 2020. "Interacting with Android Auto and Apple CarPlay When Driving: The Effect on Driver Performance." IAM RoadSmart Published Project Report PPR948.

Romeo, Javier, Julia Wärnberg, Esther Nova, and Ligia E. Díaz. 2007. "Moderate Alcohol Consumption and the Immune System: A Review." *British Journal of Nutrition* 98(S1): S111–S115.

Ronksley, Paul E., Susan E. Brien, Barbara J. Turner, Kenneth J. Mukamal, and William A. Ghali. 2011. "Association of Alcohol Consumption with Selected Cardiovascular Disease Outcomes: A Systematic Review and Meta-Analysis." *BMJ* 342: d671.

Ruhm, Christopher J., Alison Snow Jones, Kerry Anne McGeary, William C. Kerr, Joseph V. Terza, Thomas K. Greenfield, and Ravi S. Pandian. 2012. "What U.S. Data Should Be Used to Measure the Price Elasticity of Demand for Alcohol?" *Journal of Health Economics* 31(6): 851–862.

Sacks, Jeffrey J., Katherine R. Gonzales, Ellen E. Bouchery, Laura E. Tomedi, and Robert D. Brewer. 2015. "2010 National and State Costs of Excessive Alcohol Consumption." *American Journal of Preventative Medicine* 49(5): e73–e79.

Scherer, Michael, James C. Fell, Sue Thomas, and Robert B. Voas. 2015. "Effects of Dram Shop, Responsible Beverage Service Training, and State Alcohol Control Laws on Underage Drinking Driver Fatal Fatal Crash Ratios." *Traffic Injury Prevention* 16(S2): S59–S65.

Seltzer, Carl C. 1997. "'Conflicts of Interest' and 'Political Science'." *Journal of Clinical Epidemiology* 50(5): 627–629.

Siegfried, Nandi, and Charles Parry. 2019. "Do Alcohol Control Policies Work? An Umbrella Review and Quality Assessment of Systematic Reviews of Alcohol Control Interventions (2006–2017)." *PLoS ONE* 14(4): e0214865.

Sloan, Frank A., and Penny B. Githens. 1994. "Drinking, Driving, and the Price of Automobile Insurance." *Journal of Risk and Insurance* 61(1): 33–58.

Sloan, Frank A., Bridget A. Reilly, and Christoph Schenzler. 1995. "Effects of Tort Liability and Insurance on Heavy Drinking and Drinking and Driving." *The Journal of Law & Economics* 38(1): 49–77.

Sornpaisarn, Bundit, Kevin D. Shield, Esa Österberg, and Jürgen Rehm, eds. 2017. "Resource Tool on Alcohol Taxation and Pricing Policies." World Health Organization.

Stahre, Mandy, Jim Roeber, Dafna Kanny, Robert D. Brewer, and Xingyou Zhang. 2014. "Contribution of Excessive Alcohol Consumption to Deaths and Years of Potential Life Lost in the United States." *Preventing Chronic Disease* 11(6): e130293.

Stehr, Mark. 2007. "The Effect of Sunday Sales Bans and Excise Taxes on Drinking and Cross-Border Shopping for Alcoholic Beverages." *National Tax Journal* 60(1): 85–105.

Stockwell, Tim, Jinhui Zhao, Sapna Panwar, Audra Roemer, and Timothy Naimi. 2016. "Do 'Moderate' Drinkers Have Reduced Mortality Risk? A Systematic Review and Meta-Analysis of Alcohol Consumption and All-Cause Mortality." *Journal of Studies on Alcohol and Drugs* 77(2): 185–198.

Stringham, Peter. 2009. "The Catastrophe of What Passes for Alcohol Policy Analysis." Reason Foundation Policy Brief No. 78.

Subbaraman, Meenakshi S., Nina Mulia, William C. Kerr, Deidre Patterson, Katherine J. Karriker-Jaffe, and Thomas K. Greenfield. 2020. "Relationships Between US State Alcohol Policies and Alcohol Outcomes: Differences by Gender and Race/Ethnicity." *Addiction*, forthcoming. https://doi.org/10.1111/add.14937.

Teutsch, Steven M., Amy Geller, and Yamrot Negussie, eds. 2018. *Getting to Zero Alcohol-Impaired Driving Fatalities*. Washington, DC: National Academies Press.

Thacker, Paul D. 2018. "How a Flood of Corporate Funding Can Distort NIH Research." *The Washington Post*. Retrieved March 3, 2020 (https://www.washingtonpost.com/outlook/how-corporate-funding-distorts-nih-research/2018/06/22/ad0260c8-7595-11e8-9780-b1dd6a09b549_story.html).

Thom, Michael. 2017. *Tax Politics and Policy*. New York: Routledge.

van den Brandt, Piet A., and Lloyd Brandts. 2020. "Alcohol Consumption in Later Life and Reaching Longevity: The Netherlands Cohort Study." *Age and Ageing*, forthcoming. https://doi.org/10.1093/ageing/afaa003.

Vandenberg, Brian, and Anurag Sharma. 2016. "Are Alcohol Taxation and Pricing Policies Regressive? Product-Level Effects of a Specific Tax and a Minimum Unit Price for Alcohol." *Alcohol and Alcoholism* 51(4): 493–502.

van Ours, Jan C. 2004. "A Pint a Day Raises a Man's Pay; but Smoking Blows That Gain Away." *Journal of Health Economics* 23(5): 863–886.

Wagenaar, Alexander C., and Mildred M. Maldonado-Molina. 2007. "Effects of Drivers' License Suspension Policies on Alcohol-Related Crash Involvement: Long-Term Follow-Up in Forty-Six States." *Alcoholism: Clinical & Experimental Research* 31(8): 1399–1406.

Wagenaar, Alexander C., Matthew J. Salois, and Kelli A. Komro. 2009. "Effects of Beverage Alcohol Price and Tax Levels on Drinking: A Meta-Analysis of 1003 Estimates from 112 Studies." *Addiction* 104(2): 179–190.

Wagenaar, Alexander C., Amy L. Tobler, and Kelli A. Komro. 2010. "Effects of Alcohol Tax and Price Policies on Morbidity and Mortality: A Systematic Review." *American Journal of Public Health* 100(11): 2270–2278.

Wagenaar, Alexander C., Melvin D. Livingston, and Stephanie S. Staras. 2015. "Effects of a 2009 Illinois Alcohol Tax Increase on Fatal Motor Vehicle Crashes." *American Journal of Public Health* 105(9): 1880–1885.

Wagner, Richard E. 1997. "The Taxation of Alcohol and the Control of Social Costs." pp. 227–246 in *Taxing Choice: The Predatory Politics of Fiscal Discrimination*, edited by William F. Shughart II. New Brunswick, NJ: Transaction Publishers.

Wheeler, Denise R., Everett M. Rogers, J. Scott Tonigan, and W. Gill Woodall. 2004. "Effectiveness of Customized Victim Impact Panels on First-Time DWI Offender Inmates." *Accident Analysis & Prevention* 36(1): 29–35.

Whetten-Goldstein, Kathryn, Frank A. Sloan, Emily Stout, and Lan Liang. 2000. "Civil Liability, Criminal Law, and Other Policies and Alcohol-Related Motor Vehicle Fatalities in the United States: 1984–1995." *Accident Analysis & Prevention* 32(6): 723–733.

Woodfield, Alan. 1988. "Economic Cost of Alcohol-Related Health Care in New Zealand: An Interpretive Comment." *British Journal of Addiction* 83: 1031–1035.

Young, Douglas J., and Thomas W. Likens. 2000. "Alcohol Regulation and Auto Fatalities." *International Review of Law and Economics* 20(1): 107–126.

CHAPTER 4

Taxing Tobacco

Europeans may have brought sugarcane to the New World, but they carried tobacco home. Indigenous people there had used tobacco in pipe ceremonies for millennia. On the other side of the Atlantic Ocean, the novel plant was popular and quickly spread across Europe, the Middle East, and beyond. Smoking was not only a recreational activity. Like some of the other sins, tobacco was prescribed as a therapeutic. Sixteenth-century Spanish physician Nicolás Monardes claimed tobacco was an effective treatment for dozens of ailments, including cancer. English poet Anthony Chute likewise described it as something of a miracle cure in his spartan 1595 pamphlet, "Tobacco."

Thanks to that ubiquity, tobacco taxes are, much like alcohol taxes, a centuries-old method to raise government revenue. King James I ordered a tobacco tax in England in 1604. It was taxed in the Ottoman Empire as early as 1688. Those taxes were not only proposed to generate income, but also to discourage the use of a plant that, while popular, many believed injured the body and soul.[1]

---

[1] The English tobacco tax was never enforced, but a formal levy was introduced in 1660. The English position was more benign than that adopted by other governments. Some American colonies banned public smoking altogether. Emperor Chongzhen and Emperor Kangxi, who ruled China during the seventeenth century, also ordered tobacco prohibition. Violators there were punishable by death. Explorations of tobacco's history are available in Grier (2019), Goodman (1993), and Milov (2019).

© The Author(s) 2021   87
M. Thom, *Taxing Sin*,
https://doi.org/10.1007/978-3-030-49176-5_4

Although federal officials in the United States proposed a tobacco tax in 1790, it was not enacted until four years later. The levy passed despite complaints from opponents who claimed the burden would disproportionately fall on the poor. Due to evasion and administrative difficulties, the tax was suspended and repealed by 1800. Short-term tobacco taxes were reinstituted to finance the War of 1812. They came back again in 1862 alongside dozens of other taxes to fund the Civil War. Federal tobacco taxes have remained in effect ever since.

Compared to its long history of taxation, tobacco paternalism is relatively new. Because drinking was customarily regarded as more harmful than smoking tobacco, the progressive and temperance movements directed more energy to alcohol prohibition. While there was definite concern among paternalists that tobacco use jeopardized public health—enough to compel many governments to charge taxes and institute other controls, including poorly-enforced smoking bans—a significant anti-tobacco movement did not materialize in the late nineteenth or early twentieth century.[2]

Though it chafes against modern sensibilities, it was not uncommon during that time to hear arguments made against tobacco control. During World War I, many people thought smoking was necessary to boost military morale, and efforts to limit soldiers' access to cigarettes were not welcomed. Some progressive era feminist groups also fought restrictions on women's freedom to smoke in public.[3]

But attitudes evolved during and after World War II as it became more commonly understood that tobacco use was not advantageous to good health and that it imposed additional healthcare costs on society. As tobacco paternalism garnered more attention, activists called for policies to restrict its use. Even Nazi Germany implemented a robust anti-tobacco

---

[2] That's not to say there were no organized campaigns or public outcry against tobacco. Throughout the late eighteenth and early nineteenth centuries, many political cartoons depicted smoking in an unflattering light, featuring skull-and-crossbones caricatures, haggard faces, and the like (Sullum 1998, pp. 147–151). In 1914 Henry Ford published *The Case Against the Little White Slaver*, a book that warned readers "almost any criminal…is an inveterate cigarette smoker." Ford's concern was with smoking's effect on boys, who he wrote "go with other smokers to the pool rooms and saloons." Among other evidence for the perils of smoking, the book cited an experiment in which a cat died after being injected with "tobacco juice."

[3] Reiter (1996).

program, including public health messaging against smoking and funding for research on tobacco's harmful effects.[4]

Paternalists argued that taxes were an important facet of tobacco control, one that would raise prices, decrease smoking, and generate revenue to offset tobacco-related externalities. The movement gained momentum following the United States Surgeon General's landmark 1964 report on tobacco, which concluded cigarette smoking was a causal factor in lung cancer, bronchitis, and emphysema. Paternalism accumulated further support after the public grew more aware that the tobacco industry—the veritable "big tobacco"—had known for years that its products were addictive and harmful yet publicly denied it, a colossal subterfuge and public relations disaster.

Thanks in part to promotion by public health groups, tobacco paternalism continues today. Since 1998, the World Health Organization has administered the Tobacco Free Initiative, which provides resources to policymakers interested in shrinking tobacco use. Taxes are among the organization's many proposals to improve health and raise government revenue. The American Heart Association likewise "advocates for significant increases in tobacco excise taxes at the federal, state, county and municipal levels" because higher prices cause a "substantial reduction" in cigarette use.[5] Taxes have also been endorsed by the American Medical Association, the American Lung Association, and the International Union Against Tuberculosis and Lung Disease.

The American Cancer Society is perhaps the strongest advocate for tobacco paternalism among the public health community. It maintains the Tobacco Atlas, an online resource that depicts the tobacco industry as a squid-like creature emerging from a giant package of cigarettes. The Atlas's website informs readers that tobacco "costs society trillions of dollars" and that taxing it is "the most effective but the least-used tobacco control tool."[6]

For decades, experts have echoed that refrain by conducting research that reinforces tobacco paternalism and the need for government action.[7]

---

[4] Proctor (1996, 1999).

[5] American Heart Association (2019).

[6] Quoted from the website's homepage (http://tobaccoatlas.org).

[7] Some tobacco control experts worry that the rise of concern about the obesity epidemic draws attention away from tobacco control, as if paternalism is some type of zero-sum game; see Schroeder and Warner (2010).

Many are attached to think tanks at major universities, such as the Center for Tobacco Control Research and Education at the University of California, San Francisco, which publishes studies about the sins of tobacco use and the virtues of tobacco control.

Other experts promote tobacco paternalism by writing books. In 2010, one wrote a book about how to fight back against the "tobacco holocaust."[8] One year later, a book from a different expert also compared tobacco use to the holocaust.[9] Another pair of experts coauthored a book on the "war" waged against tobacco companies by public health organizations.[10] Yet another expert warned that the burden of smoking per person exceeded $100,000.[11]

Anti-tobacco experts are frequently sponsored by an array of philanthropic organizations, including Bloomberg Philanthropies and the Bill and Melinda Gates Foundation. The Robert Wood Johnson Foundation, which attempted to distance itself from its support of soda taxes, proudly declares that it "has a long history of working with national and local health organizations, faith groups, businesses, government and others to advocate for higher tobacco taxes."[12]

As with the other sins, special interest groups bolster the work done by experts and public health organizations. The Campaign for Tobacco-Free Kids—"the leading advocacy organization working to reduce tobacco use and its deadly consequences"—actively promotes control policies including taxes, which it calls "the most direct and effective method for reducing tobacco consumption."[13] Action on Smoking and Health—otherwise known as "ASH," a group with affiliates in Australia, the United Kingdom, the United States, and New Zealand—has published several commentaries favorable to higher tobacco taxes and critical of dissenting opinion. The Truth Initiative, a "nonprofit public health organization committed to making tobacco use a thing of the past," endorses

[8] Rubinoff (2010).

[9] Proctor (2011).

[10] Glantz and Balbach (2000).

[11] Sloan et al. (2006).

[12] Quoted from website (https://www.rwjf.org/en/library/collections/tobacco-control.html). As Sullum (1998, p. 125) notes, the Foundation as far back as 1994 announced $10 million in funding to bolster campaigns in favor of higher tobacco taxes.

[13] Quoted from website (https://www.tobaccofreekids.org/what-we-do/global/taxation-price).

taxes because the "research is clear: increases in tobacco taxes decrease tobacco use."[14]

The media does little to question tobacco paternalism. A review of newspaper coverage in Australia over ten years found news items were more than twice as likely to include statements favorable toward tobacco control than they were statements to the contrary.[15] Assessments of media coverage in the United States also find that the tone is biased in favor of tobacco control.[16]

Not surprisingly, public opinion strongly approves of tobacco taxes. Support is highest when revenue is dedicated to tobacco control.[17] Around the world, policy matches public sentiment. Over 100 countries have enacted taxes and other policies that raise the price of tobacco products, including cigarettes, cigars, and chewing tobacco. Federal tobacco taxes in the United States are supplemented by an additional tax in all 50 states. Some local governments, including the cities of New York, Chicago, and Philadelphia, add a third layer of taxation.

* * *

There should be no question that using tobacco products damages human health. Smokers face a higher risk of multiple types of cancer as well as heart disease and stroke. But strange as it may seem, tobacco products offer benefits to certain individuals. Nicotine, the addictive substance found within tobacco plants, is a successful treatment for conditions that cause cognitive impairment, including attention deficit hyperactivity disorder, Alzheimer's disease, and schizophrenia.[18]

Tobacco's risks are also amplified in the public imagination.[19] While smokers have a higher risk of lung cancer than nonsmokers, 85–90% will

---

[14] Quoted from website (https://truthinitiative.org/research-resources/tobacco-prevention-efforts/importance-tobacco-taxes).

[15] McLeod et al. (2009).

[16] Thrasher et al. (2014) and Wackowski et al. (2013), but see also Blake et al. (2015).

[17] Gardner and West (2010).

[18] Gray et al. (1996) and Rezvani and Levin (2001).

[19] Viscusi (1990, 1992).

never develop the disease. Smokers also have a higher risk of emphysema, but most will never develop that condition, either.[20]

Furthermore, the number of tobacco-related deaths each year—a number often quoted by public health officials, experts, and interest groups as justification for tobacco taxes—is overstated. Methods used by the Centers for Disease Control and Prevention, as well as the United States Surgeon General and the American Cancer Society, exaggerate the actual number by over 100%. Using appropriate data and controlling for confounding factors that affect mortality, such as diet, exercise, and working conditions, the real number of tobacco-related deaths in the United States is closer to 150,000 annually, not the 400,000 plus usually cited.[21]

Notwithstanding the exaggeration, that sizable number of deaths lends plausibility to the argument that, in addition to other harms, tobacco use is responsible for hundreds of thousands of deaths and illnesses that impose unnecessary healthcare costs. But like soda and alcohol, tobacco's apparent externalities warrant a closer look, if for no other reason than that the estimates offered by experts and public health groups are exorbitant.

For example, the American Cancer Society's Tobacco Atlas homepage claimed in 2020 that tobacco "costs society trillions of dollars." No source was cited for that estimate. A more credible number comes courtesy of the Truth Initiative, which noted in 2019 that "smoking-related illnesses" cost the United States $326 billion, or nearly $1000 per person.[22]

Three sources were identified for that estimate. The first was a study about tobacco's potential role in causing various illnesses. The study did

---

[20] Lung cancer, emphysema, and other respiratory disease incidence varies by sex, country, and length of time spent smoking, among other variables. Research indicates that genetics and nutrition also affect lung cancer risk among smokers; see Bach et al. (2003), Kelland (2010), and Swaminathan (2008).

[21] Levy and Marimont (1998); see also Sterling et al. (1993). Comparable exaggerations about the number of obesity-related deaths have been published and used to justify related public health interventions.

[22] See "Action Needed: Tobacco Taxes," a policy brief issued in January 2019. The $170 billion figure was specific to the United States. Estimates of smoking's burden on the healthcare systems in other countries typically fall in the billions of dollars. For example, Callum et al. (2011) claim tobacco's burden on the United Kingdom's National Health Service as far back as 1996 was nearly £2 billion annually.

not offer an accounting for tobacco's financial impact, however, so it is not clear why it was referenced.

The second source, a 2014 report from the United States Surgeon General, indicated that tobacco imposed $156 billion in "lost productivity" each year, defined as the total wages lost by individuals who died from an illness that may have been caused by tobacco use.[23] Regardless of whether that estimate is correct—like appraisals of tobacco-related deaths, it's likely overblown—lost wages are an internality borne by tobacco users, not an externality inflicted on society.[24] Recall that mixing internalities and externalities was a frequent mistake in studies that attempted to illustrate just how harmful soda and alcohol were—and why taxing them was necessary.

The third source, a study funded by the Centers for Disease Control and Prevention, estimated that tobacco was liable for "as much as" $170 billion annually in healthcare costs.[25] To arrive at that number, the study's authors made a dubious assumption: that all healthcare costs associated with smokers were attributable to tobacco use. Thus, for smokers, the cost of setting a broken bone, the cost of an annual physical, and the cost of any other routine medical procedure were ascribed to tobacco. By design, that assumption inflates estimates of tobacco-related healthcare costs.

Nevertheless, the study reported that only 3% of healthcare spending in the United States was for the 23% of the population that smoked. Nearly all healthcare spending—91%—was for the 56% of the population that never smoked.[26]

---

[23] See "The Health Consequences of Smoking – 50 Years of Progress: A Report of the Surgeon General," issued in 2014.

[24] There may be some spillover, but a smoker who dies prematurely or otherwise stops working opens their job to someone else. For that person, smoking has imposed a positive externality. If the smoker is replaced with a healthier worker, overall productivity may rise, another positive externality. However, evidence suggests that smokers are no more absent from work than non-smokers (Ault et al. 1991). Other studies with much smaller sample sizes come to the opposite conclusion (e.g., Halpern et al. 2001) as do studies funded by anti-tobacco research centers (e.g., Leigh 1995).

[25] Xu et al. (2015).

[26] The remainder are considered "former smokers." The authors state that over a four-year period, former smokers contributed to a larger share of healthcare spending than current smokers. Combined, all current and former smokers were responsible for 8.7% of healthcare spending.

That disparity stems in part from nonsmokers' longer life expectancies, which ultimately impose higher healthcare costs.[27] It's a variation of the tradeoff that occurs with the obese and with excessive drinkers. Tobacco users may generate higher healthcare costs while living, but by dying prematurely, they avoid certain other healthcare costs. Premature death may also reduce pension, social security, and long-term care expenses.[28]

This tradeoff among tobacco users is not a recent discovery. As two economists from the Congressional Research Service, a government think tank in the United States that advises members of Congress, noted in 1994, "the alternative to death from a smoking-related illness is not immortality and perfect health—it is later death, and perhaps from a more costly illness."[29] As the authors of another study observed, "If we eliminate a specific cause of death, we simply die later from another. In the meantime we grow older, become generally more disabled, and need more care."[30]

The tradeoff is also not mere theory. Multiple studies indicate that tobacco users do not impose the financial burden paternalists complain about. According to some studies, costs between users and nonusers are an even exchange. One study concluded that, on the one hand, "non-smokers subsidize smokers' medical care and group life insurance," but on the other hand, "smokers subsidize nonsmokers' pensions and nursing home payments," a finding echoed in other reports.[31]

Some studies go farther and show that tobacco users are net contributors to public treasuries. A Canadian study estimated that smokers' shorter life expectancies, combined with taxes paid on tobacco products, yielded a net contribution equal to billions of dollars annually.[32] An Australian study estimated that tobacco tax revenue exceeded tobacco's externalities in that country by over $3 billion every year.[33] A New Zealand study ventured that tobacco tax revenue exceeds associated healthcare costs,

---

[27] van Baal et al. (2008).

[28] Temple (2011).

[29] Gravelle and Zimmerman (1994).

[30] Bonneux et al. (1998).

[31] Manning et al. (1989); see also Viscusi (1995).

[32] Raynauld and Vidal (1992).

[33] Collins and Lapsley (2008).

even without considering pension savings that result from users' prema-ture death.[34] And last but not least, a Finnish study found that smokers' overall healthcare and pension costs in that country were markedly lower than non-smokers'. The study concluded that each smoker represented a net contribution of €133,800.[35]

While these studies incorporate tobacco taxes paid by users in their cost–benefit analyses, others suggest that even if taxes are excluded from consideration, tobacco users still subsidize nonusers.[36]

To better understand how different studies arrive at divergent conclu-sions about tobacco's externalities, consider two estimates for the United Kingdom. A 2010 report from Policy Change, a British think tank, esti-mated an annual figure of £13.7 billion.[37] But 69% of that estimate was tied to lost productivity—an internality, not an externality. Worse, the estimate was inflated: the report's authors assumed that employees who took smoking breaks had lower productivity, but nonsmoking employees take breaks, too. Furthermore, studies show that breaks don't reduce employee productivity.[38] A smaller proportion of the estimate was tied to lost wages—another internality—and, to exaggerate that figure, the authors assumed that, but for smoking, every employee would have worked until age 74. The authors also assumed that, but for smoking, employees "would not have been affected by any other health prob-lems."[39]

An ensuing critique from the Institute for Economic Affairs, another British think tank, applied more realistic assumptions and found that tobacco use saved that country's government nearly £10 billion each year. Although premature death reduced some revenues, such as income and other taxes paid by tobacco users, the authors found that shortened lifespans reduced spending on welfare, education, pensions, and health-care. Their estimate did not include tobacco taxes paid by smokers; if it

---

[34] O'Dea and Thomson (2007).

[35] Tiihonen et al. (2012). Nevertheless, to arrive at the conclusion that smoking was a burden on society, the authors assumed that each year of life was worth €22,200.

[36] McCormick et al. (1997).

[37] Featherstone and Nash (2010).

[38] Tucker (2003).

[39] Snowdon and Tovey (2017).

had, smokers' net contribution to British finances would have been much higher.[40]

Collectively, this evidence undermines the view—no matter how reasonable on its face, and no matter how deeply ingrained in the conventional wisdom—that tobacco products deserve taxation because of their externalities. Tobacco is a lethal substance, but its lethality saves society money. The lack of externalities also undermines a key justification for the 1998 Master Settlement Agreement between tobacco companies and 46 American state governments: that those states, primarily through their Medicaid programs, were burdened by tobacco-related healthcare costs. On that principle, tobacco companies agreed to pay states over $200 billion.

* * *

Paternalists do not welcome evidence that casts skepticism on the belief that tobacco imposes net harm on society. Their faith in tobacco's harms is not easily shaken. The same is true of their faith in tobacco taxes, which paternalists assume are an effective policy to communicate tobacco's harms, minimize use, raise government revenue, and improve public health.

That's not just paternalistic rhetoric. A Chinese study estimated that using a tax to increase cigarette prices by 50% would reduce the number of tobacco-related premature deaths in that country.[41] The authors of a study on cigarette taxes in Mexico concluded that they were "an effective tool for generating government revenue" and that they "can also be a useful measure to improve population health."[42] Summarizing the literature, a review of eight studies concluded that tobacco taxes "generate substantial healthcare cost savings" and also "generate large revenues."[43]

But like soda and alcohol research, many tobacco tax studies depend on simulation models to arrive at their conclusions. The study that determined tobacco taxes would improve public health in China utilized a simulation, and so did the study of taxes in Mexico. All eight studies

[40] Ibid.
[41] Verguet et al. (2015).
[42] Jimenez-Ruiz et al. (2007).
[43] Contreary et al. (2015).

in the review article were simulations. Countless other simulation models purport to demonstrate tobacco tax efficacy.[44]

In addition to their other faults, tobacco-related simulations are not necessarily designed to be an objective research method. The "original intent" behind SimSmoke, a model developed with funding from the Robert Wood Johnson Foundation, was—according to its creator—"to provide justification for tobacco control to policymakers."[45] That model is the basis for quite literally hundreds of seemingly unbiased studies on the advantages of tobacco taxes and other control policies.

Observational studies tell a different story about tobacco taxes—namely, that users are not that responsive to higher prices. One study that evaluated both reported smoking levels and data gathered from blood tests found that each $1 cigarette tax increase in the United States reduced smoking by only about 2%.[46] Another estimated that large tobacco tax increases between 1992 and 2008 reduced smoking by no more than 5.2%.[47] According to a different study, the relationship between tobacco taxes and "smoking participation or smoking intensity is negative, small, and not usually statistically significant." The study's authors concluded that doubling taxes might reduce smoking by between 2 and 4%.[48] A study of 27 European nations concluded elevated prices did not have a substantial impact on smoking.[49]

Observational research also casts doubt on whether tobacco taxes have other positive public health effects. Paternalists often justify taxes by arguing that higher prices deter youth smoking, but their impact on tobacco use among minors is negligible to nonexistent.[50] Others claim that taxes increase the chance that a smoker quits, but that's

---

[44] Levy et al. (2000) and Goodchild et al. (2016); see also Rhoads (2012) and Tauras et al. (2005).

[45] Levy et al. (2002, 2006).

[46] Nesson (2017); despite a small impact, the author described cigarette taxes as "an effective policy tool."

[47] MacLean et al. (2016).

[48] Callison and Kaestner (2014).

[49] Bogdanovica et al. (2012).

[50] DeCicca et al. (2002, 2008) and Hansen et al. (2017), which find that while taxes may have reduced youth smoking in the past, there's no reason to believe that's true after 2007.

mostly among individuals who report an easier time achieving goals—like smoking cessation—in the first place.[51]

Paternalists also argue that tobacco taxes encourage the poor, who can scarcely afford higher prices, to quit smoking. But studies show that low-income smokers are less responsive to price increases.[52] When they spend more money on tobacco products, less money is available to spend on food. Tobacco taxes thus contribute to the unintended consequence of food insecurity.[53]

* * *

The primary shortcoming in simulation models and other studies that purport to show the benefits of tobacco taxes is a failure to incorporate elements of the real world where individuals make choices about whether, and how, to use tobacco. By neglecting those elements, studies too often arrive at flawed conclusions—conclusions that inevitably diffuse unchecked into the public imagination, and eventually into public policy.

Many studies fail to capture the extent to which smokers modify their behavior in response to higher tobacco taxes. That mistake occurs despite a mountain of evidence that shows most smokers do not simply accept higher prices and reduce smoking. Several studies find that when prices increase, some users switch to a less expensive brand.[54] Others find that users switch to a higher-quality brand.[55] Higher prices push some toward more harmful products with higher tar and nicotine content.[56] Smokers may also buy packs instead of cartons or change from cigarettes to smokeless tobacco or loose tobacco.[57] Many respond with increased smoking efficiency by extracting more nicotine from each cigarette.[58]

[51] Ferrer and Orehek (2018).

[52] Franks et al. (2007).

[53] Cutler-Triggs et al. (2008).

[54] Hyland et al. (2005), Tsai et al. (2005), Wangen and Biørn (2006), and White et al. (2013).

[55] Nesbit (2018) and Sobel and Garrett (1997).

[56] Evans and Farrelly (1998) and Farrelly et al. (2004).

[57] Espinosa and Evans (2013), Hanewinkel et al. (2008), and Ohsfeldt et al. (1997).

[58] Adda and Cornaglia (2006, 2013); see also Benowitz et al. (1986) and Scherer (1999).

Tobacco users also seek other means to avoid taxes. At least a dozen studies report evidence that users counter higher taxes by purchasing tobacco products in areas with lower prices.[59] That might include neighboring cities, regions, countries, or, in the United States, Native American reservations where taxes are often inapplicable. Users also buy tobacco products on the illicit market.[60]

Not surprisingly, tax avoidance is more prevalent in areas with higher tobacco taxes.[61] According to one study, over 75% of discarded cigarette packs in New York City evade appropriate state and local taxes, meaning they were purchased illegally or in a jurisdiction outside the city.[62] Another study found a remarkably similar percentage among discarded cigarette packs in Chicago.[63]

But the errors in tobacco research go much deeper than ignoring behavioral responses. Far too many studies rely on flawed data, often drawn from self-reported consumption by tobacco users. Given the stigma associated with smoking, there is clear social pressure to underreport, making such data sources inaccurate. Some experts wisely attempt to circumvent the problems inherent to self-reporting by using retail sales data instead. While that's a more objective source of information, it fails to capture the impact of tax avoidance. A better approach taken in recent studies draws on data collected from blood tests. Compared to

---

[59] Lakhdar et al. (2016), LaFaive (2018), Lovenheim (2008), and Luccasen et al. (2005).

[60] That is not a modern response. The Ottoman Empire's tobacco taxes were so high that they were widely believed to have encouraged smuggling, leading authorities to cut the tax.

[61] DeCicca et al. (2013). Smuggling tobacco products across state lines is sometimes an exercise in behavior more nefarious than tax avoidance. In 2000, United States authorities arrested several individuals tied to a cigarette smuggling operation that ran between North Carolina and Michigan. Members of the group purchased thousands of cartons of cigarettes in low-tax North Carolina and drove them to high-tax Michigan, where they took advantage of higher market prices and sold the products to gas stations. The group did not pay Michigan tobacco taxes. Instead, a portion of the profits was funneled to the Islamic terrorist group Hezbollah. It was later revealed that the operation's ringleader, Mohamad Youssef Hammoud, entered the United States illegally in 1992 and initiated the scheme about three years later. In 2002 he was found guilty of multiple crimes, including providing support to terrorists.

[62] Kurti et al. (2013).

[63] Merriman (2010).

earlier findings, those studies tend to report that smoking behavior is less responsive to price.[64]

Like alcohol research, another frequent error in tobacco research is the assumption that correlation proves causation. A study on the impact of tobacco tax increases in Massachusetts—funded with revenues from the tax—concluded "a strongly implemented, comprehensive tobacco control programme can significantly reduce tobacco use."[65] Yet the study's authors did nothing more than compare smoking rates in Massachusetts to other states that earmarked less funding for tobacco control, and since higher taxes correlated with a decline in smoking, the authors assumed the taxes were the cause. They did not control for confounding factors that may have contributed to lower smoking. Two additional studies funded by tobacco tax revenue used the same correlation-is-causation method to arrive at the same conclusion.[66]

A later study that controlled for confounding factors like demographics, cigarette smuggling, and the smoking decline well at hand before the tax increase—a study that was not funded by any outside group—came to a different conclusion. It found that sales of taxed cigarettes continued to fall after tax-induced price increases but likely would have anyway. It also reported that the state's higher prices encouraged interstate smuggling.[67]

The propensity to automatically credit any decline in tobacco use to public policy without exploring alternative explanations is a hallmark of tobacco research.[68] Consider a study published in the *Journal of the American Medical Association* that concluded California's anti-tobacco policies successfully lowered tobacco use. Not only did the study's authors fail to control for demographics and other confounding factors, but their data suggested an alternative explanation: smoking prevalence was in sharp decline well before the control policies and would have continued to fall without government intervention. Perhaps accidentally, the study also

[64] Gallet and List (2003).

[65] Biener et al. (2000).

[66] Robbins et al. (2002) and Weintraub and Hamilton (2002).

[67] Marlow (2012).

[68] Marlow (2009).

showed that the rate of decline in tobacco use only slowed *after* California committed hundreds of millions of dollars to tobacco control.[69]

Tobacco research studies also tend to ignore or overlook unintended consequences. While it may not be because of taxation, fewer individuals use tobacco products now than in the past. But that trend has likely contributed to another: the rise in obesity. Although findings on the relationship between tobacco use and obesity are mixed, many studies report at least an association between smoking and weight gain.[70] Using data on Canadian adults, for example, one study found that a 10% increase in cigarette taxes led to a 4–5% increase in the obese population because the taxes reduced smoking and the faster metabolism it causes.[71] On a related note, studies have also shed light on another unintended consequence of diminished smoking: lower levels of exercise.[72]

But perhaps the most expensive unintended consequence associated with lower tobacco use is higher spending on healthcare and other government programs. Reduced cigarette sales have contributed to increasing life expectancy—and to rising healthcare costs that balloon with a larger, aging population.[73] A 1997 study published in *The New England Journal of Medicine* offered this succinct prediction: "If all smokers quit, health care costs would be lower at first, but after 15 years they would become higher than at present."[74] Several studies report precisely that.[75]

* * *

Paternalists blanch at evidence that undermines their argument for the necessity of tobacco taxes. Some attack critics with hyperbole. When an analysis funded by Philip Morris, a multinational tobacco company and a

---

[69] Pierce et al. (1998).

[70] Flegal et al. (1995) and see discussion in Gruber and Frakes (2006). While claiming to disprove the hypothesis that lower smoking leads to increased weight, the study relies on self-reported height, weight, and smoking levels rather than objectively collected data. Au et al. (2013) find that the relationship varies by gender; see also Courtemanche (2009).

[71] Sen et al. (2010). Relatedly, Cawley et al. (2004) find that women looking to lose weight are more likely to initiate smoking.

[72] Conway and Niles (2017).

[73] Lippiatt (1990).

[74] Barendregt et al. (1997).

[75] Leu and Schaub (1983) and Temple (2011); see also Schelling (1986).

charter member of "big tobacco," concluded that smokers in the Czech Republic were a net contributor to that nation's finances, a local newspaper compared the company to Nazis—a strange insult, given that actual Nazis were firmly anti-tobacco.[76]

Other paternalists charge that studies contradicting their beliefs cannot be trusted because the study's authors or funding sponsors are somehow linked to the tobacco industry.[77] But it's not clear whether industry sponsorship has much of an impact on tobacco research. The experts behind one assessment of that question concluded that articles from other experts with ties to the industry were indeed biased in the industry's favor.[78] But an assessment from the same experts published a year earlier found no evidence that studies with industry funding were of lesser quality than studies without it.[79] More importantly, the experts behind both assessments were not neutral on the question of bias. Both had written books that attacked tobacco companies, and both received grant funding from anti-tobacco groups.

If anything, the concerning bias is just the opposite. Acceptance of funding from anti-tobacco groups is a common trait among those who allege that the tobacco industry manipulates research. A 2018 review

---

[76] See Green (2001). A rebuttal study (Ross 2004) claimed that tobacco use bled money from the Czech treasury and implied that the Philip Morris-sponsored analysis was insufficiently paternalistic. The rebuttal received little notice, perhaps because it had several methodological flaws of its own. It estimated that tobacco use "drains at least $373 million from the state budget annually" but that figure's source is not clear. The rebuttal includes no empirical models or sensitivity checks. The author claimed that lost wages and productivity were an externality, even though they aren't—an ironic mistake, given that one of the author's complaints about the Philip Morris report was sloppy handling of externalities and internalities. The author also complained that the report failed to incorporate several costs of tobacco use, including "grief," and argued for tobacco paternalism.

[77] Cohen (1996).

[78] Barnes and Bero (1998). The authors applied a liberal interpretation of "industry ties" that included a person who had ever received any industry funding or supported the industry during its fight with the Environmental Protection Agency over its flawed report on secondhand smoking.

[79] Barnes and Bero (1997). The authors conceded that few of the studies they reviewed disclosed industry funding, making it difficult to evaluate the potential bias it may impose—but, in so conceding, provided evidence that the tobacco industry has not inundated academic journals with pro-tobacco or anti-tax research.

concluded that the industry's data on illicit tobacco sales was exaggerated, a strategy consistent with what the authors called "the tobacco industry's long history of manipulating research, including its extensive efforts to undermine and cause confusion on science showing the negative health impacts of smoking."[80] The authors arrived at their conclusion of industry bias by consulting "tobacco control experts" and comparing their personal evaluations of the quality of industry-funded data. They proposed a solution to tobacco industry bias: "tax tobacco companies and administer the resulting funds to experts, independent of the tobacco industry." Not coincidentally, the authors were affiliated with anti-tobacco research centers funded by grants from government agencies and nonprofit organizations.

There are other biases in tobacco research. Some experts reveal their prejudice by offering conclusions that contradict their findings. After reporting that higher cigarette prices corresponded with weight gain and obesity, the authors of one study wrote that "in no way" should their findings imply that a reduction to cigarette taxes was necessary.[81] After presenting evidence of tobacco tax avoidance, undoubtedly encouraged by high taxes, the authors of another study concluded that tobacco taxes should nevertheless rise.[82]

Bias also poisons government research. The United States Environmental Protection Agency issued a report in 1993 that claimed secondhand smoke was responsible for thousands of deaths every year. Consequently, the agency classified it as a carcinogen—a decision that reverberated nationwide, lending support to anti-tobacco groups that demanded public smoking bans. A tobacco cooperative, joined by Philip Morris and R. J. Reynolds, another tobacco company, sued the Agency for violating administrative procedures and failing to engage in "reasoned decision-making." They won the lawsuit, in part because the Agency—in the words of a federal judge—"committed to a conclusion before research had begun," "disregarded information and made findings on selective

[80] Gallagher et al. (2018).

[81] Baum (2009).

[82] Fix et al. (2014).

information," and "adjusted established procedure and scientific norms" to "influence public opinion."[83]

Far worse than mistake-filled research and bias is the length to which some paternalists will go to attack legitimate science that undermines tobacco paternalism. One of the most extensive peer-reviewed studies on the relationship between secondhand smoke, heart disease, and lung cancer found that the relationship was "considerably weaker than generally believed." For challenging tobacco paternalism, the study's authors were the subject of a coordinated public relations campaign teeming with *ad hominem* attacks and false claims about their methods and findings. The campaign was advanced by anti-tobacco experts and the American Cancer Society. While critics complained that the study was funded by the tobacco industry, it was also funded by tobacco tax revenue and—ironically—the American Cancer Society. The campaign was part of a larger pattern of paternalists and interest groups spreading false claims about the effects of secondhand smoke.[84] Some went so far as to call for a boycott of a session at an academic conference on secondhand smoke's health effects.[85]

Instead of calling their critics Nazis, paternalists would be better served by focusing attention on their own bias—and improving their social science. A review of 27 studies on how tobacco price impacts use found that they are characterized by several problems, including "recall bias, a general failure to apply diagnostic tests ... and to conduct sensitivity analysis," and "a reliance on empirical approaches that are methodologically weak." Overall, the authors wrote that "existing studies do not provide strong evidence that tobacco prices or taxes affect smoking onset."[86]

* * *

[83] Quoted from the decision in *Flue-Cured Tobacco Cooperative Stabilization Corporation v. United States EPA and Carol Browner* (1998).

[84] Siegel (2007). Other studies also question the relationship between secondhand smoke exposure and lung cancer (e.g., Peres 2013).

[85] Phillips (2007). A 2005 review funded by the American Cancer Society documented the tobacco industry's strategies to "manipulate" information about the risks of tobacco use, including publishing studies that support their position, attacking studies that don't, and funding research centers (Bero 2005). The strategies used by tobacco paternalists and groups like the American Cancer Society are no different.

[86] Guindon (2014).

The many problems with research used to justify tobacco paternalism could be disregarded if tobacco tax revenue was earmarked for productive use. But like revenue from soda and alcohol taxes, that rarely occurs.

Federal tobacco tax revenue in the United States is far greater than the budget of the agency that collects it, the Alcohol and Tobacco Tax and Trade Bureau. But the surplus is not allocated to tobacco cessation programs, nor does it reimburse healthcare providers—or nonsmokers—for their share of tobacco's ostensible burden. Instead, it subsidizes the State Children's Health Insurance Program, which provides healthcare for middle- and low-income families with children.

The same arrangement persists all over the world. Tobacco tax revenue within a particular jurisdiction more than pays for the cost of collecting it, and the excess is transferred to public healthcare programs. In Ecuador, tobacco taxes subsidize the Solidarity Fund for Health, known as FOSAULD. Jamaican taxes likewise support that country's National Health Fund.[87]

But in some countries, tobacco tax revenue drifts away from healthcare. Lithuanian revenues support the country's Physical Education and Sport Support Fund. Romania also uses tobacco tax revenue to subsidize sports programs. In Estonia, some revenue is earmarked for the Cultural Endowment, which uses funding on "projects which promote, introduce and popularize the arts, folk culture, physical fitness and sport."

Among American states, a small percentage of tobacco tax revenue is earmarked for prevention and health programs. For example, less than 25% of revenue from a tobacco tax increase approved by Massachusetts voters in 1992 was allocated for tobacco cessation.[88] But that fraction was generous. According to a report from the Centers for Disease Control and Prevention, less than 4% of the $245 billion collected by state governments from tobacco taxes and settlements with the industry between 1998 and 2010 was spent on tobacco control.[89]

That may not be a bad thing, however, because tobacco control programs are generally ineffective. Several studies have found that

---

[87] See "WHO report on the global tobacco epidemic 2017: Monitoring tobacco use and prevention policies," issued in July 2017. Tobacco tax earmarks are reported in Appendix IX, Table 9.4.

[88] Ritch and Begay (2001).

[89] See the Centers for Disease Control and Prevention's Morbidity and Mortality Weekly Report for May 25, 2012.

government-sponsored anti-tobacco initiatives have little to no effect on smoking prevalence.[90] Some studies do find that such programs are effective, but their reported impact is often small. A study that found "increases in funding for state tobacco control program reduce tobacco use" actually determined that, for an average state government, tobacco control spending reduced the number of cigarettes bought per capita by 0.16.[91] But given widespread behavioral shifts and tax avoidance, cigarette sales are a poor indicator of tobacco consumption. Many other studies that purport to show the efficacy of tobacco control programs fail to account for confounding factors that may explain reductions in use.[92]

A more concerning facet of tobacco control efforts is that rent-seeking interest groups receive millions of dollars in government funding, even if it is not always directly earmarked from tobacco tax revenue. From 2012 to 2017 government grants provided $31 million in funding to the pro-tax American Lung Association, equal to about 10% of the organization's total revenue.[93] From 2016 to 2018, government funding contributed over $16 million to the pro-tax American Cancer Society.[94] The Truth Initiative, a $1 billion nonprofit organization funded initially with proceeds from the Master Settlement Agreement, received $12.1 million in government funding from 2013 through 2018.[95] From 2014 to 2017, government funding contributed to $1.1 million to the American Nonsmokers' Rights Foundation, about 13% of its revenue.[96]

How nonprofit organizations spend government funding is a matter of some contention. A coalition of interest groups, including the American Cancer Society, the American Heart Association, and the American Lung Association, lobbied for California Proposition 99, an initiative

---

[90] Ciecierski et al. (2011), Goel (2008), and Marlow (2010).

[91] Farrelly et al. (2003). The average state spent $0.31 per capita on tobacco control programs. The coefficient is −0.53. Multiply them to get −0.1643. The average per capita cigarette consumption was 106.55.

[92] Marlow (2007).

[93] Based on figures reported in the American Lung Association's 2012 through 2017 Form 990.

[94] Based on figures reported in the American Cancer Society's 2016 through 2018 Form 990.

[95] Based on figures reported in the Truth Initiative's 2013 through 2018 Form 990.

[96] Based on figures reported in the American Nonsmokers' Rights Foundation's Form 990s.

approved by voters in 1988 that more than tripled the state's cigarette tax and added new taxes on other tobacco products. The same groups then applied for grants funded by those new taxes. Some received grants for education programs but used the funding for political activities forbidden by state law. Others used the money for prizes and pool parties.[97]

Worthy as it may or may not be, spending tobacco tax revenue on healthcare programs—or sports programs, or pool parties—has two major problems. First, the burden has a larger impact on the poor, who are more likely to use tobacco products. Second, it leaves funding for those programs dependent on maintaining a large population of tobacco users. If tobacco use drops to zero—the stated goal of nearly every tobacco paternalist—then program funding also drops. Healthcare programs would simultaneously have to grapple with lower revenue and higher costs associated with longer life expectancies facilitated by reduced smoking. Ironically, tobacco is a sin healthcare programs cannot afford to live without.

* * *

Tobacco tax necessity is so ingrained in the conventional wisdom—and so vigorously defended by experts and interest groups—that the taxes are almost certainly here to stay. But absent repeal, tobacco taxes need reform. Individuals, interest groups, and research centers that collect money from tobacco tax revenue should not be able to lobby for them. Existing tobacco taxes should be also be converted to temporary taxes that require periodic voter reauthorization. Taxpayers should also hold paternalists to account by demanding healthcare spending cuts equal to whatever savings are supposed to accrue as a result of higher tobacco taxes—a test of just how deeply paternalists believe their own claims.

Still, none of those reforms changes the fact that tobacco use is not the vast burden on society that most believe it is, nor do they change the fact that tobacco taxes are counterproductive. Paternalists should stop demanding tax increases. They should also avoid stigmatizing tobacco use, which motivates some individuals—like adolescents and teenagers—to want to smoke more, the same type of reactance that occurs when

---

[97] A coalition of interest groups sued the state for diverting revenue earmarked for anti-tobacco programs toward prenatal care and other health services for the poor. See DiLorenzo (1997).

paternalists condemn soda. Denouncing tobacco also has unintended, negative consequences for smokers' mental health and delays their seeking medical care.[98]

Other tobacco control policies should be reconsidered, too. Studies show that smoking bans have had little to no public health impact in the United States, the United Kingdom, Germany, and Scotland.[99] Instead, they have unleashed a torrent of unintended consequences. One study found that smoking bans have had the perverse effect of increasing nonsmokers' exposure to cigarette smoke, because the bans displace smokers to nonregulated areas where they smoke and consequently expose even more people.[100] Smoking bans have also been shown to jeopardize tobacco users' physical safety, especially women, who have to exit the security of a building to smoke outside, thereby exposing them to a higher risk of assault.[101] There is also compelling evidence that alcohol-related motor vehicle accidents occur more often in areas that have smoking restrictions because tobacco users drive longer distances to find establishments that allow smoking, perhaps outdoors or through noncompliance, or to areas without a ban in place.[102]

A more prudent approach to tobacco control would concentrate public policy on achieving two objectives. The first is to focus on tobacco education programs on minors. Messaging is more effective when it highlights tobacco's negative health effects than when it attacks the tobacco industry.[103] Other policies, like banning tobacco advertisements, are not effective.[104] Likewise, although mandating graphic warning labels on tobacco products is a popular strategy, studies that purport to show their

[98] Burgess et al. (2009).

[99] Gao and Baughman (2017), Jones et al. (2015), Kvasnicka et al. (2018), and Shetty et al. (2011). Substitution can be partly blamed for smoking bans' lack of health efficacy. Some tobacco users react to smoking prohibition by switching to smokeless tobacco (Adams et al. 2013).

[100] Adda and Cornaglia (2010).

[101] Moore et al. (2010).

[102] Adams and Cotti (2008). Another study—funded by the National Institute on Alcohol Abuse and Alcoholism—found no such consequences, but only looked at data in two states (Bernat et al. 2013).

[103] Pechmann and Reibling (2006).

[104] Boddewyn (1994).

effectiveness are marred by methodological problems that overstate the labels' true impact.[105]

The second objective is a focus on harm reduction. To that end, the best approach is to avoid strict tobacco controls. Tobacco paternalists only have one aim: total cessation. But just as abstinence only sex education curricula are derided for ignoring the realities of human behavior, so do draconian limits on tobacco use. Many users have no interest in quitting, so governments should instead focus on harm reduction—acknowledging, however, that lower tobacco use now will come at the cost of higher healthcare and retirement spending in the future.

Luckily, the marketplace is full of tobacco substitutes that reduce harm. The obvious alternative to smoking is an e-cigarette. The benefits are many. A 2015 report from Public Health England concluded that e-cigarette use is about 95% less harmful than smoking.[106] E-cigarettes may also help smokers reduce their dependence on traditional cigarettes.[107] That is especially true for flavored e-cigarettes.[108] Despite fears that vaping could serve as a gateway to smoking, e-cigarette availability appears to have accelerated the decline in tobacco use already occurring, especially among young adults.[109]

Unfortunately, e-cigarettes face increasing resistance from tobacco paternalists.[110] By 2020, the American Cancer Society's website warned visitors about the potential for "serious lung disease" from vaping, and the American Heart Association called the "vaping epidemic" an "emergency situation." The American Lung Association issued a warning to concerned parents: "Big tobacco is back. And it's trying to hook your kids." Many policymakers got the message. Several American states issued bans on vaping products, and the Food and Drug Administration issued sweeping regulations.

And there were predictable calls to charge a sin tax on vaping products.

---

[105] Beleche et al. (2018).

[106] Public Health England (2015).

[107] Hajek et al. (2019).

[108] Buu et al. (2018).

[109] Levy et al. (2018).

[110] Phillips (2009).

But vaping fears are, like so many other things, rooted in bad science. In 2020, the *Journal of the American Heart Association* retracted a prominent study that concluded that e-cigarettes substantially increased users' heart attack risk. The study was coauthored by a leading anti-tobacco expert from the Center for Tobacco Control Research and Education and was funded by the National Institute on Drug Abuse, the Food and Drug Administration, and the National Heart, Lung, and Blood Institute. The retraction was forced by the discovery that the study included individuals who had a heart attack before they started vaping. A subsequent critique reran the analysis without those individuals and found "vapers were much less likely to have had a heart attack."[111]

Predictably, the study's lead author responded by calling his chief critic a "tobacco industry apologist."[112]

Paternalists are not likely to embrace a recalibrated approach to tobacco control, especially if it comes at the expense of reduced or eliminated tobacco taxes, because their underlying motive is not necessarily to improve public health. The number of interest groups, public health organizations, and anti-tobacco experts who cite "more government revenue" as a benefit of tobacco taxes is quite revealing about the movement's true impulse. They need this sin to pay for their politics.

REFERENCES

Adams, Scott, and Chad Cotti. 2008. "Drunk Driving After the Passage of Smoking Bans in Bars." *Journal of Public Economics* 92(5–6): 1288–1305.

Adams, Scott, Chad D. Cotti, and Daniel M. Fuhrmann. 2013. "Smokeless Tobacco Use Following Smoking Bans in Bars." *Southern Economic Journal* 80(1): 147–161.

Adda, Jérôme, and Francesca Cornaglia. 2006. "Taxes, Cigarette Consumption, and Smoking Intensity." *American Economic Review* 96(4): 1013–1028.

Adda, Jérôme, and Francesca Cornaglia. 2010. "The Effects of Bans and Taxes on Passive Smoking." *American Economic Journal: Applied Economics* 2(1): 1–32.

Adda, Jérôme, and Francesca Cornaglia. 2013. "Taxes, Cigarette Consumption, and Smoking Intensity: Reply." *American Economic Review* 103(7): 3102–3114.

[111] Rodu and Plurphanswat (2019) and Sullum (2020).
[112] O'Donnell (2019).

American Heart Assocation. 2019. "Higher Prices for Better Health: Raising Tobacco Excise Taxes. Fact Sheet." Retrieved March 16, 2020 (https://www.heart.org/-/media/files/about-us/policy-research/fact-sheets/tobacco-and-clean-air/tobacco-excise-taxes-2019.pdf).

Au, N., K. Hauck, and B. Hollingsworth. 2013. "The Relationship Between Smoking, Quitting Smoking and Obesity in Australia: A Seemingly Unrelated Probit Approach." *Applied Economics* 45(16): 2191–2199.

Ault, Richard W., Robert B. Ekelund Jr., John D. Jackson, Richard S. Saba, and David S. Saurman. 1991. "Smoking and Absenteeism." *Applied Economics* 23(4): 743–754.

Bach, Peter B., Michael W. Kattan, Mark D. Thornquist, Mark G. Kris, Ramsey C. Tate, Matt J. Barnett, Lillian J. Hsieh, and Colin B. Begg. 2003. "Variations in Lung Cancer Risk Among Smokers." *Journal of the National Cancer Institute* 95(6): 470–478.

Barendregt, Jan J., Luc Bonneux, and Paul J. van der Maas. 1997. "The Health Care Costs of Smoking." *The New England Journal of Medicine* 337: 1052–1057.

Barnes, Deborah E., and Lisa A. Bero. 1997. "Scientific Quality of Original Research Articles on Environmental Tobacco Smoke." *Tobacco Control* 6(1): 19–26.

Barnes, Deborah E., and Lisa A. Bero. 1998. "Why Review Articles on the Health Effects of Smoking Reach Different Conclusions." *Journal of the American Medical Association* 279(19): 1566–1570.

Baum, Charles L. 2009. "The Effects of Cigarette Costs on BMI and Obesity." *Health Economics* 18(1): 3–19.

Beleche, Trinidad, Nellie Lew, Rosemarie L. Summers, and J. Laron Kirby. 2018. "Are Graphic Warning Labels Stopping Millions of Smokers? A Comment on Huang, Chaloupka, and Fong." *Econ Journal Watch* 15(2): 129–157.

Benowitz, Neal L., Peyton Jacob, Lynn T. Kozlowski, and Lisa Yu. 1986. "Influence of Smoking Fewer Cigarettes on Exposure to Tar, Nicotine, and Carbon Monoxide." *The New England Journal of Medicine* 315: 1310–1313.

Bernat, Debra H., Mildred Maldonado-Molina, Andrew Hyland, and Alexander C. Wagenaar. 2013. "Effects of Smoke-Free Laws on Alcohol-Related Crashes in California and New York: Time Series Analysis from 1982 to 2008." *American Journal of Public Health* 103(2): 214–219.

Bero, Lisa A. 2005. "Tobacco Industry Manipulation of Research." *Public Health Reports* 120(2): 200–208.

Biener, Lois, Jeffrey E. Harris, and William Hamilton. 2000. "Impact of the Massachusetts Tobacco Control Programme: Population Based Trend Analysis." *BMJ* 321(7257): 351–354.

Blake, Kelly D., Annette R. Kaufman, Joshua Lorenzo, and Erik M. Auguston. 2015. "Coverage of Tobacco in the United States: Frequency of Topics,

Frames, Exemplars, and Efficacy." *Journal of Health Communication International Perspectives* 20(12): 1415–1421.

Boddewyn, Jean J. 1994. "Cigarette Advertising Bans and Smoking: The Flawed Policy Connection." *International Journal of Advertising* 13(4): 311–332.

Bogdanovica, Ilze, Rachael Murray, Ann McNeill, and John Britton. 2012. "Cigarette Price, Affordability and Smoking Prevalence in the European Union." *Addiction* 107(1): 188–196.

Bonneux, Luc, Jan J. Barendregt, Wilma J. Nusselder, and Paul J. Van der Maas. 1998. "Preventing Fatal Diseases Increases Healthcare Costs: Cause Elimination Life Table Approach." *BMJ* 316: 26–29.

Burgess, Diana J., Steven S. Fu, and Michelle van Ryn. 2009. "Potential Unintended Consequences of Tobacco-Control Policies on Mothers Who Smoke." *American Journal of Preventative Medicine* 37(2): S151–S158.

Buu, Anne, Yi-Han Hu, Megan E. Piper, and Hsien-Chang Lin. 2018. "The Association Between E-Cigarette Use Characteristics and Combustible Cigarette Consumption and Dependence Symptoms: Results from a National Longitudinal Study." *Addictive Behaviors* 84: 69–74.

Callison, Kevin, and Robert Kaestner. 2014. "Do Higher Tobacco Taxes Reduce Adult Smoking? New Evidence of the Effect of Recent Cigarette Tax Increases on Adult Smoking." *Economic Inquiry* 52(1): 155–172.

Callum, Christine, Seán Boyle, and Amanda Sandford. 2011. "Estimating the Cost of Smoking to the NHS in England and the Impact of Declining Prevalence." *Health Economics, Policy and Law* 6(4): 489–508.

Cawley, John, Sara Markowitz, and John Tauras. 2004. "Lighting Up and Slimming Down: The Effects of Body Weight and Cigarette Prices on Adolescent Smoking Initiation." *Journal of Health Economics* 23(2): 293–311.

Ciecierski, Christian Czart, Pinka Chatterji, Frank J. Chaloupka, and Henry Wechsler. 2011. "Do State Expenditures on Tobacco Control Programs Decrease Use of Tobacco Products Among College Students?" *Health Economics* 20(3): 253–272.

Cohen, Jon. 1996. "Tobacco Money Lights Up a Debate." *Science* 272(5261): 488–494.

Collins, David J., and Helen M. Lapsley. 2008. "The Costs of Tobacco, Alcohol, and Illicit Drug Abuse to Australian Society in 2004/05." Commonwealth of Australia Report.

Contreary, Kara A., Sajal K. Chattopadhyay, David P. Hopkins, Frank J. Chaloupka, Jean L. Forster, Victoria Grimshaw, Carissa B. Holmes, Ron Z. Goetzel, Jonathan E. Fielding. 2015. "Economic Impact of Tobacco Price Increases Through Taxation: A Community Guide Systematic Review." *American Journal of Preventative Medicine* 49(5): 800–808.

Conway, Karen Smith, and David P. Niles. 2017. "Cigarette Taxes, Smoking— And Exercise?" *Health Economics* 26(8): 1019–1036.

Courtemanche, Charles. 2009. "Rising Cigarette Prices and Rising Obesity: Coincidence or Unintended Consequence?" *Health Economics* 28(4): 781–798.

Cutler-Triggs, Cynthia, George E. Fryer, and Thomas J. Miyoshi. 2008. "Increased Rates and Severity of Child and Adult Food Insecurity in Households with Adult Smokers." *Archives of Pediatric and Adolescent Medicine* 162(11): 1056–1062.

DeCicca, Philip, Donald Kenkel, and Alan Mathios. 2002. "Putting Out the Fires: Will Higher Taxes Reduce the Onset of Youth Smoking?" *Journal of Political Economy* 110(1): 144–169.

DeCicca, Philip, Donald Kenkel, Alan Mathios, Yoon-Jeong Shin, and Jae-Young Lim. 2008. "Youth Smoking, Cigarette Prices, and Anti-smoking Sentiment." *Health Economics* 17: 733–749.

DeCicca, Philip, Donald Kenkel, and Feng Liu. 2013. "Excise Tax Avoidance: The Case of State Cigarette Taxes." *Journal of Health Economics* 32(6): 1130–1141.

DiLorenzo, Thomas J. 1997. "Taxing Choice to Fund Politically Correct Propaganda." Pp. 117–138 in *Taxing Choice: The Predatory Politics of Fiscal Discrimination*, edited by William F. Shughart II. New Brunswick, NJ: Transaction Publishers.

Espinosa, Javier, and William N. Evans. 2013. "Excise Taxes, Tax Incidence, and the Flight to Quality: Evidence from Scanner Data." *Public Finance Review* 41(2): 147–176.

Evans, William N., and Matthew C. Farrelly. 1998. "The Compensating Behavior of Smokers: Taxes, Tar, and Nicotine." *RAND Journal of Economics* 29(3): 578–595.

Farrelly, Matthew C., Terry F. Pechacek, and Frank J. Chaloupka. 2003. "The Impact of Tobacco Control Program Expenditures on Aggregate Cigarette Sales: 1981–2000." *Health Economics* 22(5): 843–859.

Farrelly, Matthew C., C.T. Nimsch, A. Hyland, and M. Cummings. 2004. "The Effects of Higher Cigarette Prices on Tar and Nicotine Consumption in a Cohort of Adult Smokers." *Health Economics* 13(1): 49–58.

Featherstone, Henry, and Robert Nash. 2010. "Cough Up: Balancing Tobacco Income and Costs in Society." Policy Exchange Research Note.

Ferrer, Rebecca A., and Edward Orehek. 2018. "Cigarette Tax Rates, Behavioral Disengagement, and Quit Ratios." *Journal of Economic Psychology* 66: 13–21.

Fix, Brian V., Andrew Hyland, Richard J. O'Connor, K. Michael Cummings, Geoffrey T. Fong, Frank J. Chaloupka, and Andrea S. Licht. 2014. "A Novel Approach to Estimating the Prevalence of Untaxed Cigarettes in the USA: Findings from the 2009 and 2010 International Tobacco Control Surveys." *Tobacco Control* 23(S1): i61–i66.

Flegal, Katherine M., Richard P. Troiano, Elsie R. Pamuk, Robert J. Kuczmarski, and Stephen M. Campbell. 1995. "The Influence of Smoking Cessation on the Prevalence of Overweight in the United States." *The New England Journal of Medicine* 333(18): 1165–1170.

Franks, Peter, Anthony F. Jerant, J. Paul Leigh, Dennis Lee, Alan Chiem, Ilene Lewis, and Sandy Lee. 2007. "Cigarette Prices, Smoking, and the Poor: Implications of Recent Trends." *American Journal of Public Health* 97(10): 1873–1877.

Gallagher, Allen W.A., Karen A. Evans-Reeves, Jenny L. Hatchard, and Anna B. Gilmore. 2018. "Tobacco Industry Data on Illicit Tobacco Trade: A Systematic Review of Existing Assessments." *Tobacco Control* 28(3): 334–345.

Gallet, Craig A., and John A. List. 2003. "Cigarette Demand: A Meta-Analysis of Elasticities." *Health Economics* 12(10): 821–835.

Gao, Jia, and Reagan A. Baughman. 2017. "Do Smoking Bans Improve Infant Health? Evidence from U.S. Births: 1995–2009." *Eastern Economic Journal* 43(3): 472–495.

Gardner, Benjamin, and Robert West. 2010. "Public Support in England for Raising the Price of Cigarettes to Fund Tobacco Control Initiatives." *Tobacco Control* 19(4): 331–333.

Glantz, Stanton A., and Edith D. Balbach. 2000. *Tobacco War*. Berkeley, CA: University of California Press.

Goel, Rajeev K. 2008. "Smoking Prevalence in the United States: Differences Across Socioeconomic Groups." *Journal of Economics and Finance* 32(2): 195–205.

Goodchild, Mark, Anne-Marie Perucic, and Nigar Nargis. 2016. "Modelling the Impact of Raising Tobacco Taxes on Public Health and Finance." *Bulletin of the World Health Organization* 94: 250–257.

Goodman, Jordan. 1993. *Tobacco in History: The Cultures of Dependence*. New York, NY: Routledge.

Gravelle, Jane, and Dennis Zimmerman. 1994. "The Marlboro Math." *The Washington Post*. Retrieved March 5, 2020 (https://www.washingtonpost.com/archive/opinions/1994/06/05/the-marlboro-math/23b12c26-f915-4e5a-a0e5-71474ac77d84/).

Gray, Richard, Arun S. Rajan, Kristofer A. Radcliffe, Masuhide Yakehiro, and John A. Dani. 1996. "Hippocampal Synaptic Transmission Enhanced by Low Concentrations of Nicotine." *Nature* 383: 713–716.

Green, Peter S. 2001. "Czechs Debate Benefits of Smokers' Dying Prematurely." *The New York Times*. Retrieved March 5, 2020 (https://www.nytimes.com/2001/07/21/business/international-business-czechs-debate-benefits-of-smokers-dying-prematurely.html).

Grier, Jacob. 2019. *The Rediscovery of Tobacco: Smoking, Vaping, and the Creative Destruction of the Cigarette*. Kindle Direct.

Gruber, Jonathan, and Michael Frakes. 2006. "Does Falling Smoking Lead to Rising Obesity?" Journal of *Health Economics* 25(2): 183–197.

Guindon, Godefroy Emmanuel. 2014. "The Impact of Tobacco Prices on Smoking Onset: A Methodological Review." *Tobacco Control* 23(2): e5.

Halpern, Michael T., Richard Shikiar, Anne M. Rentz, and Zeba M. Khan. 2001. "Impact of Smoking Status on Workplace Absenteeism and Productivity." *Tobacco Control* 10(3): 233–238.

Hajek, Peter, Anna Phillips-Waller, Dunja Przulj, Francesca Pesola, Katie Myers Smith, Natalie Bisal, Jinshuo Li, Steve Parrott, Peter Sasieni, Lynne Dawkins, Louise Ross, Maciej Goniewicz, Qui Wu, and Hayden McRobbie. 2019. "A Randomized Trial of E-Cigarettes Versus Nicotine-Replacement Therapy." *The New England Journal of Medicine* 380: 629–637.

Hanewinkel, Reiner, Christian Radden, and Tobias Rosenkranz. 2008. "Price Increase Causes Fewer Sales of Factory-Made Cigarettes and Higher Sales of Cheaper Loose Tobacco in Germany." *Health Economics* 17(6): 683–693.

Hansen, Benjamin, Joseph J. Sabia, and Daniel I. Rees. 2017. "Have Cigarette Taxes Lost Their Bite? New Estimates of the Relationship Between Cigarette Taxes and Youth Smoking." *American Journal of Health Economics* 3(1): 60–75.

Hyland, A., J.E. Bauer, Q. Li, S.M. Abrams, C. Higbee, L. Peppone, and K.M. Cummings. 2005. "Higher Cigarette Prices Influence Cigarette Purchase Patterns." *Tobacco Control* 14(2): 86–92.

Jimenez-Ruiz, J.A., B. Saenz de Miera, L.M. Reynales-Shigematsu, H.R. Waters, M. Hernandez-Avila. 2007. "The Impact of Taxation on Tobacco Consumption in Mexico." *Tobacco Control* 17(2): 105–110.

Jones, Andrew M., Audrey Laporte, Nigel Rice, and Eugenio Zucchelli. 2015. "Do Public Smoking Bans Have an Impact on Active Smoking? Evidence from the UK." *Health Economics* 24(2): 175–192.

Kelland, Kate. 2010. "Nutrients May Be Why Some Smokers Avoid Cancer." Reuters. Retrieved March 1, 2020 (https://www.reuters.com/article/us-cancer-lung-nutrients/nutrients-may-be-why-some-smokers-avoid-cancer-idUSTRE65E5JW20100615).

Kurti, Marin K., Klaus von Lampe, and Douglas E. Thompkins. 2013. "The Illegal Cigarette Market in a Socioeconomically Deprived Inner-City Area: The Case of the South Bronx." *Tobacco Control* 22(2): 138–140.

Kvasnicka, Michael, Thomas Siedler, and Nicolas R. Ziebarth. 2018. "The Health Effects of Smoking Bans: Evidence from German Hospitalization Data." *Health Economics* 27(11): 1738–1753.

LaFaive, Michael. 2018. "Prohibition by Price: Cigarette Taxes and Unintended Consequences." Pp. 327–350 in *For Your Own Good: Taxes, Paternalism, and Fiscal Discrimination in the Twenty-First Century*, edited by Adam Hoffer and Todd Nesbit. Arlington, VA: Mercatus Center.

Lakhdar, Christian Ben, Nicolas Gerard Vaillant, and Francoise-Charles Wolff. 2016. "Does Smoke Cross the Border? Cigarette Tax Avoidance in France." *European Journal of Health Economics* 17(9): 1073–1089.

Leigh, J. Paul. 1995. "Smoking, Self-Selection and Absenteeism." *The Quarterly Review of Economics and Finance* 35(4): 365–386.

Leu, Robert E., and Thomas Schaub. 1983. "Does Smoking Increase Medical Care Expenditure?" *Social Science & Medicine* 17(23): 1907–1914.

Levy, Robert A., and Rosalind B. Marimont. 1998. "Lies, Damned Lies, & 400,000 Smoking-Related Deaths." *Regulation* 21(4): 24–29.

Levy, David T., K. Michael Cummings, and Andrew Hyland. 2000. "Increasing Taxes as a Strategy to Reduce Cigarette Use and Deaths: Results of a Simulation Model." *Preventative Medicine* 31(3): 279–286.

Levy, David T., Frank Chaloupka, Joseph Gitchell, David Mendez, and Kenneth E. Warner. 2002. "The Use of Simulation Models for the Surveillance, Justification, and Understanding of Tobacco Control Policies." *Health Care Management Science* 5(2): 113–120.

Levy, David T., Joseph E. Bauer, and Hye-ryeon Lee. 2006. "Simulation Modeling and Tobacco Control: Creating More Robust Public Health Policies." *American Journal of Public Health* 96(3): 494–498.

Levy, David T., Kenneth E. Warner, K. Michael Cummings, David Hammond, Charlene Kuo, Geoffrey T. Fong, James F. Thrasher, Macie Lukasz Goniewicz, and Ron Borland. 2018. "Examining the Relationship of Vaping to Smoking Initiation Among US Youth and Young Adults: A Reality Check." *Tobacco Control* 28(6): 629–635.

Lippiatt, Barbara C. 1990. "Measuring Medical Cost and Life Expectancy Impacts of Changes in Cigarette Sales." *Preventive Medicine* 19(5): 515–532.

Lovenheim, Michael F. 2008. "How Far to the Border? The Extent and Impact of Cross-Border Casual Cigarette Smuggling." *National Tax Journal* 61(1): 7–33.

Luccasen, R. Andrew, R. Morris Coats, and G. Karahan. 2005. "Cigarette Smuggling Mitigates the Public Health Benefits of Cigarette Taxes." *Applied Economic Letters* 12(12): 769–773.

MacLean, Johanna Catherine, Asia Sikora Kessler, and Donald S. Kenkel. 2016. "Cigarette Taxes and Older Adult Smoking: Evidence from the Health and Retirement Study." *Health Economics* 25(4): 424–438.

Manning, Willard G., Emmett B. Keeler, and Joseph P. Newhouse. 1989. "The Taxes of Sin: Do Smokers and Drinkers Pay Their Way?" *Journal of the American Medical Association* 261(11): 1604–1609.

Marlow, Michael L. 2007. "Do Tobacco-Control Programs Lower Tobacco Consumption? Evidence from California." *Public Finance Review* 35(6): 689–709.

Marlow, Michael L. 2009. "Anatomy of Public Health Research: Tobacco Control as a Case Study." *Journal of American Physicians and Surgeons* 14(3): 79–80.

Marlow, Michael L. 2010. "Do Expenditures on Tobacco Control Decrease Smoking Prevalence?" *Applied Economics* 42(11): 1331–1343.

Marlow, Michael L. 2012. "Effectiveness of Massachusetts' Comprehensive Tobacco Control Program." *Applied Economics* 44(3): 373–385.

McCormick, Robert E., Robert Tollison, and Richard E. Wagner. 1997. "Smoking, Insurance, and Social Cost." *Regulation* 20(3): 33–37.

McLeod, K., M. Wakefield, S. Chapman, K. Clegg Smith, and S. Durkin. 2009. "Changes in the News Representation of Smokers and Tobacco-Related Media Advocacy from 1995 to 2005 in Australia." *Journal of Epidemiology & Community Health* 63(3): 215–220.

Merriman, David. 2010. "The Micro-Geography of Tax Avoidance: Evidence from Littered Cigarette Packs in Chicago." *American Economic Journal: Economic Policy* 2(2): 61–84.

Milov, Sarah. 2019. *The Cigarette: A Political History*. Cambridge, MA: Harvard University Press.

Moore, Roland S., Rachelle M. Annechino, and Juliet P. Lee. 2010. "Unintended Consequences of Smoke-Free Bar Policies for Low-SES Women in Three California Counties." *American Journal of Preventative Medicine* 37(2): S138–S143.

Nesbit, Todd. 2018. "Excise Taxation and Product Quality Substitution." Pp. 143–165 in *For Your Own Good: Taxes, Paternalism, and Fiscal Discrimination in the Twenty-First Century*, edited by Adam Hoffer and Todd Nesbit. Arlington, VA: Mercatus Center.

Nesson, Erik. 2017. "Heterogeneity in Smokers' Responses to Tobacco Control Policies." *Health Economics* 26(2): 206–225.

O'Dea, Des, and George Thomson. 2007. "Report on Tobacco Taxation in New Zealand." The Smokefree Coalition and ASH New Zealand Report.

O'Donnell, Jayne. 2019. "Study Linking Vaping to Heart Attacks Muddied Amid Spat Between Two Tobacco Researchers." *USA Today*. Retrieved August 1, 2019 (https://www.usatoday.com/story/news/health/2019/07/17/vaping-heart-attacks-false-claims-sexual-harassment-allegations/1676473001/).

Ohsfeldt, Robert L., Raymond G. Boyle, and Eli Capilouto. 1997. "Effects of Tobacco Excise Taxes on the Use of Smokeless Tobacco Products in the USA." *Health Economics* 6(5): 525–531.

Pechmann, Cornelia, and Ellen T. Reibling. 2006. "Antismoking Advertisements for Youths: An Independent Evaluation of Health, Counter-Industry, and Industry Approaches." *American Journal of Public Health* 96(5): 906–913.

Peres, Judy. 2013. "No Clear Link Between Passive Smoking and Lung Cancer." *Journal of the National Cancer Institute* 105(24): 1844–1846.

Phillips, Carl V. 2007. "Warning: Anti-tobacco Activism May Be Hazardous to Epidemiologic Science." *Epidemiologic Perspectives & Innovations* 4(13).

Phillips, Carl V. 2009. "Debunking the Claim That Abstinence Is Usually Healthier for Smokers than Switching to a Low-Risk Alternative, and Other Observations About Anti-Tobacco-Harm-Reduction Arguments." *Harm Reduction Journal* 6:29.

Pierce, John P., Elizabeth A. Gilpin, Sherry L. Emery, Martha M. White, Brad Rosbrook, and Charles C. Berry. 1998. "Has the California Tobacco Control Program Reduced Smoking?" *Journal of the American Medical Association* 280(10): 893–899.

Proctor, Robert N. 1996. "The Anti-tobacco Campaign of the Nazis: A Little Known Aspect of Public Health in Germany, 1933–45." *British Medical Journal* 313: 1450–1453.

Proctor, Robert N. 1999. *The Nazi War on Cancer*. Princeton, NJ: Princeton University Press.

Proctor, Robert N. 2011. *Golden Holocaust: Origins of the Cigarette Catastrophe and the Case for Abolition*. Berkeley, CA: University of California Press.

Public Health England. 2015. "E-Cigarettes: A New Foundation for Evidence-based Policy and Practice." Report. Retrieved March 1, 2020 from (https://assets.publishing.service.gov.uk/government/uploads/system/uploads/att achment_data/file/454517/Ecigarettes_a_firm_foundation_for_evidence_based_policy_and_practice.pdf).

Raynauld, André, and Jean-Pierre Vidal. 1992. "Smokers' Burden on Society: Myth and Reality in Canada." *Canadian Public Policy* 18(3): 300–317.

Reiter, Jendi B. 1996. "Citizens or Sinners? The Economic and Political Inequity of Sin Taxes on Tobacco and Alcohol Products." *Columbia Journal of Law and Social Problems* 29: 443–468.

Rezvani, Amir H., and Edward D. Levin. 2001. "Cognitive Effects of Nicotine." *Biological Psychiatry* 49(3): 258–267.

Rhoads, Jennifer K. 2012. "The Effect of Comprehensive State Tobacco Control Programs on Adult Cigarette Smoking." *Journal of Health Economics* 31(2): 393–405.

Ritch, Wendy A., and Michael E. Begay. 2001. "Smoke and Mirrors: How Massachusetts Diverted Millions in Tobacco Tax Revenues." *Journal of Epidemiology & Community Health* 56(7): 522–528.

Robbins, H., M. Krakow, and D. Warner. 2002. "Adult Smoking Intervention Programmes in Massachusetts: A Comprehensive Approach with Promising Results." *Tobacco Control* 11(Supplement 2): ii4–ii7.

Rodu, Brad, and Nantaporn Plurphanswat. Letter to Barry London, Daniel T. Eitzman, Janice Weinberg, and Robert Harrington, July 11, 2019. Retrieved from (https://reason.com/wp-content/uploads/2020/02/Letter-to-JAHA-re-Bhatta-Glantz-20-Jan-2020-Final.pdf).

Ross, Hana. 2004. "Critique of the Philip Morris Study of the Cost of Smoking in the Czech Republic." *Nicotine & Tobacco Research* 6(1): 181–189.

Rubinoff, Michael. 2010. *Ending the Tobacco Holocaust: How Big Tobacco Affects Our Health, Pocketbook and Political Freedom—And What We Can Do About It*. Santa Rosa, CA: Elite Books.

Schelling, Thomas C. 1986. "Economics and Cigarettes." *Preventative Medicine* 15(5): 549–560.

Scherer, Gerhard. 1999. "Smoking Behaviour and Compensation: A Review of the Literature." *Psychopharmacology* 145(1): 1–120.

Schroeder, Steven A., and Kenneth E. Warner. 2010. "Don't Forget Tobacco." *The New England Journal of Medicine* 363: 201–204.

Sen, Anindya, Mahdiyeh Entezarkheir, and Alan Wilson. 2010. "Obesity, Smoking, and Cigarette Taxes: Evidence from the Canadian Community Health Surveys." *Health Policy* 97(2–3): 180–186.

Shetty, Kanaka D., Thomas DeLeire, Chapin White, and Jayanta Bhattacharya. 2011. "Changes in U.S. Hospitalization and Mortality Rates Following Smoking Bans." *Journal of Policy Analysis and Management* 30(1): 6–28.

Siegel, Michael. 2007. "Is the Tobacco Control Movement Misrepresenting the Accurate Cardiovascular Health Effects of Secondhand Smoke Exposure? An Analysis of the Scientific Evidence and Commentary on the Implications for Tobacco Control and Public Health Practice." *Epidemiologic Perspectives & Innovations* 4: 12.

Sloan, Frank A., Jan Ostermann, Gabriel Picone, Christopher Conover, and Donald H. Taylor. 2006. *The Price of Smoking*. Cambridge, MA: MIT Press.

Snowdon, Christopher, and Mark Tovey. 2017. "Smoking and the Public Purse." Institute of Economic Affairs Report.

Sobel, Russell, and Thomas Garrett. 1997. "Taxation and Product Quality: New Evidence from Generic Cigarettes." *Journal of Political Economy* 105(4): 880–887.

Sterling, T.D., W.L. Rosenbaum, and J.J. Weinkam. 1993. "Risk Attribution and Tobacco-Related Deaths." *American Journal of Epidemiology* 138(2): 128–139.

Sullum, Jacob. 1998. *For Your Own Good: The Anti-smoking Crusade and the Tyranny of Public Health*. New York, NY: Free Press.

Sullum, Jacob. 2020. "American Heart Association Journal Finally Retracts Study Implying That E-Cigarettes Cause Heart Attacks Before People Use Them." *Reason*. Retrieved February 19, 2020 (https://reason.com/2020/02/18/american-heart-association-journal-finally-retracts-a-study-implying-that-e-cigarettes-cause-heart-attacks-before-people-use-them/).

Swaminathan, Nikhil. 2008. "Why Some Smokers Get Lung Cancer—And Others Are Spared." *Scientific American*. Retrieved February 1, 2020 (https://www.scientificamerican.com/article/why-some-smokers-get-lung/).

Tauras, John A., Frank J. Chaloupka, Matthew C. Farrelly, Gary A. Giovino, Melanie Wakefield, Lloyd D. Johnston, Patrick M. O'Malley, Deborah D. Kloska, and Terry F. Pechacek. 2005. "State Tobacco Control Spending and Youth Smoking." *American Journal of Public Health* 95(2): 338–344.

Temple, Norman J. 2011. "Why Prevention Can Increase Health-Care Spending." *European Journal of Public Health* 22(5): 618–619.

Thrasher, James F., Sei-Hill Kim, India Rose, Ashley Navarro, Mary-Kathryn Craft, Kelly J. Davis, and Sharon Biggers. 2014. "Print Media Coverage Around Failed and Successful Tobacco Tax Initiatives: The South Carolina Experience." *American Journal of Health Promotion* 29(1): 29–36.

Tiihonen, Jari, Kimmo Ronkainen, Aki Kangasharju, and Jussi Kauhanen. 2012. "The Net Effect of Smoking on Healthcare and Welfare Costs: A Cohort Study." *BMJ Open* 2: e001678.

Tsai, Yi-Wen, Chung-Lin Yang, Chin-Shyan Chen, Tsai-Hing Liu, and Pei-Fen Chen. 2005. "The Effect of Taiwan's Tax-Induced Increases in Cigarette Prices on Brand-Switching and the Consumption of Cigarettes." *Health Economics* 14(6): 627–641.

Tucker, Philip. 2003. "The Impact of Rest Breaks Upon Accident Risk, Fatigue and Performance: A Review." *Work & Stress* 17(2): 123–137.

van Baal, Pieter H.M., Johan J. Polder, G. Ardine de Wit, Rudolf T. Hoogenveen, Talitha L. Feenstra, Hendriek C. Boshuizen, Peter M. Engelfriet, and Werner B.F. Brouwer. 2008. "Lifetime Medical Costs of Obesity: Prevention No Cure for Increasing Health Expenditure." *PLoS Medicine* 5(2): e29.

Verguet, Stephane, Cindy L. Gauvreau, Sujata Mishra, Mary MacLennan, Shane M. Murphy, Elizabeth D. Brouwer, Rachel A. Nugent, Kun Zhao, Prabhat Jha, and Dean T. Jamison. 2015. "The Consequences of Tobacco Tax on Household Health and Finances in Rich and Poor Smokers in China: An Extended Cost-Effectiveness Analysis." *The Lancet Global Health* 3(4): E206–E216.

Viscusi, W. Kip. 1990. "Do Smokers Underestimate Risks?" *Journal of Political Economy* 98(6): 1253–1269.

Viscusi, W. Kip. 1992. *Smoking: Making the Risky Decision*. New York, NY: Oxford University Press.

Viscusi, W. Kip. 1995. "Cigarette Taxation and the Social Consequences of Smoking." Pp. 51–102 in *Tax Policy and the Economy*, edited by James M. Poterba. Cambridge, MA: MIT Press.

Wackowski, Olivia A., Jane Lewis, Cristine D. Delnevo, and Pamela M. Ling. 2013. "A Content Analysis of Smokeless Tobacco Coverage in U.S. Newspapers and News Wires." *Nicotine & Tobacco Research* 15(7): 1289–1296.

Wangen, Knut R., and Erik Biørn. 2006. "How Do Consumers Switch Between Close Substitutes When Price Variation Is Small? The Case of Cigarette Types." *Spanish Economic Review* 8(4): 239-253.

Weintraub, J.M. and W.L. Hamilton. 2002. "Trends in Prevalence of Current Smoking, Massachusetts and States Without Tobacco Control Programmes, 1990–1999." *Tobacco Control* 11(Supplement 2): ii8–ii13.

White, Justin S., Jing Li, The-wei Hu, Geoffrey T. Fong, and Yuan Jiang. 2013. "The Effect of Cigarette Prices on Brand-Switching in China: A Longitudinal Analysis of Data from the ITC China Survey." *Tobacco Control* 23(Supplement 1): i54–i60.

Xu, Xin, Ellen E. Bishop, Sara M. Kennedy, Sean A. Simpson, and Terry F. Pechacek. 2015. "Annual Healthcare Spending Attributable to Cigarette Smoking: An Update." *American Journal of Preventative Medicine* 48(3): 326–333.

CHAPTER 5

Taxing Marijuana

Humans have put cannabis plants to good use for approximately ten thousand years.[1] Hemp—which refers to cannabis varieties that contain low levels of the psychoactive substance tetrahydrocannabinol ("THC")—was employed for some time to manufacture paper, rope, and fabric.[2] Hemp seeds and hemp oil have just as long found value as dietary supplements. Cannabis variants with higher THC concentrations—broadly known as marijuana—have been used in a variety of applications, including veterinary medicine, pain relief, and religious ceremonies.[3]

Given its many purposes, few governments have had a consistent approach to regulating cannabis. As early as the eighteenth century, the Kingdom of Imerina, an area that includes present-day Madagascar, prohibited cannabis, alcohol, and tobacco use. In the early nineteenth century, cannabis prohibition spread to several countries, including

---

[1] Archeological evidence has yet to identify cannabis's origin but indicates that some varieties were cultivated in parts of Europe and East Asia at least ten thousand years ago (Long et al. 2017). Hashish also dates back thousands of years. More comprehensive discussions of cannabis history are available in Booth (2003) and Lee (2012).

[2] Governments within the United States typically define hemp as a type of cannabis with a THC concentration of less than 0.3%, measured according to dry weight. That concentration is assumed to be low enough to avoid intoxication. The THC threshold considered intoxicating differs outside of the United States.

[3] Butrica (2002).

© The Author(s) 2021
M. Thom, *Taxing Sin*,
https://doi.org/10.1007/978-3-030-49176-5_5

Jamaica, Mexico, and Canada. However, many of the same countries—including Jamaica, Mexico, and Canada—later overturned those bans.[4]

The United States is probably the best example of a country with a contradictory but evolving cannabis policy. During the sixteenth and seventeenth centuries many American farmers grew hemp, including George Washington at his Mount Vernon plantation. Throughout the eighteenth century, cannabis was prescribed by some doctors for medicinal purposes. But public awareness about its psychological effects rose by the mid-1850s.[5] An 1853 article in the British publication *Blackwood's Magazine*, underscored one year later in the *New York Times*, described the effects of sufficient cannabis doses as follows:

> The sun shines upon every thought that passes through the brain, and every movement of the body is a source of enjoyment.[6]

Until the progressive era, however, there were few cannabis restrictions in the United States. By the early twentieth century, paternalists argued marijuana but not necessarily cannabis in general was detrimental to public health and a gateway to more harmful drugs. Several state governments enacted laws that characterized marijuana as a poison, subjecting it to regulation.[7]

That trend grew under alcohol prohibition. Some paternalists believed marijuana was much worse than a public health threat. They saw the drug as responsible for another sin: urban crime.[8] Others blamed marijuana

[4] Jamaica reversed cannabis prohibition in 2015, and Canada followed in 2018. The Supreme Court of Mexico ruled in 2018 that laws prohibiting cannabis use were unconstitutional, effectively legalizing it.

[5] Gieringer (1999).

[6] Quoted from "The Narcotics We Indulge In," a lengthy article in *Blackwood's Magazine*, Volume 74. The piece was highlighted in an 1854 *New York Times* article, "Our Fashionable Narcotics." According to the *Times*, the author was "said to be Prof. Johnson".

[7] The success of anti-marijuana laws during this period can be traced to the anti-narcotic movement of the time and the desire for governments to act to control drug traffic, especially opium imports. California and Utah banned marijuana in 1913 and 1914, respectively. Several other states followed.

[8] Galliher and Walker (1977) argue that the perceived marijuana crisis of the era was not rooted in fact. Some say that marijuana use in the United States increased under

use and its assumed harms on Mexican immigration. Charles Goethe, a prominent progressive and eugenicist, argued in 1935:

> Marihuana, perhaps now the most insidious of our narcotics, is a direct by-product of unrestricted Mexican immigration. Easily grown, it has been asserted that it has recently been planted between rows in a California penitentiary garden. Mexican peddlers have been caught distributing sample marihuana cigarets (sic) to school children.[9]

The belief that marijuana encouraged criminal activity and entrapped children, all while jeopardizing public health, led to demands for immigration restrictions and more government control of marijuana.[10] That culminated in the Marihuana Tax Act of 1937, which amplified federal oversight but did not impose prohibition. The Act instead mandated that importers, growers, sellers, and users register with the Internal Revenue Service and pay a tax.[11] The law remained in effect until 1969 when the Supreme Court ruled it unconstitutional.[12] Congress responded in 1970 by classifying marijuana as a Schedule I drug, meaning that—in the eyes of the federal government—it had a high potential for abuse and no medical value. The classification essentially outlawed the same plant the nation's first president grew at his home.

---

alcohol prohibition because it was a cheap alternative to illegal alcoholic beverages that, as a result of prohibition, were more expensive.

[9] Quoted in a letter to the editor in the *New York Times*, published September 15, 1935. Other than his ardent support for forced sterilization, Goethe is famous for founding California State University in Sacramento.

[10] Musto (1972).

[11] Because the tax was also charged on the doctors prescribing marijuana and the pharmacists providing it, the American Medical Association opposed the Act. The law did little to curb marijuana paternalism in culture; the era gave rise to several anti-marijuana films, including *Marihuana* (1936), *Reefer Madness* (1936), *Assassin of Youth* (1937), and *Devil's Harvest* (1942). It also wasn't the United States federal government's last foray into antidrug legislation. The Boggs Act followed in 1952, and the Narcotics Control Act four years later.

[12] In resolving the lawsuit, *Leary v. United States*, the Court's majority found that requiring parties that used or were otherwise involved with marijuana to register with the Internal Revenue Service was tantamount to forcing those parties to offer self-incriminating evidence in states where marijuana was illegal, which was a violation of the Fifth Amendment to the United States Constitution.

Much of the inconsistency in American marijuana policy stems from the fact that, compared to soda, alcohol, and tobacco, marijuana paternalism is less well-defined. Some paternalists argue that it should remain illegal. Others say marijuana should be legalized but taxed heavily to compensate for the externalities it imposes on society. High prices and strict regulations are also thought to discourage marijuana's other harms, including addiction, crime, and adolescent use. Still others, but often not paternalists, support marijuana taxes not because they believe it is harmful, but because they see taxes as the political price to pay for legal access.

Muddled paternalism can be traced in part to careful appraisals from major public health groups—the same groups that are much more consistent in their posture toward the other sins. The World Health Organization has neither called for full legalization nor prohibition and instead warns policymakers of both the risk of marijuana abuse and its potential as a medical treatment. The American Cancer Society notes marijuana's potential harms and benefits but has yet to take a formal position on medical marijuana until more research is available. But the Society opposes "smoking or vaping of marijuana and other cannabinoids in public places because the carcinogens in marijuana smoke pose numerous health hazards."[13] Similarly, the American Lung Association "opposes the inhalation of smoke or aerosol of marijuana" but calls for more research on its medicinal applications.[14] In only slight contrast, the American Medical Association "believes that cannabis is a dangerous drug" and a "serious public health concern" that substantiates a prohibition of recreational—also known as "adult use"—marijuana. Yet the group also urges governments to "allocate a substantial portion" of marijuana tax revenue for "public health purposes."[15]

Expert opinion has also failed to settle on a consensus. An exhaustive 2017 report from the National Academies of Sciences, a professional organization for science experts, noted "evidence of a statistical association between cannabis use and the development of schizophrenia or other psychoses" but also acknowledged that the research on marijuana's health

[13] American Cancer Society (2017).

[14] American Lung Association (2015).

[15] Quoted from American Medical Association Policy H-95.923, "Taxes on Cannabis Products," and H-95.924, "Cannabis Legalization for Recreational Use."

impacts is weak.[16] Some experts, though, unambiguously favor marijuana paternalism. Two years after the National Academies of Sciences report, a statement signed by 41 public health experts in Massachusetts was not so cautious. "The science is clear," according to the statement, "marijuana … has the potential to do significant harm to public health."[17]

The fact that interest groups have aligned on all sides of marijuana paternalism only worsens the ambiguity surrounding its impact. The Drug Free America Foundation admits that marijuana has medical potential, but also notes that the "claim that smoked marijuana is medicinal is a tactic to legalize marijuana for any purpose and to eventually legalize other drugs for personal use." The Foundation warns that:

> There is great potential to make a lot of money through the sale of marijuana. Tobacco companies, who made a killing on cigarettes to the detriment of so many, have already patented names for marijuana products.[18]

Several other groups share that position. Citizens Against Legalizing Marijuana ("CALM"), an American organization "dedicated to defeating any effort to legalize marijuana," believes "laws against the use, cultivation, and transportation of marijuana should be maintained and enforced and should not be relaxed or softened."[19] Smart Approaches to Marijuana ("SAM"), another American group, warns that marijuana opens the door to more harmful drugs and also causes several other problems, including reduced cognitive ability and impaired driving. SAM's talking points memo on the issue states that "the move to legalize marijuana is really a move to commercialize marijuana for profit. It is today's version of Big Tobacco."[20] Still another American group, Parents Opposed to Pot, is steadfast in efforts toward "bursting the bubble of marijuana hype." They argue marijuana use is deadly—and a "common" trait among mass killers.[21]

---

[16] National Academies of Science, Engineering, and Medicine (2017).

[17] Massachusetts Prevention Alliance (2019).

[18] See information posted on https://www.dfaf.org/marijuana-qa/.

[19] See information posted on https://calmca.org/.

[20] Smart Approaches to Marijuana (2018).

[21] Parents Opposed to Pot (2018).

Other groups are more open to legalizing marijuana, especially when legalization is paired with a tax. In contrast to many of the organizations that favor other sin taxes, groups that promote a marijuana tax are less explicit about earmarking revenue to redeem its supposed sins. The Marijuana Policy Project vaguely, but favorably, notes that "adult-use marijuana programs have generated large annual surpluses from taxes and fees."[22] The National Organization for the Reform of Marijuana Laws ("NORML"), which has branches in the United States, United Kingdom, Canada, South Africa, France, and New Zealand, also reports positively on the benefits of marijuana tax revenue.[23]

Some groups are more explicit about where they believe the money should go, and it's rarely to correcting externalities. The Campaign to Regulate Marijuana Like Alcohol, which backed a decriminalization initiative in Colorado, argued that marijuana tax revenue should fund public education. The Coalition to Regulate Marijuana Like Alcohol—not to be confused with Colorado's Campaign—formed to advocate decriminalization in Michigan and garnered public support by promising tax revenue would support public schools, infrastructure, and local governments.[24]

Against that backdrop, media coverage tends to support legalization.[25] Many newspaper opinion sections have argued in favor. In 2014 the *New York Times* editorialized that the federal ban in the United States imposed "great harm on society just to prohibit a substance far less dangerous than alcohol."[26]

Public sentiment increasingly agrees. A 2019 Gallup poll found two-thirds of American adults favored legalizing marijuana, compared to just 12% in 1969.[27] That matches the findings of other surveys, which also report that adults believe marijuana is less harmful than other drugs and alcohol.[28] Support for taxing marijuana is robust and rises when revenue

---

[22] Marijuana Policy Project (2020).

[23] See information posted on https://blog.norml.org/tag/taxes/.

[24] See information posted on https://www.regulatemi.org/about/faq/.

[25] McGinty et al. (2016).

[26] The *Times'* editorial, "Repeal Prohibition, Again," was published July 27, 2014.

[27] Jones (2019).

[28] De Pinto (2019).

goes to public education, mental health programs, or to reduce other taxes.[29]

Nevertheless, by 2020, recreational marijuana remained illegal in several countries, including China, Denmark, Iceland, Ireland, Japan, Russia, and Taiwan. Many countries have less restrictive rules for medicinal marijuana, and many do not enforce prohibition consistently, if at all.

Policy in the United States has continued to evolve since 1970. Despite federal prohibition, many states decriminalized medical marijuana. Several further decriminalized recreational marijuana.[30] Each one matched decriminalization with a tax, but the amount and structure varies. Some states charge a flat tax per ounce of plant, and others charge a tax based on a percentage of the selling price, like a traditional excise or sales tax. In some states, local governments levy additional taxes.

* * *

Marijuana paternalism rests on the presumption that marijuana use inflicts a multitude of harms on society. That conviction is held by paternalists who want governments to maintain strict marijuana controls like prohibition, and by those who are willing to tolerate granting legal access to marijuana in exchange for a tax. The supposed harms are many. In adults, paternalists argue that marijuana use reduces productivity, impairs driving, creates health problems, and leads to more dangerous and addictive drugs.

They also warn about marijuana's potential influence on minors. A brochure published in 2016 by the National Institute on Drug Abuse, a federal research agency in the United States, cautioned parents that marijuana use was "linked to" several negative outcomes, including "lower grades, school failure, and poorer quality of life" as well as "some mental illnesses."[31] A 2019 book also alerted parents that marijuana use among

---

[29] A survey of 1500 New Jersey residents found 44% favored recreational marijuana and 53% support if doing so would lead to a reduction in local property taxes (Arco 2018). A survey of 1055 New Mexico residents found support for recreational marijuana if tax revenue was spent on "mental health services and public education" (Gould 2019).

[30] State decriminalization creates obvious conflict with federal law and begs more important questions about American federalism; see Adler (2020).

[31] The brochure was titled "Marijuana: Facts Parents Need to Know."

teenagers led to psychosis, violence, and crime.[32] In a *Mother Jones* article
that described the conclusions as "scary," the book's author said of the
experts he spoke with: "I believe the people I talk to. They don't have
any agenda other than trying to promote the public health."[33]

Like their peers insistent on soda, alcohol, and tobacco restrictions,
marijuana paternalists summon research to support the argument that
marijuana use is a burden on society. But compared to the other sins,
national estimates of marijuana's externalities are hard to come by.[34]
However, in the United States, some state-specific estimates have been
publicized to make the case against legalization. A 2018 study from the
Centennial Institute, a think tank based at Colorado Christian University,
reported that legalized marijuana imposed an externality of over $1 billion
per year in Colorado alone, far greater than the tax revenue generated
from marijuana purchases in that state.[35]

Paternalists point to studies that indicate externalities derive from a
variety of adverse consequences that go hand in hand with marijuana
use. For example, many studies tie broader marijuana availability to
an increased frequency of motor vehicle accidents.[36] Others link marijuana use to cardiovascular disease, school dropout, the consumption of
other illegal drugs, and mental illness.[37] Experts have paid considerable

[32] Berenson (2019).

[33] Mencimer (2019). *Mother Jones* later appended the article with this revealing correction: "An earlier version of this article overstated the connection ... between marijuana,
bipolar disorder, and the risk of suicide, depression, and social anxiety disorders. It also
overstated the connection between the increasing number of pot users and the number
of people over 30 coming into the ER with psychosis; the researchers in that case 'did
not directly examine whether marijuana had led to any psychotic diagnoses.'"

[34] There are several reasons why marijuana's alleged externalities have attracted less
attention than those for obesity, alcohol, and tobacco. Unlike the other sins, marijuana
remains illegal throughout much of the world, making research relatively scarce. Compared
to the other sins, existing research is mixed about its health impact. Marijuana is also less
frequently consumed. According to the 2018 National Survey on Drug Use and Health, a
survey administered by the Substance Abuse and Mental Health Services Administration,
only about half of American adults report ever using marijuana, compared to 66% for
tobacco and 86% for alcohol.

[35] The report, "Economic and Social Costs of Legalized Marijuana," was issued in
October 2018. It was conducted by QREM, a Colorado-based "third-party evaluation
firm serving non-profits and other organizations."

[36] Asbridge et al. (2012) and Lee et al. (2012).

[37] Hall (2015).

attention to the latter. According to the authors of one review, "evidence from epidemiologic studies provides strong enough evidence to warrant a public health message that cannabis use can increase the risk of psychotic disorders."[38]

But much like the research on other sins, these and comparable findings should be taken with a grain of tax-free salt. The Centennial Institute's appraisal of marijuana's externalities was attention-grabbing but flawed. Like so many of their colleagues researching other sins, the Institute's experts treated lost productivity as an externality. But in this case, as with the other sins, lost productivity is an internality.[39]

That was not the only blunder. The study's authors additionally claimed that marijuana use was responsible for 180 suicides and 139 traffic fatalities in Colorado, but—astonishingly—conceded in a footnote that "marijuana cannot be determined to be the cause of lives lost, especially for suicides." That theme recurs throughout the study: a correlation between two variables is assumed to mean causation. The discussion proceeds on that basis, but admission is made somewhere i n the fine print that correlation does not prove causation. That much, at least, the experts behind the study were right about.

More importantly, numerous studies challenge paternalists' other claims about marijuana. The evidence that pervasive use raises impaired driving fatalities, for instance, is repeatedly misconstrued. A review of studies that make that particular claim found that they had "substantially overestimated the effect of acute cannabis intoxication on crash risk." The review's authors instead reported that marijuana was associated with a "low to medium" risk increase. They also cautioned that it is hard to know with certainty whether marijuana is a causal factor in vehicle accidents.[40] Even conceding the argument that marijuana use increases accidents does not mean that the growth is meaningful or even permanent. A 2019 study

---

[38] Gage et al. (2016).

[39] Probably the most common stereotype of marijuana users—the one for which they are most often mocked—is that they are lazy. Research on that phenomenon, which is formally and dryly known as amotivational syndrome, is unclear. Some studies report that marijuana use contributes to diminished productivity (Lac and Luk 2018; Pacheco-Colón et al. 2018), but other studies do not (Barnwell et al. 2006; Duncan 1987; Nelson 1994). The ambiguity can be partially chalked up to weak research designs. Many studies rely on self-reported motivation; others depend on small, nonrepresentative samples.

[40] Rogeberg and Elvik (2016); note that the authors issued a subsequent correction that reduced their estimated risks.

reported that recreational marijuana in Colorado, Oregon, and Washington might have led to one additional traffic death per one million residents—a small effect that was also temporary.[41]

But worries over marijuana's effects on driving may be entirely misplaced. A study that scrutinized vehicle fatalities in Colorado and Washington found only "limited" evidence that decriminalization was responsible for more deaths in either state, partly because there were too many confounding factors.[42] A Canadian study found no significant impact of THC blood concentration on motor vehicle accidents.[43] That finding reiterates the conclusion from a review of 66 studies, which reported that marijuana use had no significant effect on the risk of injury or death from motor vehicle accidents. Although the review found a slightly higher risk of property damage, it was smaller than the increased risk imposed by driving while using anti-asthma medications.[44]

In fact, there is support for the notion that marijuana availability *increases* traffic safety. Research shows that marijuana is a substitute for alcohol—rather than drink, some individuals choose to smoke instead, resulting in fewer alcohol-related vehicle accidents.[45] Studies have also associated marijuana decriminalization with lower binge drinking among college-aged students.[46]

What about the theory that marijuana is harmful to health? Multiple studies show that it is not a causal factor behind subsequent use or abuse of other drugs, alcohol, or nicotine.[47] The evidence that marijuana causes asthma, heart disease, or bladder, cervical, esophageal, lung, prostate, and testicular cancer is practically non-existent.[48] Data and research studies

---

[41] Lane and Hall (2019).

[42] Hansen et al. (2018); see also Aydelotte et al. (2017).

[43] Brubacher et al. (2019).

[44] Elvik (2013).

[45] Anderson et al. (2013). This indicates that alcohol and marijuana are not complements—i.e., goods consumed together—but substitutes, as demonstrated in several natural experiments (Anderson and Rees 2014).

[46] Alley et al. (2020).

[47] Morral et al. (2002) and Verweij et al. (2018).

[48] Carroll (2018). Marijuana's impact on pregnant women and unborn children is unclear. A 2018 report from the American Academy of Pediatrics encouraged pregnant women to abstain from marijuana use, not because it was harmful, but because the science is unsettled. See also Thompson et al. (2019). As an anti-nausea treatment, however,

also contradict the allegation that marijuana use leads to mental illnesses, an argument implied throughout the National Academies of Sciences study and in so much of the literature that warns parents about marijuana's effect on their children.[49] Perhaps most damning to that hypothesis is that, even as marijuana use increased, rates of schizophrenia did not.[50] And it's no wonder: studies show that marijuana does not cause or exacerbate schizophrenia or related conditions.[51]

In reality, the relationship between marijuana and mental health is not as black-and-white as paternalists tend to believe. According to a 2014 study, there may be common genetic underpinnings of both schizophrenia and marijuana use, making it unclear whether the latter causes the former or vice versa.[52] That finding returned in a later study that concluded the relationship "is not causal and results from confounding due to shared familial factors"—in other words, genetics.[53] A 2016 study reiterated that marijuana use does not cause psychosis. Rather, individuals that are more susceptible to psychosis are more likely to use it, perhaps as a form of self-medication, just as they may also self-medicate with another sin: tobacco.[54] Confusing the issue further, some studies have found that long-term marijuana users are actually *less* likely to develop psychotic disorders.[55] Evidence also shows that users who experience psychotic symptoms may be *more* likely to quit.[56]

And as to marijuana's impact on crime? Research contradicts that old stereotype. One study that compared crime rates over four years in American states that decriminalized marijuana concluded that easier access

---

it may be no more harmful than prescription and other drugs approved by regulatory agencies.

[49] One member of the panel that developed the report told *Rolling Stone*, "To say that we concluded cannabis causes schizophrenia, it's just wrong, and it's meant to precipitate fear" (Lewis 2019). Yet the report notes several times that marijuana use increases the risk of developing a host of health conditions. For those in on the wrong side of the risk estimate, it would appear to be a heavily implied causal factor.

[50] Degenhardt et al. (2003) and Hill (2015).

[51] Williams et al. (2019).

[52] Power et al. (2014).

[53] Giordano et al. (2015).

[54] Ksir and Hart (2016).

[55] Bloomfield et al. (2014).

[56] Sami et al. (2019).

"failed to significantly predict property or violent crime rates."[57] Another study found no evidence of an increase in crime in areas surrounding medical marijuana dispensaries.[58] An exhaustive report commissioned by the Office of National Drug Control Policy, a federal agency that advises American presidents, found "even though marijuana is commonly used by individuals arrested for crimes, there is little support for a contemporaneous, causal relationship between its use and either violent or property crime."[59]

Despite fervent warnings to the world's parents, there is also little reason to believe that marijuana availability is harmful to minors. Several studies report that increased access, either through medical or recreational laws, has not increased usage.[60] While many studies warn that marijuana use has a relationship with school dropout, it is not likely a causal relationship. Instead, the decision to drop out of school results from an intricate combination of factors, including academic performance, peer influence, and parental attitudes toward drug use.[61]

Unfortunately, the movement to preserve marijuana prohibition, or to legalize it and use taxes to increase prices and minimize use, puts millions of people and society overall at risk of missing out on its many benefits. Marijuana is an effective treatment for epilepsy, seizures, and chronic pain, and it is a substitute for more harmful painkillers like opioids.[62] It is also a substitute for benzodiazepines, antidepressants, sleeping pills, cocaine, and heroin.[63] In what may come as a shock to the Centennial Institute, some evidence shows that marijuana availability reduced the suicide rate

[57] Maier et al. (2017); see also Lu et al. (2019).

[58] Zakrzewski et al. (2020).

[59] The report, "Improving the Measurement of Drug-Related Crime," was issued in October 2013.

[60] Anderson et al. (2015, 2019), Choo et al. (2014), Dills et al. (2017), Lynne-Landsman et al. (2013), and Melchior et al. (2019).

[61] McCaffrey et al. (2010).

[62] Boehnke et al. (2016), Boehnke et al. (2019), Bradford et al. (2018), Darkovska-Serafimovska et al. (2018), Mascal et al. (2019), and Powell et al. (2018).

[63] Chu (2015), Lucas and Walsh (2017), and Piper et al. (2017).

by about 10% among American men between ages 20 and 39.[64] And take note, soda paternalists: medical marijuana laws may reduce obesity.[65]

* * *

Although paternalists will not enjoy reading it, the research they depend on to paint marijuana as harmful to society is undermined by the same mistakes as the research that backs soda, alcohol, and tobacco taxes.

Perhaps because research is lacking compared to the other sins, many claims about marijuana's detrimental effects stem from review articles that summarize what little research is available. The review that concluded the association between marijuana use and psychotic disorders was strong enough to "warrant a public health message" is a prime example. Such analyses help identify patterns across existing research, but they are only as good as the studies they examine. If studies included in any review are not objective, perhaps due to publication bias in favor of marijuana paternalism, then so will the reviews.

That's not just a hypothetical. Evidence indicates that, just as there was for soda, alcohol, and tobacco, there is publication bias in favor of research that supports marijuana paternalism. A review of 24 studies on the relationship between marijuana use and traffic accidents found "very high" bias in favor of research that documented a positive effect.[66] Publication bias also affects research on marijuana's impact on other health and social outcomes.[67] When experts don't make adjustments for publication bias, they tend to find that marijuana is harmful.[68] But when they do make adjustments, they often find that the evidence for marijuana's risks shrinks to the point of non-significance.[69]

---

[64] Anderson et al. (2014).

[65] Sabia et al. (2017). Thus, whether true or not, the stereotype that marijuana users like to snack does not seem to have a cumulative effect on their weight.

[66] Hostiuc et al. (2018).

[67] Kraan et al. (2016) and Pizzol et al. (2019). See also discussion in chapter 5 of "The Health and Social Effects of Nonmedical Cannabis Use," a 2016 report from the World Health Organization.

[68] Gage et al. (2016) failed to correct for publication bias. The text also fails to discuss testing procedures to verify whether bias was an issue and does not acknowledge that potential bias is a limitation on the study's conclusions.

[69] Elvik (2013). Some reviews find no evidence of publication bias but concede that may be the result of examining a small number of studies (Martín-Sánchez et al. 2009).

The bias in favor of marijuana paternalism is not always deliberate. In several studies, it stems from experts' use of unsuitable data. Many experts that draw a connection between marijuana use and motor vehicle accidents rely on information gleaned from the Fatality Analysis Reporting System ("FARS"), a database maintained by the National Highway Traffic Safety Administration, a federal agency in the United States.[70] FARS data has serious limitations. There is no uniformity among jurisdictions that submit information. Worse, the data indicate only whether marijuana or other drugs were present in drivers involved in fatal accidents, not the degree of intoxication.[71] That lack of precision injects significant uncertainty into any analysis, which ultimately biases a study's results. Not surprisingly, reliance on FARS data has been found to exaggerate the risk of harm from marijuana use.[72]

Data issues are not confined to FARS. According to a 2017 study, adolescent marijuana use rose following decriminalization in Washington. Therefore, the authors argued, "investment in adolescent substance use prevention programs" may be warranted.[73] But the study drew on data from Monitoring the Future ("MTF"), a survey administered by the National Institute on Drug Abuse, the same agency that cautioned parents that marijuana leads to poor grades and mental illness. But MTF is not intended for use in state-level analysis. Using more representative data, an ensuing study—written by some of the same experts—found that adolescent use in Washington declined following decriminalization.[74]

That conclusion wasn't a one-off. When used appropriately in nationwide analyses, other MTF-based studies find marijuana liberalization has no effect on use among minors.[75]

Data limitations are a fact of life in the social sciences. But other errors in marijuana research cannot be reconciled with accepted scientific practices. In study after study, experts report a correlation between marijuana use and a particular outcome as proof that marijuana caused that outcome. A widely cited study that concluded marijuana use "is

[70] Lee et al. (2018), Salomonsen-Sautel et al. (2014), and Pollini et al. (2015).

[71] Berning and Smither (2014).

[72] Romano et al. (2017).

[73] Cerdá et al. (2017).

[74] Dilley et al. (2019).

[75] Dills et al. (2017).

associated with an increased risk of developing schizophrenia" could not resolve whether marijuana caused that condition or vice versa, despite implying a causal relationship from correlation alone. Furthermore, the study's data were drawn from a rather narrow sample: Swedish men.[76] A later study suggested marijuana was indeed the cause—but admitted that only about ten percent of marijuana users at 15 developed schizophrenia by 26. That led the authors to suggest not a ban or a tax on marijuana, but that "cannabis use among *psychologically vulnerable adolescents* should be strongly discouraged" (emphasis added).[77]

Some experts attempt to resolve whether marijuana does in fact cause adverse outcomes, but that is easier said than done, and many defaults to the simpler approach of reporting a simple correlation. Yet taking the path of least resistance only clouds marijuana research. Indeed, the failure to control for confounding factors is one explanation for the inconsistent results about marijuana's public health impact.[78] Some experts make a valiant attempt, but make mistakes in the process. The authors of a 2005 study concluded "the association between cannabis use and psychotic symptoms is unlikely to be due to confounding factors" did—admirably—examine the role of such confounders. But they failed to report any of the effects. The authors also depended on self-reported marijuana use, not an objective measure of THC concentration in users' blood, making their conclusion of questionable validity.[79]

In a point of departure from research on the other sins, some experts have taken note of the junk science behind marijuana paternalism. In 2019, one hundred experts from around the world signed a letter condemning a popular book about the risks of marijuana—the same book featured in *Mother Jones*—as "a polemic based on a deeply inaccurate misreading of science." The experts noted that the author repeatedly

---

[76] Zammit et al. (2002).

[77] Arseneault et al. (2002).

[78] Pearson (2019); see also Table 1 in Gage et al. (2016), which shows that studies that account for more confounding factors find a much smaller risk of negative outcomes from marijuana use compared to studies that account for a smaller number of confounders.

[79] Fergusson et al. (2005). Many studies that link marijuana to poor mental health outcomes are based on self-reported frequency of use, not concentration (e.g., van Os et al. 2002). As it does with alcohol, THC concentration matters—except to paternalists who view any amount of marijuana consumption as problematic.

mistook correlation for causation, cherry-picked data, relied on anecdotes, and ignored the harms associated with marijuana prohibition.[80]

* * *

Whether of the paternalistic origin or not, campaigns to legalize marijuana derive much of their support and ultimate success from convincing policymakers and voters that marijuana taxes are a lucrative source of revenue. Advocates claim that the money could support an abundance of government programs, from drug and alcohol rehabilitation to public schools—thus benefiting "the children."

It is an effective tactic with little basis in reality. Enough jurisdictions have pursued legalize-and-tax measures that it's safe to say revenue does not fulfill advocates' promises.[81] Tax collections in some areas were sluggish from the point of legalization; in others, initial surges were not sustainable, and revenue quickly reached a ceiling.[82]

Much more worrisome about the rush to tax marijuana is that the revenue often supports programs of questionable value or those that are of ostensibly societal benefit—like public education—which begs the question of why marijuana users should finance a lopsided share of the cost.

California is a perfect case study in the perils of taxing marijuana. After voters in 2016 approved recreational marijuana—medicinal marijuana passed in 1996—tax advocates and state government officials estimated revenue would amount to $1 billion annually. Before the referendum, voters were told that the revenue would fund a variety of social, education, and environmental programs statewide.

But by 2019, California's marijuana tax revenue lingered below $300 million. Several factors contributed to that unequivocally lackluster result. Despite decriminalization at the state level, many local governments kept bans on marijuana-related businesses in effect. That alone constrained the legal market's size. Even in areas without restrictive rules, businesses required approval from multiple state and local regulatory agencies. But

---

[80] See "Letter from Scholars and Clinicians who Oppose Junk Science about Marijuana," dated February 14, 2019, available at https://www.drugpolicy.org/resource/letter-scholars-and-clinicians-who-oppose-junk-science-about-marijuana.

[81] Becker (2019).

[82] Pew Charitable Trust (2019).

even clearing those hurdles was no guarantee of success. Combined state and local taxes exceeded 30%, and in some areas, the effective tax rate approached 50%. That rendered illegal marijuana far less expensive than what was sold in legal dispensaries. Small wonder that the illicit market continued to thrive in California, just as it had for decades.[83] By early 2020, state policymakers had resorted to considering a marijuana tax cut, never a popular topic in politically progressive California.[84]

Although the tax contributed hundreds of millions of dollars to California's state treasury, it is difficult to justify how policymakers spent the money. Twenty percent went to programs aimed at helping state and local agencies "assist with law enforcement, fire protection, or other local programming to address public health and safety associated with" recreational marijuana.[85] That might be reasonable if marijuana use posed a danger to public health or safety, but evidence supports neither claim. If anything, the risk of problems is higher from marijuana purchased on the illicit market. Forcing users who bought marijuana legally to pay a higher price for the issues created by those who bought it illegally does not seem fair.

Nor does forcing them to pay for environmental damage they did not cause. Another 20% of California's marijuana tax revenue went to state agencies "to clean up and prevent environmental damage resulting from the illegal growing of cannabis."[86] This included, for example, funding for the California Department of Fish and Wildlife to locate and eliminate illicit marijuana farms. Thus, in California, the cost of removing illegal marijuana farms was subsidized by those who followed the law and purchased marijuana from legal retailers.

The remaining 60% went to the state's Department of Health Care Services. The department used some of the funds for its Youth Substance

---

[83] Sullum (2019).

[84] McGreevy (2020). Continued uncertainty in the United States over whether the federal government would enforce the Controlled Substances Act—and, if so, what enforcement would look like—was an additional factor behind underwhelming marijuana tax collections in California and other states.

[85] Quoted from California Board of State and Community Corrections, Proposition 64 Grant Program Description, available at https://www.bscc.ca.gov/s_cppgrantfundedprograms/.

[86] California Legislative Analyst's Office (2017).

Use Disorder Prevention Program, which issues grants to nonprofit organizations that:

> lifts up and makes available racially and culturally responsive population-based and place-based approaches specifically for California's demographic communities disproportionately impacted by the war on drugs.[87]

That funding choice was even more peculiar than the others. It forced those who purchased marijuana legally to subsidize a restorative social justice program aimed at repairing the burden of a drug war those users did not cause or—in most cases—ever support. The cost fell disproportionately on younger generations, who are more likely to purchase marijuana products and who were not even alive when the United States' so-called war on drugs launched in the 1970s.

California is not the only American state that earmarks marijuana tax revenue to programs with dubious grounds. Following decriminalization in Oregon, the state allocated 40% of revenue to its Common School Fund, which distributes funding to local school districts. Twenty percent went to the Mental Health Alcoholism and Drug Services Account, which issues grants to organizations that administer drug and alcohol treatment programs. The remainder was divided among local governments (20%), the Oregon State Police (15%), and the Oregon Health Authority (5%).

Regardless of whether the programs are a worthwhile investment, it remains unclear why marijuana users have to subsidize a larger proportion of their cost. There is no evidence to suggest that those users burden the healthcare system with externalities, and there is no evidence that they commit more crimes—other than perhaps violating laws against marijuana use. The same critiques apply in Washington, where marijuana taxes support the state's general fund and healthcare services for low-income populations, and in Colorado, where most of the state's revenue subsidizes public education spending.

But at least the revenue in those states supports fairly broad programs. In other instances, the tax looks like little more than a money grab to fund policymakers' pet projects or fiscal cover for poorly managed budgets.

---

[87] See California Department of Health and Community Services, "Prop 64 Advisory Group," available at https://www.dhcs.ca.gov/provgovpart/Pages/Prop-64-Advisory-Group.aspx.

Portland, Oregon is a noteworthy illustration. Voters there approved a local marijuana tax in 2016 on the understanding that revenue would fund drug and alcohol treatment programs, public safety training on how to handle impaired driving, and initiatives to help small businesses, especially those owned by women and minorities. A 2019 report from the city's auditor found that just five percent of marijuana tax revenue went to drug and alcohol treatment, and only 16% went to small business support. Over $2 million covered a deficit in the city's general fund. Three million dollars went to "Vision Zero," an initiative that the city's Bureau of Transportation states is "committed to ending traffic violence" by redesigning roadways around pedestrians, not vehicles.[88] Vision Zero's unfortunate result in most cities an increase in pedestrian deaths, the opposite of its goal.[89]

Port Hueneme, California, is another good example. Local officials there used marijuana tax revenue to pay public sector pension fund expenses and to hire additional police officers. And that's not all. The city also mandated that marijuana dispensaries donate one percent of sales to local charities, a quasi-tax passed on to consumers. Some of that revenue subsidized the city's Independence Day fireworks display.[90]

Or consider Evanston, Illinois. In 2019, policymakers there voted overwhelmingly in favor of directing marijuana tax revenue toward a reparations program. According to a report in the *Chicago Tribune*, local officials viewed the money "as an opportunity to pay for a local reparations program that would address the lingering institutional effects of slavery and discrimination."[91]

* * *

There is little reason to support paternalists' claims that marijuana deserves outright prohibition or, if legalized, a tax. Overall, the evidence does not support arguments that the choice to use marijuana misses the secular mark by imposing additional healthcare costs or by causing crime and other unsavory behaviors. Research instead shows that marijuana is as harmless as the other sins, and is often beneficial for treating

[88] Portland City Auditor (2019).

[89] Bliss et al. (2019).

[90] Gillers (2020).

[91] Bookwalter (2019).

certain health conditions. That leaves little reason for any government to maintain prohibition or tax-induced higher prices.

Nevertheless, marijuana paternalists continue to focus on strict regulations. In late 2019, the Food and Drug Administration, an American regulatory agency, issued warnings to 15 companies for, in the agency's opinion, selling food, dietary supplements, and other products that contain cannabidiol, one of the active ingredients in cannabis commonly referred to as "CBD."[92] The move cascaded down the governmental chain of command. Within weeks, Oregon's Liquor Control Commission, which regulates both alcohol and marijuana, issued a ban on THC and CBD-infused beverages. They were not the first to act, however; the states of Washington, Maine, and California had already done so, and so had the cities of New York and Detroit.

Some government action concerning CBD products is justifiable. It is reasonable for regulatory agencies to act when manufacturers and sellers of CBD products—or any product, for that matter—make unsupported claims, such as that it is a miracle cure for cancer. It is also reasonable for agencies to demand consistent product labeling because CBD concentration disclosures are inconsistent.[93]

But prohibition or other regulations are unnecessary. A report from the World Health Organization in 2017 stated that CBD "exhibits no effects indicative of any abuse or dependence potential."[94] Food and beverage products infused with CBD, and even with THC, offer less intoxicating but longer-lasting effects and avoid any potential respiratory risks that go along with smoking marijuana.[95]

Yet marijuana prohibition—or, where it is legal, marijuana taxes—is not likely to disappear. Marijuana taxes in areas where they are perceived as excessive may be reduced, but not eliminated. The reason is that, compared to the other sins, many experts, and interest groups have not made a strong case for marijuana taxes on public health grounds. From

---

[92] At that time, CBD-infused food and beverage products were illegal under the Food, Drug, and Cosmetic Act, which does not allow the addition of drugs—even those approved by regulatory agencies—to foods intended for human or even animal consumption.

[93] Bonn-Miller et al. (2017).

[94] The report, "Cannabidiol (CBD) Pre-Review Report," was issued by the Expert Committee on Drug Dependence in November 2017.

[95] Cone et al. (1988) and Cooper et al. (2013).

the start, the movement has emphasized raising government revenue and imposing more regulations on the legal sale of marijuana. They may not be sure that marijuana is sinful, but to paternalists, giving up the option to tax it might be.

REFERENCES

Adler, Jonathan H., ed. 2020. *Marijuana Federalism: Uncle Sam and Mary Jane.* Washington DC: Brookings Institution Press.

Alley, Zoe M., David C.R. Kerr, and Harold Bae. 2020. "Trends in College Students' Alcohol, Nicotine, Prescription Opioid and Other Drug Use after Recreational Marijuana Legalization, 2008-2018." *Addictive Behaviors* 102: 106212.

American Cancer Society. 2017. "Marijuana and Cancer." Retrieved March 1, 2020 (https://www.cancer.org/treatment/treatments-and-side-effects/com plementary-and-alternative-medicine/marijuana-and-cancer.html).

American Lung Association. 2015. "Public Policy Position—Lung Health." Retrieved March 2, 2020 (https://www.lung.org/get-involved/become-an-advocate/public-policy-position-lung-health.html).

Anderson, D. Mark, and Daniel I. Rees. 2014. "The Legalization of Recreational Marijuana: How Likely Is the Worst-Case Scenario?" *Journal of Policy Analysis and Management* 33(1): 221–232.

Anderson, D. Mark, Benjamin Hansen, and Daniel I. Rees. 2013. "Medical Marijuana Laws, Traffic Fatalities, and Alcohol Consumption." *The Journal of Law & Economics* 56(2): 333–369.

Anderson, D. Mark, Benjamin Hansen, and Daniel I. Rees. 2015. "Medical Marijuana Laws and Teen Marijuana Use." *American Law and Economics Review* 17(2): 495–528.

Anderson, D. Mark, Daniel I. Rees, and Joseph J. Sabia. 2014. "Medical Marijuana Laws and Suicides by Gender and Age." *American Journal of Public Health* 104(12): 2369–2376.

Anderson, D. Mark, Benjamin Hansen, Daniel I. Rees, and Joseph J. Sabia. 2019. "Association of Marijuana Laws with Teen Marijuana Use: New Estimates From the Youth Risk Behavior Surveys." *JAMA Pediatrics* 173(9): 879–881.

Arco, Matt. 2018. "Most Jersey Residents Say They'd Go for Legal Weed if it Means Lower Property Taxes, Poll Shows." Retrieved March 1, 2020 (https://www.nj.com/marijuana/2018/09/a_majority_of_nj_agrees_well_take_legal_weed_for_l.html).

Arseneault, Louise, Mary Cannon, Richie Poulton, Robin Murray, Avshalom Caspi, and Terrie E Moffitt. 2002. "Cannabis Use in Adolescence and Risk for Adult Psychosis: Longitudinal Prospective Study." *BMJ* 325: 1212–1213.

Asbridge, Mark, Jill A. Hayden, and Jennifer L. Cartwright. 2012. "Acute Cannabis Consumption and Motor Vehicle Collision Risk: Systematic Review of Observational Studies and Meta-Analysis." *BMJ* 344: e536.

Aydelotte, Jayson D., Lawrence H. Brown, Kevin M. Luftman, Alexandra L. Mardock, Pedro G.R. Teixeira, Ben Coopwood, and Carlos V.R. Brown. 2017. "Crash Fatality Rates After Recreational Marijuana Legalization in Washington and Colorado." *American Journal of Public Health* 107(8): 1329–1331.

Barnwell, Sara Smucker, Mitch Earleywine, and Rand Wilcox. 2006. "Cannabis, Motivation, and Life Satisfaction in an Internet Sample." *Substance Abuse Treatment, Prevention, and Policy* 1: 2.

Becker, Bernie. 2019. "Cannabis Was Supposed to be a Tax Windfall for States. The Reality Has Been Different." *Politico.* Retrieved March 1, 2020 (https://www.politico.com/agenda/story/2019/10/14/marijuana-tax-revenue-001062).

Berenson, Alex. 2019. *Tell Your Children: The Truth About Marijuana, Mental Illness, and Violence.* New York, NY: Simon and Schuster.

Berning, Amy, and Dereece D. Smither. 2014. "Understanding the Limitations of Drug Test Information, Reporting, and Testing Practices in Fatal Crashes." Washington DC: United States Department of Transportation, National Highway Traffic Safety Administration Research Note.

Bliss, Laura, David Montgomery, and Matthew Gerring. 2019. "What Happens When a City Tries to End Traffic Deaths." *CityLab.* Retrieved February 1, 2020 (https://www.citylab.com/transportation/2019/11/vision-zero-data-traffic-deaths-pedestrians-cyclist-safety/601831/).

Bloomfield, Michael A.P., Celia J.A. Morgan, Alice Egerton, Shitij Kapur, H. Valerie Curran, and Oliver D. Howes. 2014. "Dopaminergic Function in Cannabis Users and Its Relationship to Cannabis-Induced Psychotic Symptoms." *Biological Psychiatry* 75(6): 470–478.

Boehnke, Kevin F., Evangelos Litinas, and Daniel J. Clauw. 2016. "Medical Cannabis Use is Associated With Decreased Opiate Medication Use in a Retrospective Cross-Sectional Survey of Patients with Chronic Pain." *Journal of Pain* 17(6): 739–744.

Boehnke, Kevin F., Saurav Gangopadhyay, Daniel J. Clauw, and Rebecca L. Hafajee. 2019. "Qualifying Conditions of Medical Cannabis License Holders in the United States." *Health Affairs* 38(2): 295–302.

Bonn-Miller, Marcel O., Mallory J.E. Loflin, Brian F. Thomas, Jahan P. Marcu, Travis Hyke, and Ryan Vandrey. 2017. "Labeling Accuracy of Cannabidiol Extracts Sold Online." *Journal of the American Medical Association* 318(17): 1708–1709.

Bradford, Ashley C., W. David Bradford, Amanda Abraham, and Grace Bagwell Adams. 2018. "Association between US State Medical Cannabis Laws and Opioid Prescribing in the Medicare Part D Population." *JAMA Internal Medicine* 178(5): 667–672.

Brubacher, Jeffrey R., Herbert Chan, Shannon Erdelyi, Scott Macdonald, Mark Asbridge, Robert E. Mann, Jeffrey Eppler, Adam Lund, Andrew MacPherson, Walter Martz, William E. Schreiber, Rollin Brant, and Roy A. Purssell. 2019. "Cannabis Use as a Risk Factor for Causing Motor Vehicle Crashes: A Prospective Study." *Addiction* 114(9): 1616–1626.

Bookwalter, Genevieve. 2019. "Evanston Will use Recreational Marijuana Sales Tax Proceeds to Fund Local Reparations Program." *The Chicago Tribune.* Retrieved March 1, 2020 (https://www.chicagotribune.com/suburbs/eva nston/ct-evr-evanston-reparations-marijuana-tax-tl-1205-20191126-g3ifwaikr jfmrillfv6ytvwgii-story.html).

Booth, Martin. 2003. *Cannabis: A History.* New York, NY: Picador.

Butrica, James L. 2002. "The Medical Use of Cannabis Among the Greeks and Romans." *Journal of Cannabis Therapeutics* 2(2): 51–70.

California Legislative Analyst's Office. 2017. "Proposition 64 Revenues." Retrieved March 12, 2020 (https://lao.ca.gov/handouts/crimjust/2017/ Proposition-64-Revenues-021617.pdf).

Carroll, Aaron E. 2018. "It's Time for a New Discussion of Marijuana's Risks." *The New York Times.* Retrieved May 8, 2018 (https://www.nytimes. com/2018/05/07/upshot/its-time-for-a-new-discussion-of-marijuanas-risks. html).

Cerdá, Magdalena, Melanie Wall, Tianshu Feng, Katherine M. Keyes, Aaron Sarvet, John Schulenberg, Patrick M. O'Malley, Rosalie Liccardo Pacula, Sandro Galea, and Deborah S. Hasin. 2017. "Association of State Recreational Marijuana Laws with Adolescent Marijuana Use." *JAMA Pediatrics* 171(2): 142–149.

Choo, Esther K., Madeline Benz, Nikolas Zaller, Otis Warren, Kristin L. Rising, and K. John McConnell. 2014. "The Impact of State Medical Marijuana Legislation on Adolescent Marijuana Use." *Journal of Adolescent Health* 55(2): 160–166.

Chu, Yu-Wei Luke. 2015. "Do Medical Marijuana Laws Increase Hard-Drug Use?" *The Journal of Law and Economics* 58(2): 481–517.

Cone, Edward J., Rolley E. Johnson, Buddha D. Paul, Leroy D. Mell, and John Mitchell. 1988. "Marijuana-laced Brownies: Behavioral Effects, Physiologic Effects, and Urinalysis in Humans following Ingestion." *Journal of Analytical Toxicology* 12(4): 169–175.

Cooper, Ziva D., Sandra D. Comer, and Margaret Haney. 2013. "Comparison of the Analgesic Effects of Dronabinol and Smoked Marijuana in Daily Marijuana Smokers." *Neuropsychopharmacology* 38(10): 1984–1992.

Darkovska-Serafimovska, Marija, Tijana Serafimovska, Zorica Arsova-Sarafinovska, Sasho Stefanoski, Zlatko Keskovski, and Trajan Balkanov. 2018. "Pharmacotherapeutic Considerations for Use of Cannabinoids to Relieve Pain in Patients with Malignant Diseases." *Journal of Pain Research* 11: 837–842.

De Pinto, Jennifer. 2019. "Support for Marijuana Legalization Hits New High, CBS News Poll Finds." CBS News. Retrieved April 19, 2019 (https://www.cbsnews.com/news/support-for-marijuana-legalization-hits-new-high-cbs-news-poll-finds/).

Degenhardt, Louisa, Wayne Hall, and Michael Lynskey. 2003. "Testing Hypotheses about the Relationship between Cannabis Use and Psychosis." *Drug and Alcohol Dependence* 71(1): 37–48.

Dilley, Julia A., Susan M. Richardson, Beau Kilmer, Rosalie Licardo Pacula, Mary B. Segawa, and Magdalena Cerdá. 2019. "Prevalence of Cannabis Use in Youths After Legalization in Washington State." *JAMA Pediatrics* 173(2): 192–193.

Dills, Angela K., Sietse Goffard, and Jeffrey Miron. 2017. "The Effects of Marijuana Liberalizations: Evidence from Monitoring the Future." National Bureau of Economic Research Working Paper 23779.

Duncan, David F. 1987. "Lifetime Prevalence of 'Amotivational Syndrome' among Users and Non-users of Hashish." *Psychology of Addictive Behaviors* 1(2): 114–119.

Elvik, Rune. 2013. "Risk of Road Accident Associated with the Use of Drugs: A Systematic Review and Meta-Analysis of Evidence from Epidemiological Studies." *Accident Analysis & Prevention* 60: 254–267.

Fergusson, David M., L. John Horwood, and Elizabeth M. Ridder. 2005. "Tests of Causal Linkages between Cannabis Use and Psychotic Symptoms." *Addiction* 100(3): 354–366.

Gage, Suzanne H., Matthew Hickman, and Stanley Zammit. 2016. "Association between Cannabis and Psychosis: Epidemiologic Evidence." *Biological Psychiatry* 79(7): 549–556.

Galliher, John F., and Allynn Walker. 1977. "The Puzzle of the Social Origins of the Marihuana Tax Act of 1937." *Social Problems* 24(3): 367–376.

Gieringer, Dale H. 1999. "The Forgotten Origins of Cannabis Prohibition in California." *Contemporary Drug Problems* 26(2): 237–288.

Gillers, Heather. 2020. "Is Your City's Pension Fund a Little Short? Marijuana Might Help." *The Wall Street Journal*. Retrieved February 4, 2020 (https://www.wsj.com/articles/is-your-citys-pension-fund-a-little-short-marijuana-might-help-11580812201).

Giordano, G.N., H. Ohlsson, K. Sundquist, J. Sundquist, and K.S. Kendler. 2015. "The Association between Cannabis Abuse and Subsequent Schizophrenia: A Swedish National Co-relative Control Study." *Psychological Medicine* 45(2): 404–417.

Gould, Jens. 2019. "Poll: Most New Mexicans Support Legalizing Recreational Pot." *Santa Fe New Mexican*. Retrieved January 2, 2020 (https://www.santafenewmexican.com/news/local_news/poll-most-new-mexicans-support-legalizing-recreational-pot/article_fe8aab3e-22b0-11ea-a3e9-cb717a696699.html).

Hall, Wayne. 2015. "What Has Research Over the Past Two Decades Revealed about the Adverse Health Effects of Recreational Cannabis Use?" *Addiction* 110(1): 19–35.

Hansen, Benjamin, Keaton Miller, and Caroline Weber. 2020. "Early Evidence on Recreational Marijuana Legalization and Traffic Fatalities." *Economic Inquiry* 58(2): 547–568.

Hill, Matthew. 2015. "Perspective: Be Clear about the Real Risks." *Nature* 525: S14.

Hostiuc, Sorin, Alin Moldoveanu, Ionut Negoi, and Eduard Drima. 2018. "The Association of Unfavorable Traffic Events and Cannabis Usage: A Meta-Analysis." *Frontiers in Pharmacology* 9: 99.

Jones, Jeffrey M. 2019. "U.S. Support for Legal Marijuana Steady in Past Year." Gallup. Retrieved March 12, 2020 (https://news.gallup.com/poll/267698/support-legal-marijuana-steady-past-year.aspx).

Kraan, T., E. Velhorst, L. Koenders, K. Zwaart, H.K. Ising, D. van den Berg, L. de Haan, and M. van der Gaag. 2016. "Cannabis Use and Transition to Psychosis in Individuals at Ultra-high Risk: Review and Meta-Analysis." *Psychological Medicine* 46(4): 673–681.

Ksir, Charles, and Carl L. Hart. 2016. "Cannabis and Psychosis: A Critical Overview of the Relationship." *Current Psychiatry Reports* 18: 12.

Lac, Andrew, and Jeremy W. Luk. 2018. "Testing the Amotivational Syndrome: Marijuana Use Longitudinally Predicts Lower Self-Efficacy Even After Controlling for Demographics, Personality, and Alcohol and Cigarette Use." *Prevention Science* 19(2): 117–126.

Lane, Tyler J., and Wayne Hall. 2019. "Traffic Fatalities within US States That Have Legalized Recreational Cannabis Sales and Their Neighbours." *Addiction* 114(5): 847–856.

Lee, Jaeyoung, Ahmad Abdel-Aty, and Juneyoung Park. 2018. "Investigation of Associations between Marijuana Law Changes and Marijuana-Involved Fatal Traffic Crashes: A State-Level Analysis." *Journal of Transport & Health* 10: 194–202.

Lee, Martin A. 2012. *Smoke Signals: A Social History of Marijuana—Medicinal, Recreational, and Scientific*. New York, NY: Scribner.

Lee, Mu-Chen, Joanne E. Brady, Charles J. DiMaggio, Arielle R. Lusardi, Keane Y. Tzong, and Guohua Li. 2012. "Marijuana Use and Motor Vehicle Crashes." *Epidemiologic Reviews* 34(1): 65–72.

Lewis, Amanda Chicago. 2019. "Is Alex Berenson Trolling Us With His Anti-Weed Book?" *Rolling Stone*. Retrieved February 1, 2020 (https://www.rollingstone.com/culture/culture-features/alex-berenson-marijuana-tell-your-children-trolling-777741/).

Long, Tengwen, Mayke Wagner, Dieter Demske, Christian Leipe, and Pavel E. Tarasov. 2017. "Cannabis in Eurasia: Origin of Human Use and Bronze Age Trans-Continental Connections." *Vegetation History and Archaeobotany* 26(2): 245–258.

Lu, Ruibin, Dale Willits, Mary K. Stohr, David Makin, John Snyder, Nicholas Lovrich, Mikala Meize, Duane Stanton, Guangzhen Wu, and Craig Hemmens. 2019. "The Cannabis Effect on Crime: Time-Series Analysis of Crime in Colorado and Washington State." *Justice Quarterly*, forthcoming. https://doi.org/10.1080/07418825.2019.1666903.

Lucas, Philippe, and Zach Walsh. 2017. "Medical Cannabis Access, Use, and Substitution for Prescription Opioids and Other Substances: A Survey of Authorized Medical Cannabis Patients." *International Journal of Drug Policy* 42: 30–35.

Lynne-Landsman, Sarah D., Melvin D. Livingston, and Alexander C. Wagenaar. 2013. "Effects of State Medical Marijuana Laws on Adolescent Marijuana Use." *American Journal of Public Health* 103(8): 1500–1506.

Maier, Shana L., Suzanne Manners, and Emily L. Koppenhofer. 2017. "The Implications of Marijuana Decriminalization and Legalization on Crime in the United States." *Contemporary Drug Problems* 44(2): 125–146.

Marijuana Policy Project. 2020. "Financial Impact of Legalizing and Regulating Cannabis for Adult Use." Retrieved March 12, 2020 (https://www.mpp.org/issues/legalization/financial-information-on-states-with-adult-use-legalization/).

Martín-Sánchez, Eva, Toshiaki Furukawa, and Julian Taylor. 2009. "Systematic Review and Meta-analysis of Cannabis Treatment for Chronic Pain." *Pain Medicine* 10(8): 1353–1368.

Mascal, Mark, Nema Hafezi, Deping Wang, Yuhan Hu, Gessica Serra, Mark L. Dallas, and Jeremy P.E. Spencer. 2019. "Synthetic, Non-intoxicating 8, 9-dihydrocannabidiol for the Migration of Seizures." *Scientific Reports* 9: 7778.

Massachusetts Prevention Alliance. 2019. "Get the Facts—Marijuana." Retrieved March 12, 2020 (https://www.mapreventionalliance.org/get-the-facts/get-the-facts-marijuana/).

McCaffrey, Daniel F., Rosalie Liccardo Pacula, Bing Han, and Phyllis Ellickson. 2010. "Marijuana Use and High School Dropout: The Influence of Unob-servables." *Health Economics* 19(11): 1281–1299.

McGinty, Emma E., Hillary Samples, Sachini N. Bandara, Brendan Saloner, Marcus A. Bachuber, and Colleen L. Barry. 2016. "The Emerging Public Discourse on State Legalization of Marijuana for Recreational Use in the US:

Analysis of News Media Coverage, 2010–2014." *Preventative Medicine* 90(9): 114–120.

McGreevy, Patrick. 2020. "California Lawmakers Say Pot Taxes Must Be Cut to Help an Industry 'On the Brink'." *Los Angeles Times*. Retrieved January 18, 2020 (https://www.latimes.com/california/story/2020-01-17/california-lower-pot-taxes-gavin-newsom).

Melchior, Maria, Aurélie Nakamura, Camille Bolze, Félix Hausfater, Fabienne El Khoury, Murielle Mary-Krause, and Marine Azevedo Da Silva. 2019. "Does Liberalisation of Cannabis Policy Influence Levels of Use in Adolescents and Young Adults? A Systematic Review and Meta-analysis." *BMJ Open* 9(7): e025880.

Mencimer, Stephanie. 2019. "This Reporter Took a Deep Look into the Science of Smoking Pot. What He Found is Scary." *Mother Jones*. Retrieved February 5, 2020 (https://www.motherjones.com/politics/2019/01/new-york-times-journalist-alex-berenson-tell-your-children-marijuana-crime-mental-illness-1/).

Morral, Andrew R., Daniel F. McCaffrey, and Susan M. Paddock. 2002. "Reassessing the Marijuana Gateway Effect." *Addiction* 97(12): 1493–1504.

Musto, David F. 1972. "The Marihuana Tax Act of 1937." *Archives of General Psychiatry* 26(2): 101–108.

National Academies of Sciences, Engineering, and Medicine. 2017. *The Health Effects of Cannabis and Cannabinoids: The Current State of Evidence and Recommendations for Research*. Washington DC: National Academies Press.

Nelson, Peter L. 1994. "Cannabis Amotivational Syndrome and Personality Trait Absorption: A Review and Reconceptualization." *Imagination, Cognition, and Personality* 14(1): 43–58.

Pacheco-Colón, Ileana, Jorge M. Limia, and Raul Gonzalez. 2018. "Nonacute Effects of Cannabis Use on Motivation and Reward Sensitivity in Humans: A Systematic Review." *Psychology of Addictive* Behaviors 32(5): 497–507.

Parents Opposed to Pot. 2018. "Marijuana is the Common Web between So Many Mass Killers." Retrieved February 9, 2020 (https://poppot.org/2018/07/03/marijuana-violence-know-connection/).

Pearson, Matthew R. 2019. "A Meta-analytic Investigation of the Associations between Cannabis Use and Cannabis-related Negative Consequences." *Journal of the Society of Psychologists in Addictive Behaviors* 33(3): 190–196.

Pew Charitable Trust. 2019. "Forecasts Hazy for State Marijuana Revenue." Retrieved March 12, 2020 (https://www.pewtrusts.org/en/research-and-analysis/issue-briefs/2019/08/forecasts-hazy-for-state-marijuana-revenue).

Piper, Brian J., Rebecca M. DeKeuster, Monica L. Beals, Catherine M. Cobb, Corey A. Burchman, Leah Perkinson, Shayne T. Lynn, Stephanie D. Nichols, and Alexander T. Abess. 2017. "Substitution of Medical Cannabis for Pharmaceutical Agents for Pain, Anxiety, and Sleep." *Journal of Psychopharmacology* 31(5): 569–575.

Pizzol, Damiano, Jacopo Demurtas, Brendon Stubbs, Pinar Soysal, Corina Mason, Ahmet Turan Isik, Marco Solmi, Lee Smith, and Nicola Veronese. 2019. "Relationship between Cannabis Use and Erectile Dysfunction: A Systematic Review and Meta-Analysis." *American Journal of Men's Health*, forthcoming. https://doi.org/10.1177/1557988319892464.

Pollini, Robin A., Eduardo Romano, Mark B. Johnson, and John H. Lacey. 2015. "The Impact of Marijuana Decriminalization on California Drivers." *Drug and Alcohol Dependence* 150: 135–140.

Portland City Auditor. 2019. "Recreational Cannabis Tax: Greater Transparency and Accountability Needed." Retrieved March 12, 2020 (https://www.portlandoregon.gov/auditservices/article/730292).

Powell, David, Rosalie Liccardo Pacula, and Mireille Jacobson. 2018. "Do Medical Marijuana Laws Reduce Addictions and Deaths Related to Pain Killers?" *Journal of Health Economics* 58: 29–42.

Power, R.A., K.H.J. Verweij, M. Zuhair, G.W. Montgomery, A.K. Henders, A.C. Heath, P.A.F. Madden, S.E. Medland, N.R. Wray, and N.G. Martin. 2014. "Genetic Predisposition to Schizophrenia Associated with Increased Use of Cannabis." *Molecular Psychiatry* 19(11): 1201–1204.

Rogeberg, Ole, and Rune Elvik. 2016. "The Effects of Cannabis Intoxication on Motor Vehicle Collision Revisited and Revised." *Addiction* 111(8): 1348–1359.

Romano, Eduardo, Pedro Torres-Saavedra, Robert B. Voas, and John H. Lacey. 2017. "Marijuana and the Risk of Fatal Car Crashes: What Can We Learn from FARS and NRS Data?" *Journal of Primary Prevention* 38(3): 315–328.

Sabia, Joseph J., Jeffrey Swigert, and Timothy Young. 2017. "The Effect of Medical Marijuana Laws on Body Weight." *Health Economics* 26(1): 6–34.

Salomonsen-Sautel, Stacy, Sung-Joon Min, Joseph T. Sakai, Christian Thurstone, and Christian Hopfer. 2014. "Trends in Fatal Motor Vehicle Crashes Before and After Marijuana Commercialization in Colorado." *Drug and Alcohol Dependence* 140: 137–144.

Sami, Musa, Caitlin Notley, Christos Kouimtsidis, Michael Lynskey, and Sagnik Bhattacharyya. 2019. "Psychotic-like Experiences with Cannabis Cessation and Desire to Quit: A Cannabis Discontinuation Hypothesis." *Psychological Medicine* 49(1): 103–112.

Smart Approaches to Marijuana. 2018. "Overall Talking Points." Retrieved March 12, 2020 (https://learnaboutsam.org/wp-content/uploads/2019/06/7-Sept-2018-General-TPs-v3.pdf).

Sullum, Jacob. 2019. "Heavy Taxes and Regulation Harsh California's Pot Buzz." *Reason*. Retrieved March 5, 2020 (https://reason.com/2019/05/01/heavy-taxes-and-regulation-har/).

Thompson, Rebecca, Katherine DeJong, and Jamie Lo. 2019. "Marijuana Use in Pregnancy." *Obstetrical & Gynecological Survey* 74(7): 415–428.

van Os, J., M. Bak, M. Hanssen, R.V. Bijl, R. de Graaf, and H. Verdoux. 2002. "Cannabis Use and Psychosis: A Longitudinal Population-Based Study." *American Journal of Epidemiology* 156(4): 319–327.

Verweij, Karin J.H., Jorien L. Treur, and Jacqueline M. Vink. 2018. "Investigating Causal Associations between Use of Nicotine, Alcohol, Caffeine and Cannabis: A Two-sample Bidirectional Mendelian Randomization Study." *Addiction* 113(7): 1333–1338.

Williams, Steven R., James R. Agapoff, Brett Y. Lu, Earl S. Hishinuma, and Mark Lee. 2019. "The Frequency of Hospitalization and Length of Stay Differences between Schizophrenic and Schizoaffective Disorder Inpatients Who Use Cannabis." *Journal of Substance Use* 24(1): 21–28.

Zakrzewski, William J., Andrew P. Wheeler, and Andrew J. Thompson. 2020. "Cannabis in the Capital: Exploring the Spatial Association between Medical Marijuana Dispensaries and Crime." *Journal of Crime and Justice* 43(1): 1–15.

Zammit, Stanley, Peter Allebeck, Sven Andreasson, Ingvar Lundberg, and Glyn Lewis. 2002. "Self Reported Cannabis Use as a Risk Factor for Schizophrenia in Swedish Conscripts of 1969: Historical Cohort Study." *BMJ* 325(7374): 1199.

CHAPTER 6

Taxing Twenty-First Century Sins

If one thing is clear from the preceding chapters, it is that paternalism is a robust foundation for taxing sin. Arguments about guarding public health and neutralizing externalities transformed once-temporary taxes on alcoholic beverages and tobacco products into permanent features of government budgets around the globe. The same arguments helped paternalists extend sin taxes to soda and marijuana.

There is little to no indication that their secular crusade will end anytime soon. Paternalists have realized as of late that the world is much more sinful than they previously realized. It is full of billions of individuals making a lot more choices that commit an error, fall stray, or miss the mark—all of it worthy of taxation's redeeming grace.

* * *

Paternalists have already placed much of what grocery stores sell in their crosshairs. Beer, wine, and spirits stocked on shelves in the alcohol department are taxed, often heavily, to deter drinking. Cigarettes and other tobacco products are taxed to accomplish the same goal—and that's if they are allowed for sale at all. Taxes have also begun to encroach on the soda aisle. And taxes will eventually reach whatever department sells marijuana and CBD-infused merchandise.

The deli is next. Perhaps the local sandwich shop, too.

The reason is that paternalists have recently declared that the choice to eat meat is sinful. Given that humans have eaten meat for millions of

© The Author(s) 2021
M. Thom, *Taxing Sin*,
https://doi.org/10.1007/978-3-030-49176-5_6

years, it's recent classification as detrimental to our survival is curious. Admittedly, the domestication of cattle, goats, pigs, and sheep—and the widespread meat eating that came with it—took place relatively recently, within the last ten thousand years. Meat consumption in many parts of the world surged to new highs during the twentieth century and later plateaued. Although beef's popularity peaked around 1970, pork and poultry remain an essential part of human diets worldwide.[1]

It took time, but all that meat eating finally roused paternalistic notice. Some paternalists grew apprehensive about meat's negative impact on the environment. Products made from livestock, which consume vast amounts of water, produce substantial greenhouse gasses, and require large areas of land for grazing, are said to have especially devastating effects on climate change.

Other paternalists contend that meat consumption is a threat to public health. The World Health Organization's International Agency for Research on Cancer lists processed meats, such as bacon and sausage, as "possibly carcinogenic." A 2015 report from the Agency advised that each daily meat serving increases an individual's colorectal cancer risk by 18%.[2] The same year, the Physician's Committee on Responsible Medicine—a "nonprofit that promotes a vegetarian or vegan diet"—reprimanded the United States Department of Agriculture for pushing meat into schools through the National School Lunch Program. The organization declared that meat contributes to the "childhood obesity epidemic" and stops children from eating healthier foods such as whole grains, fruits, and vegetables.[3]

Overall, paternalists locate meat at the nexus of a "diet-environment-health trilemma."[4] They increasingly seek government action to reduce meat's externalities and nudge individuals toward vegetarian choices,

---

[1] Larsen (2012). Data collected by the Organization for Economic Co-operation and Development ("OECD") reveal that meat consumption is relatively high in the United States, but not necessarily the highest compared to other countries. For example, beef consumption is markedly higher in Argentina, pork consumption is much higher across the European Union, China, Korea, and Vietnam, and Israelis consume far more poultry than others. Across the board, meat consumption is low in countries such as India, Thailand, and Nigeria. See OECD iLibrary, Agricultural Output statistics.

[2] Boseley (2015).

[3] Moodie (2015).

[4] Tilman and Clark (2014).

which paternalists believe are less sinful. That includes lobbying for taxes and other public policies that increase meat prices. It may also include treating carnivores like smokers. In 2018, a former United Nations official offered this gem: "If they want to eat meat, they can do it outside the restaurant."[5]

Meat paternalism has yet to attract the same level of attention as the other sins but enjoys the backing of notable interest groups. People for the Ethical Treatment of Animals ("PETA") calls on governments to impose a meat tax that would apply to everything from livestock to poultry, fish, and other animal flesh. "Cigarettes, alcohol, and gasoline are already federally taxed," PETA notes on its website, "but although meat consumption is a health hazard and meat production is a leading source of environmental degradation, the meat industry has gotten off easy."[6] The Food Ethics Council, a British nonprofit organization committed to environmentalism, humane treatment of animals, and eliminating hunger, declared in 2019 that it was time for society to "wake up and challenge our ultra-processed food obsession by taxing it."[7]

Experts have also supported meat paternalism. Chatham House, a British think tank, issued a report in 2015 recommending a tax on "meat and other unsustainable products" to "deliver on the public health agenda while also meeting environmental objectives."[8] A 2018 study coauthored by 23 experts predicted that humanity will struggle to feed itself and limit climate change damage unless meat consumption is drastically reduced. To that end, the study proposed that governments implement a meat tax.[9]

The doctrine of meat paternalism has been carried to public knowledge by the media. A 2012 segment on National Public Radio informed listeners that the energy required to make a quarter-pound hamburger, an American favorite, was "enough to power a microwave for 12 hours"—an estimate that the radio network later acknowledged was wrong. The

[5] Lomborg (2018).

[6] People for the Ethical Treatment of Animals (2020).

[7] The press release, "Food Policy on Trial: In the Dock—Meat Tax," was issued on May 28, 2019.

[8] Wellesley et al. (2015).

[9] Authors (2018).

real number was 18 minutes.[10] Similarly, the *Los Angeles Times* created an interactive feature for its website in 2015 that helped users visualize their diet's environmental impact by letting them create a hypothetical meal with different servings of meat, vegetables, and beverages. The feature calculated how many hundred gallons of water the meal would take to produce in real life.[11]

That coverage stopped short of condemning meat and instead provided information to inquisitive consumers. Other media coverage is distinctly more ominous about the perils of eating meat. A 2016 headline in the British *Telegraph* informed readers: "Ditch sausages for a longer life, say Harvard scientists."[12] The same year, visitors to CNN's website were told: "Meat-eaters may have a higher risk of death, but plants are the answer."[13] Not to be outdone, a CNN story in 2020 cautioned readers that "[r]ed and processed meat are not ok for health, study says, despite news to the contrary." The article began, "[i]f you've been swayed by recent reports that red and processed meat isn't harmful to your health, put down that bacon – there's bad news."[14]

Like those who focus their efforts on taxing other sins, meat paternalists offer research that corroborates their arguments about meat's impact on the environment and public health. Some aspects of their platform, such as livestock's effect on the environment, are hard to dispute. While livestock does have a negative effect, production techniques are much more efficient and less detrimental now than ever before.[15] Furthermore, discouraging meat consumption with a tax or through other public policies will have, at most, a small impact. That is because most of a person's environmental footprint is not tied to their diet, but rather to other lifestyle activities, including electricity usage and mode of transportation.[16] More importantly, discouraging meat consumption by making it more expensive or by subsidizing nonmeat products forces a tradeoff. It

---

[10] Barclay (2012).

[11] The feature is available at https://graphics.latimes.com/food-water-footprint/.

[12] Knapton (2016).

[13] Howard (2016).

[14] LaMotte (2020).

[15] Capper (2011).

[16] Hallström et al. (2015) state dietary changes "can reduce the diets GHG [greenhouse gas] emissions and land use demand by up to 50%," but as Lomborg (2018) notes, "(f)or

may save consumers money and reduce some externalities, but the savings increases consumers' disposable income that can then be spent on other activities more harmful to the environment than meat.[17]

Paternalistic claims about meat's impact on public health are also more nuanced than they initially appear. The study that compelled CNN to urge readers to "put down that bacon" did report that consuming extra servings of processed meat was associated with an increased risk of death from cardiovascular disease, but the increase was merely a few percent.[18]

Far more troubling than histrionic headlines is the fact that the research often used by meat paternalists is poor social science. Many studies merely report the findings of statistical simulations, and like the models utilized to justify soda, alcohol, and tobacco paternalism, they depend on assumptions that do not reflect reality.

Consider a simulation study that concluded a meat tax would reduce healthcare costs and lessen the "number of deaths attributable to red and processed meat." The study's authors assumed that eating meat was a causal factor in death and disease. But that assumption is, at best, debatable. They also failed to incorporate dietary changes that might transpire as a result of higher meat prices. One possibility is that individuals substitute for meat with other unhealthy foods. The authors also treated lost productivity as an externality—yet again, that is an internality—and failed to calculate the rise in healthcare and other costs that would be created by reducing premature death. Yet even with several questionable assumptions, the model estimated that a meat price increase of between seven and 47% would reduce greenhouse gas emissions by just one percent.[19]

Observational studies are not necessarily any better than simulations. One hurdle to evaluating how dietary behaviors change after public policy changes is experts' reliance on self-reported food intake data, which is often inaccurate. Bowing to social pressure, many study participants underreport consumption of foods perceived as unhealthy, just as they might underreport or lie about smoking tobacco or drinking alcohol. Self-reported food data have other flaws; many vegetarians, for instance,

---

the average person in the industrialized world, that means cutting emissions by just 4.3%." See also Lacroix (2018).

[17] Grabs (2015).

[18] Zhong et al. (2020).

[19] Springmann et al. (2018).

report buying meat.[20] Even if the data were error-free, it is next to impossible for any research method to separate the impact one aspect of a person's diet has on their health from other parts of their diet. The need to disentangle the effects of environmental and lifestyle factors introduces additional complexity.[21]

Many studies' credibility is further damaged by experts' assumption that correlation proves causation. One review of 20 studies concluded that meat consumption is associated with heart disease and diabetes, but the authors conceded that most of the studies they evaluated did not determine whether eating meat caused those problems.[22] A separate review concluded that red and processed meat consumption was also associated with other adverse health outcomes, but the authors conceded that other factors might be responsible.[23] And another review concluded that meat consumption imposes a higher risk of stroke, but the authors failed to demonstrate a causal relationship.[24]

It gets worse. Studies favorable to meat paternalism are routinely tainted by false positives and exaggerated interpretations of meat's health risks. Nutrition and health research studies are so bad, according to one commentary, that they are "difficult to reconcile with good scientific principles."[25]

Further undermining the case for meat paternalism is the fact that several studies report no reason to believe that meat consumption is a health risk.[26] In fact, more harm may come from a diet with little or no meat, because it is a good source of protein, amino acids, and certain vitamins and minerals that cannot be easily replaced with a vegetarian diet. While studies favorable to meat consumption are often afflicted by the same flaws as anti-meat studies, they warrant no less attention. For example, a 2004 study of Austrians over age 15 linked a vegetarian diet to "higher incidences of cancer, allergies, and mental health disorders" as

[20] Lusk and Norwood (2016).

[21] Leroy and Cofnas (2019).

[22] Micha et al. (2010).

[23] Wang et al. (2016).

[24] Chen et al. (2013).

[25] Ioannidis (2018).

[26] Kruger and Zhou (2018) and Lippi et al. (2015).

well as a "higher need for health care."[27] A review of 20 studies found that vegetarians and vegans had weaker bones in the neck and spine and higher rates of bone fracture.[28] Other studies tie meat-restricted diets to depression and poor mental health.[29] All things considered, it may be, as two experts observed, that "the theory that (meat) can be replaced with legumes and supplements is mere speculation."[30]

Unfortunately, because there are currently no meat taxes comparable to those on the other sins, it is impossible to evaluate their real-world impact on the environment and public health. Still, lessons can be drawn from other food-based taxes. So-called fat taxes and junk food taxes levied on foods high in saturated fat, sodium, and sugar are a clear analogue.[31] Simulation studies typically report that food taxes are a useful policy to accomplish various public health objectives.[32] But more rigorous studies show that any benefits are likely to be negated by substitution for other, less healthy foods.[33] They also show that food taxes have a disproportionate burden on the poor and the elderly.[34]

Many of those unintended consequences occurred in Denmark after policymakers in 2011 implemented a tax on foods containing over 2.3% saturated fat, including many dairy products and some meats. The levy was never popular with the public, and it ended in 2012.

Whether or not it was effective is a matter of dispute. One study reported that purchases of butter, margarine, and oil fell after the tax went into effect, but also indicated that consumers bought more from discount stores with lower prices.[35] Another study found evidence of product substitution from high- to low-fat products that, as noted in

---

[27] Burkert et al. (2014).

[28] Iguacel et al. (2019).

[29] Matta et al. (2018) and Nezlek et al. (2018).

[30] Leroy and Cofnas (2019).

[31] So-called junk food taxes are popular among some public health groups and professional organizations. For example, in 2003, the British Medical Association proposed a 17.5% value-added tax on fatty foods.

[32] Eyles et al. (2012) and Mytton et al. (2007).

[33] Epstein et al. (2012).

[34] Chouinard et al. (2007).

[35] Jensen and Smed (2013).

Chapter 2, can facilitate higher food consumption and weight gain.[36] Cross-border shopping—in Denmark's case, buying foods in neighboring Germany or Sweden—also mitigated the tax's impact. Sales of butter at one Danish retailer rose after the tax, with demand boosted thanks to a local cooking show "in which the hosts stress how desirable using butter is."[37]

Considering all of the available evidence, there is little reason to believe that meat consumption is significantly harmful to the environment or to public health, or that the benefits of a meat tax outweigh its costs and unintended consequences. Meat is another sin that does not need forgiving.

* * *

Just as it is gradually becoming impossible to exit a grocery store or restaurant without paying one or more sin taxes on foods and beverages, it is also growing more difficult to carry those purchases home without being charged another fee. That is because paternalists have added the choice to use plastic bags to the list of tax-worthy sins.

For several decades those plastic bags, also known as carryout bags and carrier bags, were a ubiquitous bookend to the shopping experience. Although first patented in the 1950s, plastic bags achieved popularity in the 1980s as an alternative to paper bags. Retailers valued the bags' lower cost and advertising potential, and customers appreciated their convenience. They also liked the bags' durability. Even though plastic bags are sometimes referred to as "single use" bags, customers often reuse them multiple times.

But paternalists argue that plastic bags' convenience carried a steep environmental cost. The high-density polyethylene ("HDPE") in some bags comes from oil, the quintessential environmentalist enemy.[38] Experts say the plastic used in some bags will take hundreds of years to biodegrade. In the meantime, bags congest water transport systems, wreak havoc on marine life, and litter public areas.

[36] Jensen et al. (2016).

[37] Bomsdorf (2012).

[38] That concern is misplaced. Most HDPE is sourced from natural gas, not oil. HDPE is used in several other consumer products, including certain types of outdoor furniture, pipes, and beverage containers that have—for now—escaped selective taxation.

By the early twenty-first century, paternalists frequently warned society about its sinful, "toxic love story" with plastic.[39] They lobbied governments to intervene with a plastic bag tax or outright prohibition. Hypothetically, either restriction would nudge people to choose less sinful, multiuse alternatives, like cotton bags, which would reduce the amount of plastic waste and its environmental externalities. Experts said taxes were an effective way to accomplish the behavioral change; one study estimated that a tax would reduce bag usage by 40%.[40]

Plastic bag paternalism was carried to the mainstream by the media and special interest groups. Media coverage of the Great Pacific Garbage Patch, a massive trash pile floating atop the Pacific Ocean, raised collective anxiety over plastic pollution. Large environmental organizations, including Earth Justice, the Nature Conservancy, the Ocean Conservancy, and the Sierra Club advocated for either plastic bag prohibition or taxes. Their advocacy was assisted by groups that focus on reducing plastic use in general, like the Plastic Pollution Coalition, which counts celebrities and several other groups among its supporters, including Greenpeace USA and the Clean Seas Coalition. Smaller, targeted organizations like California vs. Big Plastic—now known as Californians Against Waste—argue for the merits of plastic bag paternalism at the state and local level.

Plastic bag restrictions have gained a foothold worldwide. Colombia, Denmark, England, Greece, and Ireland have imposed taxes. India, Kenya, New Zealand, and Rwanda have instituted prohibition. Controls in the United States more than doubled between 2009 and 2014 alone.[41] A few states enacted prohibition, and in 2019, a statewide tax took effect in Connecticut. A growing number of American local governments pursued a combination of prohibition and taxes.

Plastic bag paternalism has even found success outside the bounds of the traditional nation-state. In 2018 the Shabab, an East African terrorist group with ties to Al Qaeda, banned plastic bags in territories under its control. According to Mohammed Abu Abdullah, a Shabab governor,

---

[39] Freinkel (2011).

[40] Homonoff (2018). Like the pattern observed with other sin taxes, initial declines may not persist over time. A study of South Africa's plastic bag tax found that although the levy initially reduced bag use, demand eventually returned to normal (Dikgang et al. 2012).

[41] Morris and Seasholes (2014).

the bags "pose a serious threat to the well-being of humans and animals alike."[42]

That is not necessarily true. Although it may come as a shock to paternalists, and Shababi leaders, most environmental plastic waste does not come from shopping bags. According to *National Geographic*, a majority of the plastic in the Great Pacific Garbage Patch is "abandoned fishing gear – not plastic bottles or packaging drawing headlines today."[43] Moreover, most of the plastic in oceans does not come from the United States or European countries, where plastic bag taxes and prohibition have gained popularity, but from the rest of the world. Two-thirds of plastic pollution comes from Asia alone. Central America, South America, and Africa are also heavy polluters.[44]

Assertions of rampant plastic bag litter on land are also mistaken. Environmental Resources Planning, an American research and consulting firm that specializes in analyzing litter's impact on the environment, notes that many litter surveys are carried out by volunteers and conducted without proper research protocols. The firm's more rigorous litter surveys show that in several large cities, including Toronto, Ontario as well as San Francisco and San Jose, California, plastic bags represent no more than two percent of litter.[45] Other items, such as food wrappers, plastic beverage bottles, and metal beverage cans, are far more commonplace.[46]

While it runs counter to conventional wisdom, another tenet of plastic bag paternalism—that plastic waste will take hundreds of years to biodegrade—is unsettled. Modern plastic bags have only existed for several decades, and there is no observational evidence of how long their breakdown actually takes. Experts' best guesses are instead based on models. But some research indicates that plastics decompose much more rapidly than experts say. A 2019 study found that polystyrene, an oft-criticized

[42] Callimachi (2018).

[43] Parker (2018).

[44] Lebreton et al. (2017).

[45] Stein (2013).

[46] See "Ocean Conservancy ICC Data—Plastic Grocery Bags in Beach Litter," a brief issued by Environmental Resources Planning in September 2017. The brief notes that 43.5% of litter is "balloons, rope, food bottles, fishing line, straps, nets, gloves, floats, buoys, tampon applicators, light bulbs, light sticks and syringes." Perhaps these should be taxed instead.

material found in Styrofoam, breaks down within decades—not, as experts often claim, hundreds or thousands of years.[47]

Far more damaging to the case for plastic bag paternalism is that taxes and prohibition are not beneficial to the environment. Studies show that plastic bag use does decline after either restriction goes into effect, but that's not necessarily a net gain for the environment or society.

One reason why is substitution. Some retailers attempt to get around plastic bag taxes and prohibition by offering customers alternatives that contain more plastic.[48] A 2019 study concluded that a plastic bag ban in California eliminated 40 million pounds worth of bags—an apparent success—but spurred a 12 million pound increase sales of larger trash bags. Sales of small trash bags that are usually thicker and contain more plastic than the prohibited bags they replace increased 120%.[49]

That is not the only kind of substitution. Some consumers utilize reusable bags made from cotton or other materials. But those bags are even worse for the environment than plastic bags. For proof, look no further than Denmark's Environmental Protection Agency, which evaluated how various kinds of bags performed across 15 measures of environmental impact. The Agency concluded that plastic bags were the best performer. Their analysis estimated that, to have a lesser environmental impact than a plastic bag, an individual would have to reuse a cotton bag 7100 times. If the bag is manufactured from organic cotton, then they would have to reuse the bag 20,000 times. Anything less, and a plastic bag has a smaller impact.[50] The Dutch study was not unique in this regard. A similar analysis by the United Kingdom's Environment Agency arrived at the same conclusion.[51]

Plastic bag restrictions also impose other unintended consequences. Reusable bags harbor bacteria and increase the risk of cross-contamination and infection. Amid the coronavirus pandemic in 2020, the governor of New Hampshire urged stores and customers to return to using

---

[47] Ward et al. (2019).

[48] Homonoff et al. (2020).

[49] Taylor (2019a).

[50] See "Life Cycle Assessment of Grocery Carrier Bags," a report issued by the Environmental Protection Agency in 2018 (Environmental Project #1985).

[51] See "Life Cycle Assessment of Supermarket Carrier Bags: A Review of the Bags Available in 2006," a report issued by the Environment Agency in 2011 (Report SC030148).

plastic bags. "It is important that shoppers keep their reusable bags at home," he tweeted, "given the potential risk to baggers, grocers and customers." To that end, he signed an order banning reusable bags. Several other policymakers, including the governor of California, signed similar measures.

Obviously, health risks can be mitigated by regularly washing reusable bags in hot water. But one survey found that just 15% of people who use reusable bags "follow recommended cleaning procedures." [52] And, just as obviously, routinely washing and disinfecting reusable bags only increases their environmental impact.[53]

There are other unintended consequences to penalizing plastic bag use. Evidence suggests that reusable bags make shopping trips less efficient. Using scanner data from a large retailer in the United States, a study found that plastic bag taxes and bans increased the amount of time it takes to check out at supermarkets by about two minutes per trip. That inefficiency amounts to a total of nearly 12 million hours of additional wait time nationwide.[54] That lost productivity is an internality. But applying the same logic experts use in research on soda, alcohol, tobacco, and marijuana—which conflates internalities and externalities—then reusable bags should be taxed, not plastic bags.

It thus comes as no surprise that, according to one study, policies to tax or ban plastic bags "may result in negative impact on the environment rather than positive."[55] Like so much of analysis of the other sins, experts and paternalists vouching for plastic bag taxes and prohibition have conveniently forgotten to address substitution and unintended consequences.

Nevertheless, plastic bag taxes may be justifiable if the revenue they generate went to effective programs. But little of the money raised goes to environmental cleanup, where harm is said to occur. Sixty percent of bag tax revenue in Denver, Colorado, is retained by the city to administer the tax and provide "education, outreach and to offer customers reusable bags." The remaining revenue is kept by stores "as a way of offsetting

[52] Kimmel et al. (2014).
[53] Williams et al. (2011).
[54] Taylor (2019b).
[55] Kimmel et al. (2014).

any costs they incur" due to the tax.[56] Revenue in Chicago, Illinois, is similarly divided between the city and retailers. The city's share is used to subsidize the cost of public safety and other city services. How those services will be funded in the future if plastic bag use ceases altogether is not known.

Curiously, the public has yet to embrace plastic bag paternalism. A 2013 Reason Foundation poll found that 60% of American adults opposed a plastic bag ban. Only 15% felt the government should dictate the type of bag consumers can use.[57] Whether paternalists take that to heart—or feel this is another choice where individuals do not know what is in their best interest—remains to be seen.

* * *

Sin taxes may soon escape the confines of grocery stores and other retailers and alight on a new target: robots.

Growth of robots, artificial intelligence, and other emerging technologies has brought to the fore proposals for a so-called robot tax, a new and very different type of sin tax. Whereas the other taxes apply to ostensibly harmful products consumed by individuals, a robot tax theoretically applies to business entities guilty of the sin of automation. Using technology to displace workers from their jobs is thought to impose externalities, including lost wages and increased demand for social services. Paternalists argue that such a transition cannot transpire apart from government intervention, including taxes and other regulations to ensure an orderly process.

Robot-imposed economic calamity is no longer the purview of science fiction writers. Surveys show that the public is concerned about automation-induced job displacement.[58] That may result from a recognition that automation has already occurred and has already eliminated some jobs.[59] Its rise in manufacturing has also contributed to lower wages in that sector.[60] By extension, it may have contributed to rising

[56] Swanson (2019).
[57] Ekins (2013).
[58] Geiger (2019).
[59] Acemoglu and Restrepo (2019a).
[60] DeCanio (2016).

income inequality, which is not likely to dissipate for some time.[61] A robot tax could, in theory, counteract that inequality.[62] Such a tax could also replace lost revenue to diminished income and payroll tax collections if job displacement accelerates.[63]

Robot tax advocacy has gained mainstream notice. Microsoft cofounder Bill Gates floated the idea of a robot tax in a 2017 interview.[64] A 2019 feature in the *New York Times* argued that a robot tax would generate revenue to cover the higher cost of social programs likely to result if a substantial number of jobs were automated.[65]

But taxing robots is complicated. One immediate difficulty is how the tax would "work." It could be a government fee added to the price of robots, leaving policymakers the arduous task of defining which technologies are and are not considered a "robot." A more plausible approach promoted by some experts is a reform of existing tax codes that would remove all tax credits, deductions, and other incentives that encourage businesses to invest in capital equipment that may automate jobs. That would render tax codes human–robot neutral by eliminating tax preferences for automation, thereby leveling the playing field.[66]

While understandable, fears of boundless automation and attendant social chaos are misplaced. According to an analysis of 21 developed countries, just nine percent of jobs are a t isk of elimination due to automation.[67] Contemporary fears of automation also ignore its economic history. As a 2020 piece in the *Wall Street Journal* noted:

> The advent of PCs and computing power in the 1980s and 1990s boosted productivity and destroyed the jobs of typists and file clerks. But software designers and social-media influencers rose to take their place, and U.S. unemployment today is at a 50-year low. If that history repeats, there will

---

[61] Berg et al. (2018).

[62] Zhang (2019).

[63] Oberson (2017).

[64] Delaney (2017). As for what to do with robot tax revenue, Gates offered, "you can amp up social services for old people and handicapped people and you can take the education sector and put more labor in there."

[65] Porter (2019).

[66] Abbott and Bogenschneider (2017).

[67] Anrtz et al. (2016).

be difficult short-term disruptions but little to warrant upending the whole tax system.[68]

Evidence of automation's benefits to society appears in research that undermines the belief that it imposes externalities. Several studies note that while there may be a difficult transition period as some jobs are eliminated, automation's long-term economic impact is positive. Benefits include improved productivity and lower prices for consumers.[69] Studies also show that the net effect on employment and wages is negligible to positive.[70] There may be fewer jobs in manufacturing, for example, but more in business services.[71] One study found that manufacturing companies that pursued automation had lower labor costs and ultimately created more jobs.[72]

A robot tax would jeopardize those benefits and impose unintended consequences. Forcing businesses to pay the tax would likely result in less innovation, a less than ideal outcome that would ripple through the economy. A robot tax in one area would almost certainly displace investment from that area—not to mention jobs—to areas where the tax is not charged.[73] That, in turn, could lead to lower economic growth.[74]

Policymakers should thus resist proposals to impose a robot tax. In the future, automation will displace some jobs; indeed, it already has. But automation is not a substitute for human labor; it is more often a complement. And as the nature of employment changes, education and training programs should, too.[75] There's no need for policymakers and experts— never skilled in the art of central planning—to nudge the process with a

---

[68] Rubin (2020).

[69] Graetz and Michaels (2018).

[70] Doms et al. (1997) and Feenstra and Hanson (1999).

[71] Dauth et al. (2018); see also Gregory et al. (2018).

[72] Koch et al. (2019).

[73] As Gasteiger and Prettner (2017) note, "From a policy perspective, the successful implementation of a robot tax is only feasible if it is introduced by many countries because of the possibility that capital moves to jurisdictions in which there is no robot tax."

[74] Zeira (1998).

[75] Autor (2015).

tax.[76] Robot tax advocates will continue to argue the need for government revenue to make up for income taxes lost when jobs disappear, but the evidence does not suggest that will happen. Even if it did, that points to the need for a much more comprehensive reform: a new tax system that doesn't rely on taxing labor.[77] It should also avoid taxing sin—personal, business, or otherwise.

* * *

The next target of paternalist ire is hard t o dvine, but carbon is the most likely candidate. While a carbon tax is not a selective tax in the spirit of the other sins—it is relatively easy to avoid the other sins taxes, but it's not easy to avoid consuming carbon—supporters have proposed the levy as needed to redeem carbon's environmental harm. The externalities largely stem from burning fossil fuels, which pollute the air with carbon dioxide and other greenhouse gasses. A carbon tax is arguably the most consistent with Pigou's original argument for sin taxes; indeed, his signature example was an industrial factory that pollutes the air.

Carbon taxes and other restrictions have been implemented around the world. Several nations impose some form of a carbon tax, including Argentina, France, Singapore, and Zimbabwe. Some Canadian provinces, including British Columbia and Quebec, have also instituted a tax. Other governments attempt to regulate carbon emissions with other policies, including cap-and-trade systems.

Carbon restrictions enjoy diverse support. Environmental groups, including the Sierra Club, support carbon taxes. So do large oil companies, including British Petroleum, ExxonMobil, and Royal Dutch Shell. In 2019, a group of 45 economists signed a statement published in the *Wall Street Journal* that said a "carbon tax offers the most cost-effective lever to reduce carbon emissions at the scale and speed that is necessary." They argued that the tax should replace existing environmental regulations and that any revenue should be distributed to citizens "through equal lump-sum rebates."[78]

---

[76] Some experts argue governments should oversee the implementation of automation. Acemoglu and Restrepo (2019b) argue that "we should not assume that, left to its own devices, the *right types* of AI will be developed and implemented" (emphasis added).

[77] Mazur (2019).

[78] Authors (2019b).

Some research shows that carbon taxes work as intended. A study of Sweden's carbon tax found that it reduced harmful emissions by nearly 11 percent.[79] Studies also show that the tax does not have the adverse effects alleged by some critics, like job losses. A report on British Columbia's carbon tax concluded that it led to a small increase in employment.[80]

But there is cause for skepticism. Many studies that report positively on carbon taxes draw on models instead of observational evidence.[81] As much as proponents may claim that all revenue will be returned to the public, that is impossible; some revenue would have to be siphoned to pay for tax administration and oversight. Critics also warn about the potential for rent-seeking, such as through interest groups seeking a share of revenue generated by a carbon tax, as they have so often sought funding provided by other sin taxes.[82] Depending on how carbon tax revenue is earmarked, the tax's impact can be regressive.[83]

The paternalism surrounding carbon and the other twenty-first century sins exemplifies the same pitfalls as the old sins. The social science is dubious or weak, and the harms exaggerated or non-existent. Yet the calls for taxes remain, even in the face of contradictory evidence.

Like the others, the new sin taxes are not necessarily about redeeming externalities, but about advancing progressivism through more government revenue and regulation of individual and corporate decisions. Some have admitted as much. One prominent backer of carbon taxes said in 2019 that raising taxes on the wealthy and allocating the money to "Green New Deal" would actually be more effective than a carbon tax.[84] The same year, a report signed by over 40 experts advocated solving the interconnected challenges of obesity, undernutrition, and climate change with "taxes on unhealthy foods" like meat. But that was not the experts' only recommendation. They also advised society to rethink the "structures, practices, and beliefs that underpin capitalism."[85]

---

[79] Andersson (2019).

[80] Yamazaki (2017).

[81] Kirchner et al. (2019).

[82] Mills (2019).

[83] Mathur and Morris (2014).

[84] Sarlin (2019).

[85] Authors (2019a).

REFERENCES

Abbott, Ryan, and Bret Bogenschneider. 2017. "Should Robots Pay Taxes? Tax Policy in the Age of Automation." *Harvard Law & Policy Review* 12: 145–175.

Acemoglu, Daron, and Pascual Restrepo. 2019a. "Automation and New Tasks: How Technology Displaces and Reinstates Labor." *Journal of Economic Perspectives* 33(2): 3–30.

Acemoglu, Daron, and Pascual Restrepo. 2019b. "The Wrong Kind of AI? Artificial Intelligence and the Future of Labour Demand." *Cambridge Journal of Regions, Economy and Society*, forthcoming. https://doi.org/10.1093/cjres/rsz022.

Andersson, Julius J. 2019. "Carbon Taxes and CO_2 Emissions: Sweden as a Case Study." *American Economic Journal: Economic Policy* 11(4): 1–30.

Arntz, Melanie, Terry Gregory, and Ulrich Zierahn. 2016. "The Risk of Automation for Jobs in OECD Countries: A Comparative Analysis." OECD Social, Employment and Migration Working Papers No. 189.

Authors. 2018. "Options for Keeping the Food System Within Environmental Limits." *Nature* 562: 519–525.

Authors. 2019a. "The Global Syndemic of Obesity, Undernutrition, and Climate Change: *The Lancet* Commission Report." *The Lancet Commissions* 393(10173): 791–846.

Authors. 2019b. "Economists' Statement on Carbon Dividends." *The Wall Street Journal*. Retrieved January 16, 2019 (https://www.wsj.com/articles/economists-statement-on-carbon-dividends-11547682910).

Autor, David H. 2015. "Why Are There Still So Many Jobs? The History and Future of Workplace Automation." *Journal of Economic Perspectives* 29(3): 3–30.

Barclay, Eliza. 2012. "A Nation of Meat Eaters: See How It All Adds Up." *National Public Radio*. Retrieved March 1, 2020 (https://www.npr.org/sections/thesalt/2012/06/27/155527365/visualizing-a-nation-of-meat-eaters).

Berg, Andrew, Edward F. Buffie, and Luis-Felipe Zanna. 2018. "Should We Fear the Robot Revolution? (The Correct Answers Is Yes)." *Journal of Monetary Economics* 97: 117–148.

Bomsdorf, Clemens. 2012. "Denmark Scraps Much-Maligned 'Fat Tax' After a Year." *The Wall Street Journal*. Retrieved March 1, 2020 (https://www.wsj.com/articles/SB10001424127887323894704578113120622763136).

Boseley, Sarah. 2015. "Processed Meats Rank Alongside Smoking as Cancer Causes—WHO." *The Guardian*. Retrieved February 1, 2020 (https://www.theguardian.com/society/2015/oct/26/bacon-ham-sausages-processed-meats-cancer-risk-smoking-says-who).

Burkert, Nathalie T., Johanna Muckenhuber, Franziska Großschädl, Éva Rásky, and Wolfgang Freidl. 2014. "Nutrition and Health—The Association Between Eating Behavior and Various Health Parameters: A Matched Sample Study." *PLoS ONE* 9(2): e88278.

Callimachi, Rukmini. 2018. "Al Qaeda-Backed Terrorist Group Has a New Target: Plastic Bags." *The New York Times*. Retrieved July 5, 2018 (https://www.nytimes.com/2018/07/04/world/africa/somalia-shabab-plastic-bags.html).

Capper, Judith L. 2011. "The Environmental Impact of Beef Production in the United States: 1977 Compared with 2007." *Journal of Animal Science* 89(12): 4249–4261.

Chen, G-C, D-B Lv, Z. Pang, and Q-F Liu. 2013. "Red and Processed Meat Consumption and Risk of Stroke: A Meta-analysis of Prospective Cohort Studies." *European Journal of Clinical Nutrition* 67(1): 91–95.

Chouinard, Hayley H., David E. Davis, Jeffrey T. LaFrance, and Jeffrey M. Perloff. 2007. "Fat Taxes: Big Money for Small Change." *Forum for Health Economics & Policy* 10(2). Online publication.

Dauth, Wolfgang, Sebastian Findeisen, Jens Suedekum, and Nicole Woessner. 2018. "Adjusting to Robots: Worker-Level Evidence." Federal Reserve Bank of Minneapolis, Opportunity & Inclusive Growth Institute Working Paper #13.

DeCanio, Stephen J. 2016. "Robots and Humans—Complements or Substitutes?" *Journal of Macroeconomics* 49: 280–291.

Delaney, Kevin J. 2017. "The Robot that Takes Your Job Should Pay Taxes, Says Bill Gates." *Quartz*. Retrieved March 1, 2020 (https://qz.com/911968/bill-gates-the-robot-that-takes-your-job-should-pay-taxes/).

Dikgang, Johane, Anthony Leiman, and Martine Visser. 2012. "Elasticity of Demand, Price and Time: Lessons from South Africa's Plastic-Bag Levy." *Applied Economics* 44(26): 3339–3342.

Doms, Mark, Timothy Dunne, and Kenneth R. Troske. 1997. "Workers, Wages, and Technology." *The Quarterly Journal of Economics* 112(1): 253–290.

Ekins, Emily. 2013. "60 Percent of Americans Oppose Plastic Bag Ban." *Reason*. Retrieved March 1, 2020 (https://reason.com/2013/08/19/60-percent-of-americans-oppose-plastic-b/).

Epstein, Leonard H., Noelle Jankowiak, Chantal Nederkoorn, Hollie A. Raynor, Simone A. French, and Eric Finkelstein. 2012. "Experimental Research on the Relation Between Food Price Changes and Food-Purchasing Patterns: A Targeted Review." *American Journal of Clinical Nutrition* 95(4): 789–809.

Eyles, Helen, Cliona Ni Mhurchu, Nhung Nghiem, and Tony Blakely. 2012. "Food Pricing Strategies, Population Diets, and Non-Communicable Disease: A Systematic Review of Simulation Studies." *PLoS Medicine* 9(12): e1001353.

Feenstra, Robert C., and Gordon H. Hanson. 1999. "The Impact of Outsourcing and High-Technology Capital on Wages: Estimates for the United States, 1979–1990." *The Quarterly Journal of Economics* 114(3): 907–940.

Freinkel, Susan. 2011. *Plastic: A Toxic Love Story*. New York: Houghton Mifflin Harcourt.

Gasteiger, Emanuel, and Klaus Prettner. 2017. "Automation, Stagnation, and the Implications of a Robot Tax." Unpublished manuscript. Retrieved January 31, 2020 (http://www.urleiwand.com/docs/Research/olgauto.pdf).

Geiger, A.W. 2019. "How Americans See Automation and the Workplace in 7 Charts." Pew Research Center. Retrieved March 1, 2020 (https://www.pew research.org/fact-tank/2019/04/08/how-americans-see-automation-and-the-workplace-in-7-charts/).

Grabs, Janina. 2015. "The Rebound Effects of Switching to Vegetarianism. A Microeconomic Analysis of Swedish Consumption Behavior." *Ecological Economics* 116: 270–279.

Graetz, Georg, and Guy Michaels. 2018. "Robots at Work." *The Review of Economics and Statistics* 100(5): 753–768.

Gregory, Terry, Anna Salomons, and Ulrich Zierahn. 2018. "Racing with or Against the Machine? Evidence from Europe." Center for European Economic Research Discussion Paper No. 16-053.

Hallström, E., A. Carlsson-Kanyama, and P. Börjesson. 2015. "Environmental Impact of Dietary Change: A Systematic Review." *Journal of Cleaner Production* 91: 1–11.

Homonoff, Tatiana A. 2018. "Can Small Incentives Have Large Effects? The Impact of Taxes versus Bonuses on Disposable Bag Use." *American Economic Journal: Economic Policy* 10(4): 177–210.

Homonoff, Tatiana, Lee-Sien Kao, Javiera Selman, and Christina Seybolt. 2020. "Skipping the Bag: The Relative Effectiveness of Bans versus Taxes." Unpublished manuscript. Retrieved March 1, 2020 (https://wagner.nyu.edu/impact/research/publications/skipping-bag-relative-effectiveness-bans-versus-taxes).

Howard, Jacqueline. 2016. "Meat-eaters May Have a Higher Risk of Death, but Plants Are the Answer." *CNN*. Retrieved March 1, 2020 (https://www.cnn.com/2016/08/01/health/meat-eaters-risk-of-death-plant-protein/index.html).

Iguacel, Isabel, María L. Miguel-Berges, Alejandro Gómez-Bruton, Luis A. Moreno, and Cristina Julián. 2019. "Veganism, Vegetarianism, Bone Mineral Density, and Fracture Risk: A Systematic Review and Meta-Analysis." *Nutrition Reviews* 77(1): 1–18.

Ioannidis, John P.A. 2018. "The Challenge of Reforming Nutritional Epidemiologic Research." *Journal of the American Medical Association* 320(10): 969–970.

Jensen, Jørgen Dejgård, and Sinne Smed. 2013. "The Danish Tax on Saturated Fat—Short Run Effects on Consumption, Substitution Patterns and Consumer Prices of Fats." *Food Policy* 42: 18–31.

Jensen, Jørgen Dejgård, Sinne Smed, Lars Aarup, and Erhard Nielsen. 2016. "Effects of the Danish Saturated Fat Tax on the Demand for Meat and Dairy Products." *Public Health Nutrition* 19(17): 3085–3094.

Kimmel, Robert M., Kay D. Cooksey, and Allison Littman. 2014. "Life Cycle Assessment of Grocery Bags in Common Use in the United States." Clemson University Environmental Studies Paper. Retrieved from https://tigerprints.clemson.edu/cgi/viewcontent.cgi?article=1006&context=cudp_environment.

Kirchner, Mathias, Mark Sommer, Kurt Kratena, Daniela Kletzan-Slamanig, and Claudia Kettner-Marx. 2019. "CO_2 Taxes, Equity and the Double Dividend—Macroeconomic Model Simulations for Austria." *Energy Policy* 126: 294–314.

Knapton, Sarah. 2016. "Ditch Sausages for a Longer Life, Say Harvard Scientists." *The Telegraph.* Retrieved March 1, 2020 (https://www.telegraph.co.uk/science/2016/08/01/ditch-sausages-for-a-longer-life-say-harvard-scientists/).

Koch, Michael, Ilya Manuylov, and Marcel Smolka. 2019. "Robots and Firms." CESifo Working Paper #7608.

Kruger, Claire, and Yuting Zhou. 2018. "Red Meat and Colon Cancer: A Review of the Mechanistic Evidence for Heme in the Context of Risk Assessment Methodology." *Food and Chemical Toxicology* 118: 131–153.

Lacroix, Karine. 2018. "Comparing the Relative Mitigation Potential of Individual Pro-environmental Behaviors." *Journal of Cleaner Production* 195: 1398–1407.

LaMotte, Sandee. 2020. "Red and Processed Meat Are Not Ok for Health, Study Says, Despite News to the Contrary." *CNN.* Retrieved February 14, 2020 (https://www.cnn.com/2020/02/03/health/red-meat-processed-meat-chicken-fish-health-risks-wellness/index.html).

Larsen, Janet. 2012. "Peak Meat: U.S. Meat Consumption Falling." Earth Policy Institute. Retrieved March 17, 2020 (http://www.earth-policy.org/data_highlights/2012/highlights25).

Lebreton, Laurent C.M., Joost van der Zwet, Jan-Willem Damsteeg, Boyan Slat, Anthony Andrady, and Julia Reisser. 2017. "River Plastic Emissions to the World's Oceans." *Nature Communications* 8:15611. Online publication.

Leroy, Frédéric, and Nathan Cofnas. 2019. "Should Dietary Guidelines Recommend Low Red Meat Intake?" *Critical Reviews in Food Science and Nutrition,* forthcoming. https://doi.org/10.1080/10408398.2019.1657063.

Lippi, Giuseppe, Camilla Mattiuzzi, and Fabian Sanchis-Gomar. 2015. "Red Meat Consumption and Ischemic Heart Disease: A Systematic Literature Review." *Meat Science* 108: 32–36.

Lomborg, Bjørn. 2018. "Ban the Beef?" *New Europe*. Retrieved March 1, 2020 (https://www.neweurope.eu/article/ban-the-beef/).

Lusk, Jayson L., and F. Bailey Norwood. 2016. "Some Vegetarians Spend Less Money on Food, Others Don't." *Ecological Economics* 130: 232–242.

Mathur, Aparna, and Adele C. Morris. 2014. "Distributional Effects of a Carbon Tax in Broader U.S. Fiscal Reform." *Energy Policy* 66(3): 326–334.

Matta, Joane, Sébastien Czernichow, Emmanuelle Kesse-Guyot, Nicolas Hoertel, Frédéric Limosin, Marcel Goldberg, Marie Zins, and Cedric Lemogne. 2018. "Depressive Symptoms and Vegetarian Diets: Results from the Constances Cohort." *Nutrients* 10: 1695. Online publication.

Mazur, Orly. 2019. "Taxing the Robots." *Pepperdine Law Review* 46(2): 277–330.

Micha, Renata, Sarah K. Wallace, and Dariush Mozaffarian. 2010. "Red and Processed Meat Consumption and Risk of Incident Coronary Heart Disease, Stroke, and Diabetes Mellitus: A Systematic Review and Meta-Analysis." *Circulation* 121(21): 2271–2283.

Mills, Mark P. 2019. "Have We Got a Carbon Tax 'Dividend' for You." *The Wall Street Journal*. Retrieved January 10, 2020 (https://www.wsj.com/articles/have-we-got-a-carbon-tax-dividend-for-you-11546992477).

Moodie, Alison. 2015. "Watchdog Group Calls for Less Processed Meats in School Cafeterias." *The Guardian*. Retrieved March 17, 2020 (https://www.theguardian.com/sustainable-business/2015/aug/31/usda-tyson-foods-american-beefpackers-michelle-obama-national-lunch-program).

Morris, Julian, and Brian Seasholes. 2014. "How Green Is that Grocery Bag Ban? An Assessment of the Environmental and Economic Effects of Grocery Bag Bans and Taxes." Reason Foundation Report. Retrieved March 2, 2020 (https://reason.org/policy-study/how-green-is-that-grocery-bag-ban/).

Mytton, Oliver, Alastair Gray, Mike Rayner, and Harry Rutter. 2007. "Could Targeted Food Taxes Improve Health?" *Journal of Epidemiology and Community Health* 61(8): 689–694.

Nezlek, John B., Catherine A. Forestell, and David B. Newman. 2018. "Relationships Between Vegetarian Dietary Habits and Daily Well-being." *Ecology of Food and Nutrition* 57(5): 425–438.

Oberson, Xavier. 2017. "How Taxing Robots Could Help Bridge Future Revenue Gaps." OECD. Retrieved March 1, 2020 (http://www.oecd.org/employment/how-taxing-robots-could-help-bridge-future-revenue-gaps.htm).

Parker, Laura. 2018. "The Great Pacific Garbage Patch Isn't What You Think It Is." *National Geographic*. Retrieved March 4, 2020 (https://www.nationalgeographic.com/news/2018/03/great-pacific-garbage-patch-plastics-environment/).

People for the Ethical Treatment of Animals. 2020. "Tax Meat." Retrieved March 17, 2020 (https://www.peta.org/features/tax-meat/).

Porter, Eduardo. 2019. "Don't Fight the Robots. Tax Them." *The New York Times*. Retrieved March 17, 2020 (https://www.nytimes.com/2019/02/23/sunday-review/tax-artificial-intelligence.html).

Rubin, Richard. 2020. "The 'Robot Tax' Debate Heats Up." *The Wall Street Journal*. Retrieved March 17, 2020 (https://www.wsj.com/articles/the-robot-tax-debate-heats-up-11578495608).

Sarlin, Benjy. 2019. "Defeated Twice, A Top Climate Change Crusader Has a Wake-Up Call Some Democrats Won't Want to Hear." NBC News. Retrieved March 4, 2020 (https://www.nbcnews.com/politics/2020-election/defeated-twice-top-climate-change-crusader-has-wake-call-some-n957691).

Springmann, Marco, Daniel Mason-D'Croz, Sherman Robinson, Keith Wiebe, H. Charles J. Godfray, Mike Rayner, and Peter Scarborough. 2018. "Health-Motivated Taxes on Red and Processed Meat: A Modelling Study on Optimal Tax Levels and Associated Health Impacts." *PLoS ONE* 13(11): e0204139.

Stein, Steven R. 2013. "ER Planning Report Brief: Plastic Retail Bags in Litter." Environmental Resources Planning. Retrieved March 1, 2020 (https://www.erplanning.com/uploads/Plastic_Retail_Bags_in_Litter.pdf).

Swanson, Conrad. 2019. "Denver City Council Passes Bag Fee, Mayor Hancock Expected to Sign into Law." *The Denver Post*. Retrieved March 4, 2020 (https://www.denverpost.com/2019/12/23/denver-city-council-passes-plastic-bag-fee/).

Taylor, Rebecca L.C. 2019a. "Bag Leakage: The Effect of Disposable Carryout Bag Regulations on Unregulated Bags." *Journal of Environmental Economics and Management* 93: 254–271.

Taylor, Rebecca L.C. 2019b. "A Mixed Bag: The Hidden Costs of Regulating Consumer Behavior." Unpublished manuscript. Retrieved March 5, 2020 (https://papers.ssrn.com/sol3/papers.cfm?abstract_id=3186504).

Tilman, David, and Michael Clark. 2014. "Global Diets Link Environmental Sustainability and Human Health." *Nature* 515: 518–522.

Wang, Xia, Xinying Lin, Ying Y. Ouyang, Jun Liu, Gang Zhao, An Pan, and Frank B. Hu. 2016. "Red and Processed Meat Consumption and Mortality: Dose-Response Meta-analysis of Prospective Cohort Studies." *Public Health Nutrition* 19(5): 893–905.

Ward, Collin P., Cassia J. Armstrong, Anna N. Walsh, Julia H. Jackson, and Christopher M. Reddy. 2019. "Sunlight Converts Polystyrene to Carbon

Dioxide and Dissolved Organic Carbon." *Environmental Science & Technology Letters* 6(11): 669–674.

Wellesley, Laura, Catherine Happer, and Anthony Froggatt. 2015. "Changing Climate, Changing Diets: Pathways to Lower Meat Consumption." Chatham House. Retrieved February 14, 2020 (https://www.chathamhouse.org/pub lication/changing-climate-changing-diets).

Williams, David L., Charles P. Gerba, Sherri Maxwell, and Ryan G. Sinclair. 2011. "Assessment of the Potential for Cross-contamination of Food Products by Reusable Shopping Bags." *Food Protection Trends* 31(8): 508–513.

Yamazaki, Akio. 2017. "Job and Climate Policy: Evidence from British Columbia's Revenue-Neutral Carbon Tax." *Journal of Environmental Economics and Management* 83(5): 197–216.

Zeira, Joseph. 1998. "Workers, Machines, and Economic Growth." *The Quarterly Journal of Economics* 113(4): 1091–1117.

Zhang, Pengqing. 2019. "Automation, Wage Inequality and Implications of a Robot Tax." *International Review of Economics & Finance* 59(1): 500–509.

Zhong, Victor W., Linda Van Horn, Philip Greenland, Mercedes R. Carnethon, Hongyan Ning, John T. Wilkins, Donald M. Lloyd-Jones, and Norrina B. Allen. 2020. "Associations of Processed Meat, Unprocessed Meat, Poultry, or Fish Intake with Incident Cardiovascular Disease and All-Cause Mortality." *JAMA Internal Medicine*, forthcoming. https://doi.org/10.1001/jamainter nmed.2019.6969.

CHAPTER 7

Conclusion: Don't Tax Sin, Forgive It

Theologians have invested a lot of effort into understanding sin. But the questions they and all believers face now are much the same as when religious texts introduced the concept long ago. Which choices commit an error, go astray, or miss the mark? What is the path to reconciliation? Can sinful individuals become sinless?

Dogma on who is responsible for answering those questions, how they should arrive at the answers, and what forgiveness demands varies over time and by religious tradition. At one point, forgiveness had a literal price in Christianity. During the sixteenth century, Catholic authorities sold indulgences, which were a means for believers to pay to relieve the spiritual debt incurred by their sin. Widespread abuse highlighted by Martin Luther helped trigger the Reformation. Pope Pius V barred the sale of indulgences for money in 1567, but to this day, the Christian faith remains split between Catholics and Protestants.

Still, the process of knowing right from wrong and how to turn wrongs into rights is more common across people of all faiths. The believer must learn from experience, contemplate their choices, commune with the divine, and learn to forgive and be forgiven. Penance is a spiritual exercise, not a financial one. The process is voluntary, not coercive.

Since the progressive era, governmental approaches to secular sin have taken a distinctly different trajectory. The period reframed the state's role in society around a paternalistic notion that freedom of choice must be restrained to advance society as a whole. Responsibility for passing

© The Author(s) 2021
M. Thom, *Taxing Sin*,
https://doi.org/10.1007/978-3-030-49176-5_7

judgment on individual choices rests with policymakers and experts, especially in economics, public health, and other social sciences. Choices that commit an error, go astray, or miss the mark are those that experts claim inflict externalities on society or internalities on the sinner. Expert testimony is amplified by public health organizations, special interest groups, philanthropists, and, more often than not, by the press.

The process of identifying secular sin has a consistent point of origin. Experts conduct research and publish studies that identify the many harms a specific choice imposes. Their reasoning is not about morality, and it is not theological. Instead, it is cloaked in the language of economics, uttered by unassailable experts who maintain that their only intention is to "do the right thing" and promote public health by helping individuals overcome their ignorance and cognitive biases to make better choices. Although experts say that the consequences of sin are dire—up to and including death—their dark narrative has a flicker of optimism. Sinful choices enact severe harm, they point out, but a tax redeems it. For government, forgiveness has a price. Sin taxes are a secular indulgence.

How the process unfolds is predictable from that point forward. Media highlight the experts' findings and warn individuals about the hazards of their choice to drink soda or alcohol, smoke tobacco or marijuana, eat meat, or use a plastic bag. Pundits caution about the existential threat posed by automation and carbon emissions. Public health organizations communicate the same information and urge policymakers to take action through taxes and regulations. Special interest groups frame sin taxes as a way to fund programs that help "the children" or "the environment." They may also frame sin taxes as a way to achieve some measure of justice by inflicting punishment on big soda, big sugar, big alcohol, big tobacco, big plastic, and—before long—big weed and big robot. Philanthropic organizations offer funding support to these groups and like-minded experts.

For their part, policymakers dutifully respond with new taxes, increases to existing taxes, and additional regulations. The sometimes explicit, but more often implicit message is that only government paternalism can save society from itself. Professional retaliation, accusations of bias, and name-calling await those who question that orthodoxy.

But the secular approach to sin, deeply rooted in paternalism and the progressive era drive to expand the role of government in society, is profoundly flawed.

The manner in which paternalistic arguments about what is the secularly sinful collapse is consistent from one sin to another. Cracks in the figurative edifice appear when scrutinizing claims of massive externalities and other harms allegedly imposed by choices that, in most cases, have been part of human existence for thousands of years. To make a case for taxing this sin or that sin, experts and other paternalists engage in a maddening comedy of errors that makes one wonder whether the choice is truly a bad as they say.

It starts with many experts' combination of internalities that impose no harm on society with externalities that do. They compound that error with faulty externality figures. Paternalists insist that obesity creates added healthcare costs yet ignore the fact that the non-obese have longer life expectancies that impose even more healthcare costs, not to mention additional expenses for age-related government programs, including pensions, social security, and long-term care. Their assessments of the alleged externalities tied to drinking alcohol, smoking tobacco, and eating meat betray the same mistake.

Paternalists embellish some sins' other harms to a degree best described as fearmongering. Parents are alerted that increasing marijuana access may turn children into criminals and schizophrenics. Bacon lovers are warned that they are one slice away from cancer or massive heart attack. Workers are told that unemployment is on the horizon because robots are coming for their jobs. Soda drinkers are advised that one more gulp could turn them into a corpulent diabetic.

The net result is a dishonest conventional wisdom about the risks associated with choices that are either not harmful at all, or that are nowhere near as sinful as paternalists claim—a conventional wisdom that supports an ever-expanding list of sin taxes that supposedly reduce the risks and undo the harms.

But a closer look at the research methods used to demonstrate the redemptive power of sin taxes undermines that narrative. As Friedrich Hayek observed some time ago, economists prefer simple models that fail to capture every aspect of the real world. Experts favor simulation models that predict how a hypothetical sin tax might have changed individuals' behavior in the past or how it might change behavior in the future. But no expert, and no statistical model, can move back and forth across time. Reality, in turns out, cares little for what models have to say about it.

Reality also shows that simulations are appallingly inaccurate at describing sin taxes' impact on behavior. Simulation studies predicted soda taxes would have a sizeable effect on obesity in Mexico and Chile, but more practical observational studies there and elsewhere showed that the models were wrong. Simulation models also overstate the benefits of alcohol, marijuana, and meat taxes. Some models are not merely wrong; they are deliberately biased. One model used to evaluate tobacco taxes was specifically designed to substantiate taxes and other anti-tobacco policies, not to offer unbiased, scientific findings.

A review of the assumptions that go into simulations and other pro-tax research weakens the narrative about the benefits of sin taxes even more. Experts often assume that individuals will respond to a tax in a manner that does not comport with the real world. Study after study overlooks the fact that when something becomes more expensive, individuals adapt, often in strategic ways. Tax a sinful food or beverage, and consumers are likely to find an alternative. They might switch from soda to a milk-shake, from one type of meat to another, or from an expensive brand of tobacco or alcohol to a cheaper one. Many individuals will choose to eat, drink, and smoke as much they want, and avoid taxes by making purchases in lower-tax areas or from illicit markets. Many that neverthe-less give their government more money to redeem their sins have less to spend on everything else, including necessities.

Those are many of even more unintended consequences imposed by taxing sin that paternalists disregard. Some studies show that soda taxes eventually lead to higher sugar and calorie intake, outcomes unlikely to deflate ballooning weights. Raising alcohol prices with taxes and other control measures reduces consumption among light and moderate drinkers, who subsequently miss out on alcohol's health benefits. High tobacco taxes worsen food insecurity among low-income populations. Plastic bag taxes and prohibition spike demand for reusable bags that are not only worse for the environment, but also more likely to spread viruses and bacteria as well as reduce checkout efficiency.

Faith in paternalism and the redeeming quality of sin taxes nears total collapse when one considers other, more distressing problems with the research used to support it. The data fed into simulations and other statistical models is often incomplete or flawed. Experts report short-term effects as long-term effects, as if the way individuals immediately respond to a new tax is permanent, unwavering compliance. Some experts misin-terpret or exaggerate statistical measures, usually in a pro-tax direction. Many experts report correlations as proof of causation, an inexcusable error for any person with even a rudimentary knowledge of statistics.

Many more publish studies that ignore confounding factors, such as assessing alcohol taxes without untangling the parallel impact of drunk driving laws. Some experts publish a study that says one thing, only to later contribute to another study that says something different, while doing little to reconcile the contradiction.

Any remaining support for sin taxes vanishes when experts' bias comes into focus. The research they produce is not just weak science; it is weak science designed to support a political end. Systematic assessments reveal publication bias in favor of studies that demonstrate the benefits of soda, alcohol, and marijuana taxes. Bias also surfaces in individual studies. The experts behind a study that concluded a soda tax would have little impact on obesity argued that governments should impose one anyway. The team behind a study that found higher tobacco taxes may increase obesity remained firmly against any cut to those taxes. The authors of a study that found high tobacco taxes encourage smuggling concluded the same.

The process of defining the choices that commit a secular sin is fraught with overstated claims, shoddy social science, and bias—sins of a different variety that are not redeemed by policymakers' stewardship of sin tax revenue. Policymakers earmark significant sums of money for special interest groups that, in addition to their standard list of often commendable accomplishments, can certainly add "successful rent-seeking." Astoundingly, some sin tax revenue is allocated to groups that vouch for the benefits of sin taxes, a titanic conflict of interest. Likewise, some sin tax revenue also goes to grants awarded to experts who write studies that inevitably conclude sin taxes provide many benefits to society. Policymakers spend the balance on a medley of suspicious, ineffective programs. Gardening books and gardening programs in Colorado. Sports programs in Lithuania and Romania. Public employee pensions and fireworks display in California. Vision Zero in Oregon. Alcohol promotion programs in Washington. And nearly everywhere, sin taxes provide a generous subsidy for basic government largess.

The reaction to those who question paternalism—who call attention to the problems inherent to allowing experts and policymakers to identify and penalize our sinful choices—is disturbing. Paternalists assert that their critics are ignorant, misinformed, biased, or lack credentials. Pointing out a glaring mistake in a study critical of e-cigarettes is sufficient to be called an "apologist for the tobacco industry." Questioning the effects of secondhand smoke incites outrage from a phalanx of professional organizations and special interest groups. Raising the possibility that tobacco users are not a burden on public treasuries earns one the Nazi label. Resist a sin tax, and one may be surprised to learn that they care neither for "the children" nor "the environment."

It is hard to believe that paternalists' hyperbolic deflection strategies are anything other than an admission of guilt—an acknowledgment that the social science they use as a soapbox is weak, and that they are as biased as anyone else. It may also result from an unspoken recognition that identifying and penalizing others' sin is a messy affair, especially for the fallible, and that basing definite policy on indefinite science creates more problems than it solves.

Paternalists should, therefore, learn a lesson from the world's great religions. They stopped charging for forgiveness centuries ago and leave the untidy business of final judgment to the divine.

Yet paternalists are not likely to follow that path. They are slow to embrace reforms to current sin taxes and are reluctant to agree to reduce those taxes in exchange for other harm reduction policies. To borrow a phrase from Jesus Christ, it is easier for a camel to pass through the eye of a needle than it is for a paternalist to let go of a sin tax.

Simply put, the ritual of taxing sin—classifying a choice as harmful and deserving of a government penalty—is too rooted in paternalists' beliefs about human nature and society. It is not about, or not only about, improving public health. It is about changing the balance of power between individuals and their government in a way consistent with progressive philosophy. Paternalists may deny it and claim they have no political bias, but given the evidence presented in this book, concluding otherwise is problematic. It is safe to say that no conservative or libertarian academic or interest group would author a study that proclaims more government revenue is a benefit of sin taxes, on par with saving lives. Yet many studies and interest groups discussed throughout the preceding chapters did exactly that. What does that indicate about their political tilt?

Individuals tired of having their choices taxed should call out the crusade's evident partisanship. They should also ask paternalists why making experts the high priests over our choices has yet to live up to progressive era promises. After over a century of experimentation, and a growing array of taxes, utopia—that "boundless vista for possible human betterment" Irving Fisher promised in 1907—remains elusive. Perhaps the folly of modern governance was not unchecked freedom of choice, but a belief that experts and policymakers could choose better. Another reformation may be in order.

INDEX

A
Alcohol Change UK, 58, 73
Alcohol Justice, 58, 73
Alzheimer's disease, 60, 91
American Academy of Pediatrics, 24, 132
American Cancer Society, 27, 89, 92, 104, 106, 109, 126
American Heart Association, 24, 27, 38, 89, 106, 109
American Lung Association, 89, 106, 109, 126
American Medical Association, 24, 89, 125, 126
Australia/Australian, 32, 65, 90, 91, 94

B
Behavioral economics, 10, 12
Berkeley (California), 26, 41
Bloomberg Philanthropies, 25, 90
Boulder (Colorado), 26, 42

C
Calhoun, John C., 4
California, 25, 26, 58, 72, 73, 90, 100, 101, 106, 124, 125, 138–142, 162–164, 181
Canada/Canadian, 57, 94, 101, 124, 128, 132, 168
Cancer, 23, 60, 65, 87, 89, 91, 92, 104, 132, 142, 154, 158, 179
Cannabidiol (CBD), 142, 153
Cardiovascular disease, 23, 60, 70, 71, 130, 157
Center on Addiction, 70, 73
Center on Alcohol Marketing and Youth, 58, 71
Centers for Disease Control and Prevention, 27–30, 61–64, 70, 71, 75, 92, 93, 105
Chicago (Illinois), 165
Chile, 27, 34, 35, 180
China, 55, 87, 96, 129, 154
Coase, Ronald, 15
Cognitive bias, 10, 12, 13, 24, 31, 32, 178

© The Editor(s) (if applicable) and The Author(s), under exclusive license to Springer Nature Switzerland AG 2021
M. Thom, *Taxing Sin*,
https://doi.org/10.1007/978-3-030-49176-5